D0160364

BETHEL SEMINARY WEST
LIBRARY
6116 Arosa Street
San Diego, CA 92115-3902

EXIT
INTERVIEWS

EXIT INTERVIEWS

WILLIAM D. HENDRICKS

MOODY PRESS
CHICAGO

BETHEL SEMINARY WEST
LIBRARY
6116 Arosa Street
San Diego, CA 92115-3902

© 1993 by
WILLIAM D. HENDRICKS

All rights reserved. No part of this book may be reproduced in any form without permission in writing from the publisher, except in the case of brief quotations embodied in
critical articles or reviews.

All Scripture quotations, unless indicated, are taken from the *Holy Bible: New International Version*®. NIV®. Copyright © 1973, 1978, 1984, International Bible Society.
Used by permission of Zondervan Publishing House. All rights reserved.

Scripture quotations marked (NASB) are taken from the *New American Standard Bible,* © 1960, 1962, 1963, 1968, 1971, 1972, 1973, 1975, and 1977 by The Lockman
Foundation, and are used by permission.

Scripture quotations marked (KJV) are taken from the King James Version.

The use of selected references from various versions of the Bible in this publication
does not necessarily imply publisher endorsement of the versions in their entirety.

Note: Throughout this book, wherever the masculine or feminine pronouns are used,
they should be understood as indicating both genders unless the context implies otherwise.

ISBN: 0-8024-2319-1

1 3 5 7 9 10 8 6 4 2

Printed in the United States of America

*This book is dedicated
to the memory of Robert P. Manning,
as well as to disillusioned Christians everywhere.*

Contents

Preface

This will be my eighth book to be published. Each of the previous seven has had its distinctive personality. None of them, however, has gripped me in quite as emotional a way as *Exit Interviews*.

One reason is the nature of the subject. Almost by definition, a book about people leaving churches has to be a book about disappointment, loss, and trouble. And so this is—a dark book, which has not been easy for me to write and for many will not be easy to read.

So why write it? The short answer is, because it's the truth, a truth that for the most part goes unspoken in church circles—that some Christians, having grown disillusioned with the church and other institutions of Christianity, and having lost the energy and enthusiasm they once had for programs of spiritual development, are now looking elsewhere to meet their deepest spiritual needs.

By presenting the stories of some of these disaffected believers, I know I run the risk of being misunderstood by some. So let me make a disclaimer here at the outset. The fact that I report on what the people in this book have said or the choices they have made in no way implies either endorsement or disapproval. In some cases, I disagree with what they have to say, but I may or may not challenge it. On the other hand, sometimes I agree wholeheartedly with what is said, but I may give no indication of that.

However, in a number of places I do offer my opinion or comment on the issues involved. My purpose is not to pass judgment on the person being interviewed, but to arrive at understanding by pointing out issues for the reader, showing why the issues are important, and in some cases suggesting ways that the reader might think about the issues.

I applaud Moody Press for its courage in publishing this book. I hope I have lived up to the trust they have placed in me to collect and tell these stories, a trust I value highly and have appreciated greatly. Even so, nothing here—neither the interviews nor my comments—should be construed as necessarily representing the views of Moody.

Having said that, I want to assure readers that they are reading true stories of actual, living persons as told directly to me. In other words, none of these interviews is fiction. However, there will be no way for anyone to "check out" these people as I have guaranteed them anonymity. To protect their privacy, I have taken the liberty of changing their names and in some cases masking identifying features. But their statements are direct quotes.

Along these lines, some readers will wonder whether I bothered to check "the other side" of what I was told. I did not, although giving both sides might have made an interesting book, albeit a very different one. No, I took the statements of my interviewees at face value. That may make some readers uncomfortable. They will be concerned that perhaps I have been duped by some of the people I spoke with, that some of them lied to me.

That's certainly a possibility. But I would recall the words that the professor spoke to the older siblings of Lucy in *The Lion, the Witch, and the Wardrobe*: "There are only three possibilities. Either your sister is telling lies, or she is mad, or she is telling the truth. You know she doesn't tell lies and it is obvious that she is not mad. For the moment then and unless any further evidence turns up, we must assume that she is telling the truth" (C. S. Lewis, *The Lion, the Witch, and the Wardrobe*. New York: Collier/Macmillan, 1950, 45).

To my knowledge, none of my interviewees was known as a habitual liar. None was a mental case. For now, then, and unless any further evidence turns up, I assume they were telling me the truth—the truth that was in them. (For the record, I did check out a number of "facts" related to these stories and the people in them.)

By the way, after reading the book, a few people will probably wish that I had taken the professor's other advice: "There is one plan which no one has yet suggested and which is well worth trying. . . . We might all try minding our own business." I'm afraid I've never had much success at doing that.

I could never have produced this book on my own. Dozens of people helped in the process. Some of the most important I must leave unnamed, either because they would not want to be identified or because I would jeopardize the anonymity of my interviewees. I think most of them know who they are and will accept my generic appreciation here, knowing that later I will thank them personally.

One person I will mention is my brother, Bob, who believed in this project from Day One and has frequently shown me the way when my own eyes could not make it out. Another encourager was my brother-in-law, Dr. Dale Godby, who suggested a number of psychological insights that I would have overlooked. I also thank Pete Hammond, mostly for his belief in me and the energy that that has released for this project.

The project required quite a bit of travel, and many friends across the country made that part of it special. Among them were Bob and Jerrie, Bill and Sally, and Michael and his cohorts.

Another group of people to whom I wish to express thanks are the numerous sociologists, demographers, and other experts whose research and insights provide a framework for this discussion. We all owe a great deal to Reginald Bibby, Wade Clark Roof, Dean Hoge, James Davison Hunter, Dean Kelly, George Barna, George Gallup, John Savage, William Kirk Kilpatrick, John Sloat, Art Miller, Jr., and Ray Bakke.

On the technical side, I wish to thank several people at Moody Press by name for their continued help, wisdom, and skill: Jim Bell, Greg Thornton, Anne Scherich, Cheryl Dunlop, and Bill Thrasher. I also want to thank Laura for her assistance in transcribing scores of hours of interview tapes.

Perhaps the key group to be thanked is my two dozen or so interviewees. Each of you has my respect for your honesty, candor, and willingness to let me visit that very personal place inside you, your spirituality. You have done the body of Christ an invaluable service by speaking up. And I feel especially privileged that you have trusted me with your story.

Finally, this book has demanded more of my family than any of my others. So I close with words of love and gratitude to Nancy, Brittany, Kristin, and Amy. Though my name appears on the cover, they have as much ownership in this book as I do, as they have endured with me the process of producing it.

WILLIAM HENDRICKS

1

The Back Door

I used to go with the multitude,
leading the procession to the house of God,
with shouts of joy and thanksgiving
among the festive throng.
Why are you downcast, O my soul?
Why so disturbed within me?

Psalm 42:4–5

When I was a boy, my family belonged to a small, independent church in Dallas, Texas. The dozen or so families that started the church put up a standard A-frame sanctuary and tacked a shotgun wing on the western end of it for Sunday school. After church on Sundays and prayer meetings on Wednesdays, everyone ended up mingling in the lobby between the sanctuary and the classrooms (only they didn't call it a lobby; they had a church-word for it, the *vestibule*).

As a boy, though, I wasn't a mingler; I was a carouser, a frolicker, a mischief-maker (some would say a terror). So it was that my pals and I often took off into the field to the west of the building, which brought us around to the back door of the Sunday school wing.

And there we'd always find him, a man I'll call Mr. Walker. What fixes him in my memory was that he always seemed to be out the back door of the church, puffing on a cigarette.

Mr. Walker was lean and tall—at least he would have been tall if he hadn't been stoop shouldered. Maybe he was born with a bent back; maybe he was wounded in the war. But I wonder if he hadn't ruined his posture through his habit of bending over to light his smokes and then holding them in his hand rather than his mouth, so that he dipped his head whenever he took a drag.

It was a lonely spot for Mr. Walker. Everyone else was up in that vestibule, talking about whatever people in Dallas talked about in 1961. But he'd be out back in the Texas sun with his Camels, an occasional jackrabbit, and a gang of seven-year-old boys tearing by in search of adventure.

I wonder why he bothered to come to church? If he wanted privacy, he could have had it at home, or in a park, or on a golf course. If he wanted friendship (or fellowship), he wasn't making much effort to find it; though amiable, he said very little, joined no committees, and mostly kept to himself. What was it, then, that kept him coming to church rather than go someplace else?

Only Mr. Walker could tell us for sure, and he's gone—yes, the smoking finally got him. But looking back, I feel certain that he showed up week after week for only one reason: he wanted to get near God and he figured church was the place to do it. I don't think he enjoyed his nicotine habit. He turned away when he bowed his head to inhale. I don't say he was ashamed of himself, but he was alienated by his addiction. Nevertheless, he brought himself—smoking and all—to a place that stood for God. He wanted to be with God. And now he is (I believe).

Fast-forward with me three decades later to 1993. A great deal of noise is now being made about what's going on at the "front door" of the church—not the church in which I grew up, but The Church, the universal church, the body of Christ. If you picture the church as a building (never a good thing to do), the front door represents one's entry into the faith, the moment of salvation or conversion or, as many put it, of being "born again."[1]

A lot is happening today to get people near, if not through, the front door of the church, to get them saved—or at least "churched," as the jargon now goes. In North America, both conservative and mainline churches are taking aggressive steps to recruit new members. The Episcopal Church has gone so far as to call the 1990s the Decade of Evangelism. Likewise, the Presbyterian Church (U.S.A.) has targeted evangelism and church development as its priority goals for this decade. Similar objectives have been set by other groups.[2]

This new evangelistic fervor hopes to catch a perceived wave of renewed interest in religion now sweeping the land. If one believes the popular press, the United States is undergoing a virtual revival, led by

Baby Boomers returning to the church. (Later we'll examine the extent to which those reports are valid. But for now, let's assume they are true.)

One survey even suggested that faith in God is now the most important thing in Americans' lives, followed by good health and a happy marriage—an "astounding" result in the opinion of one sociologist, representing nothing less than a "cultural shift." "The Age of the Yuppie is dying," trumpeted the Associated Press.[3]

As I say, a lot of noise is being made about what's going on at the "front door" of the church. But hearing it all, I wonder: what's going on around back? Not to take anything away from evangelistic outreach or attempts to make the church's programs more "relevant" to a contemporary generation. By no means!

But I've known this building all my life, and I'm still a bit mischievous and contrary. So while others may celebrate newcomers in the vestibule, my instinct is to take off for adventures out back. And what do I find at the rear of the church? Something very different from the days of my youth. Instead of a solitary figure or two like Mr. Walker, I find quite a few people—leaving! It hardly makes sense. While countless "unchurched" people are flocking in the front door of the church, a steady stream of the "churched" is flowing quietly out the back.

Moreover, talking with people who are still inside the church—especially some of the old-timers who have been in the faith for a while—I find that a growing number have lost the energy and enthusiasm they once had for programs of spiritual development such as worship services, discipleship groups, prayer meetings, Bible studies, and so on.

This "dark side" of church growth is not something that has been either widely reported or carefully studied. But it's there. In fact, I believe it is growing. Despite glowing reports of surging church attendance, more and more Christians in North America are feeling *disillusioned* with the church and other formal, institutional expressions of Christianity.

That's not to say that these "back-door believers" have given up on the faith. On the contrary, they may be quite articulate regarding spiritual matters. Indeed, some have remarkably vibrant spiritual lives and touchingly close friendships with a kindred spirit or two. But in the main, they tend to nurture their relationship with God apart from the traditional means of church and parachurch.

"Impossible!" some will reply. "One simply cannot grow as a Christian unless one is part of a church, a local body of believers." So conventional wisdom would have it. But as we'll see, many who are leaving churches have given up on conventional wisdom. There was a time when they participated in a faith community for all the reasons given for participation: worship, instruction, fellowship, service, community, accountability, and so on. But now, for a variety of reasons, they look elsewhere to meet those needs.

Actually, the issue is not really church attendance, though I don't want to discount what "going to church" means—or is supposed to mean—for Christians.[4] The issue is something toward which church attendance points—the nature of spirituality in a deeply secular age. Bill Moyers describes it well: "The search for meaning is the most stubborn trait of humanity. . . . The real story [behind political and religious strife in the world] is the struggle to define what it means today to be spiritual. The search for what it means to be spiritual is the story, not just of the decade, but of the century."[5]

This book attempts to tell part of that story. If significant numbers of Christians are growing disillusioned with churches and ministries, if they are looking elsewhere to meet their deepest spiritual needs, then someone ought to examine that. Someone needs to ask, What's going on here?

Of course, the best people to ask are disillusioned Christians themselves. That's why this is a book of interviews, a collection of stories told by individual believers about their experience in the faith. That is the most direct way to gain understanding. I agree wholeheartedly with Boston College professor William Kirk Kilpatrick that we not only need stories in our lives, but that life *is* a story, that the best way to interpret and explain a life is in a narrative way.[6]

However, this book does not pretend to tell the whole story. Indeed, it cannot. Were we to talk with two dozen other believers, we would hear different accounts. Yet always we would come back to that larger story of which Bill Moyers speaks—of people searching for what it means to be spiritual today. The search, or journey, that my interviewees are on has led them outside the programs and away from the structures. That's because they didn't find what they were looking for or what they expected in the communities of faith of which they were a part.

But is it really necessary to dwell on this subject? Sure, there may be disaffected people in the church. There may be problems. But so what? Hasn't that always been the case? And won't it always be? Why dredge up something that puts a negative face on Christianity? As believers, shouldn't we dwell on the positive, on the edifying things that God is doing among and through His people?

Yes, but the questions assume that nothing edifying is taking place, when in many cases that's exactly what is happening: God is doing His marvelous work in someone's life, even apart from the church —believe it or not. I don't want to be accused of implying that believers don't need churches. They certainly do. And in fact, none of the people with whom I spoke wanted to do away with the church or parachurch. But like most of us, they found themselves in the gap between the ideals of the New Testament and the realities of actual groups of Christians. After languishing for a while where they were, they chose to get out and find a better way. Less than ideal? You bet.

As for edification, I believe their stories stand to help the body far more than hinder it. After all, God always wants us to deal with reality. He tells us to consider "whatever is true."[7] Truth may be positive or negative, we may like it or dislike it, but whatever the case we need to face it squarely. Otherwise we walk in darkness, as unwise people.

So if many of those who traditionally have been among the churches' most loyal members are now turning elsewhere to meet their spiritual needs, that ought to give all believers pause for reflection. That's a truth that we dare not ignore or deny.

Perhaps I can illustrate why by changing my metaphor of the church from a building to a business (again, not the best thing to do; the church is not a business, and evangelism is more than marketing; nevertheless, churches ignore the principles of business and marketing to their peril).

It is not enough for the church to attract new "customers." It must also hold onto the ones it has. Why? Because that's the *purpose* of the church—*people development.*[8] The church exists "to prepare God's people for works of service, so that the body of Christ may be built up until we all reach unity in the faith and in the knowledge of the Son of God and become mature, attaining to the whole measure of the fullness of Christ.

In other words, attracting new customers (outreach and evangelism) is vital, but to use sales guru Carl Sewell's term, the church is also in business to *cultivate customers for life* (discipleship and spiritual maturity). The loss of even one previously satisfied customer is worth examining, because it suggests a breakdown somewhere, a disappointment of expectations. Such an examination, painful as it may be, might hold crucial clues as to how the church can improve its core business of bringing every believer to maturity in Christ.[9]

But let's return from analogy to reality. The church is neither a building nor a business, but a *body*—the body of Christ. We are members one of another. The tragedy is that in most cases when people put distance between themselves and the body, no one bothers to find out why. Dr. John Savage of L.E.A.D. Consultants has studied the problem of "dropouts" and advised churches in this area for more than seventeen years. In 1973 he studied the dropout patterns of four congregations, each with between 400 and 800 members.

Dr. Savage found an interesting phenomenon. After someone decides to stop attending church, she typically waits for about six to eight weeks to see if anyone will come visit her to find out why she has left. She stays in a sort of "holding pattern," not reinvesting time or energy in other areas but waiting to see how her former church will respond. If no one contacts her, she eventually crosses off her old church and looks for other options.

What stunned me in Dr. Savage's research was the finding that *100 percent* of the inactive members he interviewed said that no one had ever come to visit them![10] They had just been ignored and even viewed by some with the attitude "Good riddance!" One person told him, "I have not been active in my church for ten years, and no one has ever asked me why."[11]

That statement stops me in my tracks. We have churches and denominations today literally doing *whatever it takes* to attract "unchurched" people to the front door of the faith. Meanwhile, people who have been in the program for years can slip out the back for a variety of reasons and go six or eight weeks—or even ten years—without so much as a phone call or a visit. Surely, then, a book like this one, that gives voice to a few of those "back-door believers," is not uncalled for.

No, if the church is a body, then we owe it to the disillusioned member—we *owe* it to him or her—to listen. To really *listen*. Scripture exhorts us to "mourn with those who mourn,"[12] and many of those who leave churches feel a sense of mourning. Disillusionment involves a grief process, a struggle with feelings of loss. So if we ignore or abandon someone in that condition, we violate the explicit teaching of the New Testament.

Yet people who leave churches are rarely listened to. Instead they are preached at and, frequently, judged. Not that there are many resources that deal with these issues. But of the few that do, many seem to blame the person for whatever problems exist: "If only *you* would be more forgiving." "If only *you* would adopt a different perspective." "If only *you* would be more submissive." "If only *you* would quit your belly-aching."

"If only . . . " Messages like these do little to fulfill the church's mission to "build people up" in the faith. Instead, since they are at heart messages of condemnation rather than compassion, and of legalism rather than grace, they tear people down and eventually drive them away. Not all churches communicate that. And not all Christians are disillusioned. But many believers choose to go it alone rather than subject themselves to a community of Pharisees.

You may wonder how I came to write this book. I'm not an ordained minister. I don't lead a parachurch organization. I'm not lobbying for a cause or raising money or starting some sort of "recovery" outreach to ex-Christians. Nor do I have a personal ax to grind. The short answer, and perhaps the best, is that the issue of "what it means today to be spiritual" is one that I've been personally involved with all my life.

At four-and-a-half I prayed a prayer to Jesus for salvation. I knew exactly what I was doing—with a four-year-old's faith, to be sure, and a four-year-old's understanding. But the gospel as it was explained to me made sense, and I took it. I'm convinced that my conversion was genuine, as evidenced by the fact that my childlike faith took root and flourished and, along with mind and body, grew into adult form.

Have I ever thought seriously of turning away from the faith? I certainly have. Yet here I am. However, in the past several years, for whatever reason, I've heard person after person express private doubts about his own spirituality. Not doubts about the basic truths of the faith—the deity of Christ, the resurrection, the existence of God, and so on—but *doubts about the various programs put forth for living out that gospel* in this crazy world of ours. Christianity is true; they remain convinced of that. But how does one make it work?

I'd been clipping articles and jotting down thoughts on these matters for a number of years when I was asked whether I'd consider writing a book of interviews with "disillusioned Christians." Things took off from there.

I had no trouble finding people to interview. Virtually everyone to whom I mentioned the project knew immediately what I was talking about, and easily half of them said either, "Boy, you should interview me!" or else, "I know just the person you should talk to!" I thought that was pretty significant. It suggested that I was dealing with something that lies close to the surface, an experience that must be fairly common.

I approached this issue more from a journalist's perspective than a sociologist's. I have not worked with a scientific sample or a demographic cross-section of the church, so my findings and conclusions ought not to be construed as definitive. But then, my purpose is not to provide the last word on this subject. I'm satisfied to provide any word on it—that is, to create a vehicle for discussion, reaction, and, hopefully, insight.

I should warn any readers who have picked up this book in hopes of finding juicy tidbits of gossip that you will be disappointed. This is not an exposé. There's a time, a place, and a way to bring sin and evil to light, but that is not my purpose here.

Nor was it the motive of the people who were courageous enough to sit down with a total stranger and talk about one of the most personal things one can talk about—their relationship with God. Each one agreed to an interview on the condition that I would protect his or her identity and privacy and the privacy of those around him or her.

Nevertheless, I will not be surprised if readers approach me insisting that I have interviewed one of their acquaintances. I almost anticipate it, because, as I've suggested, virtually every believer either has or knows someone who has a story like one of my interviewees. Look carefully and you may find that disillusioned Christians are among your friends, your neighbors, your coworkers, your fellow churchgoers—even your own family. Perhaps that even describes you.

You can find out by reading the next section, which contains about two dozen "exit interviews" with people who have left the church. Following that I have added a handful of interpretive chapters that look at these conversations in light of the context in which the church finds itself today. I've also included a chapter on what I think these stories are saying to churches and church leaders. And finally I've offered a word to anyone who identifies with the people in this book.

The thing to keep in mind is that every life is a story. "If you are not looking at life poetically and dramatically, then you are not looking at it properly. And this, it seems to me, is also the way Christianity instructs us to look at life. After all, Christianity has come to us as a story, not as a theory or a philosophy or a science. . . . Despite the spirit of the age, we feel there must be a point to our lives. One of the great services which a story may render then is to help us see what that point may be. Stories may help us to recognize a moral or spiritual meaning in a personal situation that might otherwise seem chaotic or pointless."[13]

See if that is not the case with the revealing stories that follow of everyday people who have decided to leave the church.

NOTES

1. Why the metaphor of being "born again" should become the normative term for conversion is odd. A friend of mine points out that Jesus told only one man, an aristocratic Jewish leader, that he needed to be "born again" (John 3:3,5,7). By contrast, the gospels record more than thirty occasions when He told people, "Follow me." Maybe we should adopt that as the term of conversion. That would at least reflect the true nature of the Christian life for what it is—discipleship as well as salvation.

2. See Russell Chandler, *Racing Toward 2001: The Forces Shaping America's Religious Future* (Grand Rapids: Zondervan, 1992), 156.

3. Associated Press, "Faith in God Valued Highly, Poll Finds," *Dallas Morning News* (April 4, 1991): 4A. I had reasons to dispute the findings of this poll—and did so. See William D. Hendricks, "What's Wrong with This Picture?" *Wall Street Journal* (August 1, 1991): A12; or *Christianity Today* (November 25, 1991): 12.

4. "Going to church" means many things to many people, but I think most would agree that ideally it describes Christians gathering together to share life in Christ in the various ways mentioned—worship, instruction, fellowship, service, community, accountability, etc. See chapter 20 for more on my view of the church.

5. Religious News Service, "Moyers says TV must make viewers 'philosophers at large,'" *Dallas Morning News* (April 28, 1990): 46A.

6. William Kirk Kilpatrick, "Why Secular Psychology Is Not Enough," Hillsdale College *Imprimis*, vol. 15, no. 4, (April 1986): 2. Dr. Kilpatrick is professor of educational psychology at Boston College. This paper, presented at a seminar at Hillsdale College, presents the most articulate and insightful discussion of personhood and personality that I've ever come across. Interested readers may obtain a copy by contacting *Imprimis*, Hillsdale College, Hillsdale, Michigan, 49242.

7. Philippians 4:8.

8. Ephesians 4:12–13.

9. To my mind, Ephesians 4 is the P & L (profit and loss) statement by which God will evaluate the work of apostles, prophets, evangelists, and pastor-teachers (mentioned in verse 11). So if I'm one of those leaders, it behooves me to be as effective as I can be in helping people toward spiritual maturity. One way to do that is to listen carefully to those who, for a variety of reasons, have grown dissatisfied with the means of growth that I *thought* would be so helpful, but apparently were not.

   One thing's for sure: it makes no sense to write off such people as "spiritual losers." In the business world, one would soon be out of business with such an attitude. As Peter Drucker says, "Management has to ask which of the customer's wants are not adequately satisfied by the products or services offered him today. The ability to ask this question and to answer it correctly usually makes the difference between a growth company and one that depends for its development on the rising tide of the economy or of the industry. But whoever contents himself to rise with the tide will also fall with it" (*Management*, 91).

Churchgoing in America is to some extent on the rise—for now. But when the tide falls . . . ?

By the way, attracting new customers and holding on to old ones are very different tasks (see p. 276).

10. John S. Savage, *The Apathetic and Bored Church Member: Psychological and Theological Implications* (Reynoldsburg, Ohio: L.E.A.D. Consultants, 1976), 60–61. Readers can contact Dr. Savage at L.E.A.D. Consultants, Inc., P.O. Box 664, Reynoldsburg, OH 43068.

11. Ibid., 79.

12. Romans 12:15.

13. Kilpatrick, "Why Secular Psychology Is Not Enough," 4.

2

Diana

Vocatus adque, non vocatus, Deus aderit.
[Called or not called, God will be present.]
Delphic Oracle[1]

T he late Ray Stedman is reported to have said that when you boil down the Christian life, one virtue proves decisive in whether one ever arrives at spiritual maturity: perseverance. The New Testament lends support to that idea. "Let us not become weary in doing good," Paul told a group of Christians ready to give up the faith, and then added the promise (along with a *condition*), "for at the proper time we will reap a harvest *if we do not give up.*"[2]

Persistence counts for a lot. But that being the case, the strong-willed person enjoys a definite advantage. In times of spiritual drought, when faith falters and sometimes fails, she somehow keeps going, though nourished only by a reservoir of resolve.

However, stubbornness is as much a liability as an asset. It keeps one on the journey; it also causes one to fight every step of the way.

For Diana, the struggle—and the journey—began in early childhood. Alas for her conservative Presbyterian parents, predestination rewarded their faith with a stouthearted contrarian who challenged every attempt at limits and control.

"As a child I was always pretty rebellious," Diana recalled. "I did not like any kind of discipline. I would fight my parents. They had to chase me to spank me, and even then I wouldn't move my hands away from my bottom. I was so stubborn—a really strong-willed child."

When she was seven, her parents sent their little felon to a church camp where, from the sounds of it, she did not exactly fit with the program. "I didn't want to be there. Several things happened to make me feel kind of uncomfortable and unsettled, and I didn't feel good about my counselor." Nonetheless, "I really listened to what she was saying about asking Jesus into your heart."

I asked Diana what it was in the gospel that made her think, "Hey, I need to pay attention to this and do something"?

"It could have been fear that if I didn't ask Him into my heart, I was going to hell." She paused, weighing the incident in retrospect. "I'm sure that was there, and I don't appreciate that. I don't feel that needs to be the main thing you hear when you hear the gospel."

So did she respond out of fear? Not totally. "There was probably something tender about the way I felt, too, in spite of the way the message was delivered. The Spirit of Christ was actually there. Fortunately, God's bigger than how we deliver the message."

Even so, Diana was not about to give her counselor any satisfaction. Her decision was made in secret, "while I was in my little bunk bed and the counselor was talking. But I didn't let her know about it. I remember crying and I went to sleep."

Was it a genuine conversion? "My mom said she began to notice a real difference in me, independent of realizing I had done this. We had a Sunday school teacher that began talking about the old self and new self, and my mom said that I really seemed to respond to that. It began making a difference in my behavior."

In other words, she learned to please her parents. Later in high school, that would include accompanying them to a popular seminar aimed at teens. "I probably wasn't able to say it at the time, but I hated going. I thought it was ridiculous. I just sat there bored out of my mind. And I disagreed with what was being said. There was so much about authority in it, and I had always been against that anyway."

Her feelings were no different about church. "I found it interesting that people could repeat the same things over and over again with such an absence of meaning and penetration from reality—even within the church. Everyone seemed to be just kind of going along dead, and not alive—not what I would expect for people filled with the Spirit or moving in the direction of the Spirit. None of that seemed to be happening. Just words and . . . phraseology . . . spiritual jargon that had no correspondence to reality. I was mad about it!"

Yet, although she scorned empty religion, she also knew that she herself was no model of spirituality. "I was living a life of duplicity," she admitted to me, and I could tell that in her mind she was reviewing a catalog of adolescent sins. "I had a couple of years there where I was very curious about drinking. I definitely had scruples and was trying to be upstanding in some ways. But I was really curious about marijuana and things like that, all the while trying to maintain a promising image on the outside to my teachers and parents."

At this point I almost expected a tale of some crisis—a drug bust, an overdose, a car accident—that had served as a turning point in Diana's spiritual journey. And, in fact, she did make what she described as a "rededication" of her life to God during her senior year in high school. But ironically, the catalyst for change turned out to be none other than several significant authority figures, beginning with her pastor.

"We got a new pastor when I was a junior who began to communicate to me a little more. He was very articulate and he seemed to have thought out what he was saying more than other people I had heard speak.

"Also about that time I had a Sunday school teacher who became real interested in my spiritual growth. He was about six years older, a real seeker and a strong spiritual leader in our church. He told me later that he began praying for me when I was a junior because he could tell that I was rebellious in my spirit and really not on track spiritually."

Then one day, "My tennis coach came up to me and said, 'I've heard some talk that some really good kids are getting mixed up in the wrong things, and your name came up. I don't want to hear this anymore.' Tennis was a big deal to me. We had a really good team and I had aspirations to do something with my life.

"I began seeing that the track I was on—of experimenting with drinking and drugs—that that's really not the way I wanted to go. People were getting caught up in it, and their futures were going to be really affected.

"The culminating factor was that about that time my parents caught on to the fact that I was not their sweet daughter. I was doing some things that they would never have thought, and that really hurt them. We had a long talk and it really affected me. I thought, 'This is not something that I want.'

"I remember praying for a long time, 'I want to turn this around. I don't know what it means really to be a Christian, but I'd like to commit myself to finding out.' So I started on a search."

The theme of searching was one I was to run into often in listening to my interviewees, and it calls into question a common view of salvation which holds that conversion is the end of the journey. An oft-heard prayer for the unsaved implies as much: "Let them find no rest until they find their rest in Thee."

But Diana's experience, and that of many others, suggests that true spirituality may be anything but peaceful, and that conversion is not the end of the search but merely the entrance onto the right road. The journey goes on. At least that was the view set forth in *Pilgrim's Progress,* which once inspired generations of Christians in the spiritual path.

Diana's pilgrimage to find out "what it means really to be a Christian" got off to a rough start. The fall semester found her at a fiercely competitive college that managed to "knock her socks off at first." A driven and successful student from a small-town high school where she had always made A's, she now found herself up against equally if not more talented kids. "I ended up flailing a little bit there. That first semester was really hard for me, very disillusioning."

Part of the struggle was to find an acceptable peer group. The hall in her freshman dorm was divided between what she described as "really wild girls" at one end and a group of "geek-type" Christian girls at the other—nice girls, but not a lot of fun, "not cool at all." "So I really struggled, because here were the Christian girls and here were the people that I really hung out with, and I had made that switch over to what I thought I wanted to base my life on."

For two years she waffled back and forth. But during her junior year, friends recruited her to work at a summer camp. In light of where she started out in the faith, I thought it ironic that she would end up on the staff of a Christian camp. Once again, that environment was to play an important role in her spiritual search.

"I had a lot of positive feedback from what I did at camp. I did a lot of music there and played a lot of stuff. It really fed my sense of myself and who I was."

It was feeding of a kind she desperately needed. "My little self was emerging. I had a real strong sense of myself in high school, but I really became uneasy about who I was and where my place was going to be those first two years in college. I finally built it back a little bit as I got older, especially with the positive experiences at camp. I liked to play sports there and played well. I taught sports and music, which were what I used to draw people in."

She also attracted people for another reason. "I had a lot of abilities to be a spiritual leader, someone who people would want to talk to about their questions about God and stuff. I liked that. I liked being known as someone that people would say, 'Hey, she'd be good to talk to; she prays a lot.'"

But although Diana may have had answers for others, she had nothing but questions herself, especially as she approached graduation. "All the time, in college and even after college—and I'm *still* plagued with it and dealing with it—the question was what my direction was and how I was going to use what I love doing, vocationally. I graduated and didn't know what I was going to do."

After working at the camp in the summer following graduation, she took a position at a nearby private secondary school in the fall. Then, to her delight, she learned that the camp needed someone to do public relations. Her degree was in communications, so she immediately signed up. "Nothing sounded better to me than a year where I had a job that I could do and also have some real, still quiet to think about what I wanted to do with my life."

The setting was ideal. "I lived in a log cabin by myself on a lake in the mountains. It was very conducive to reflection. I was ready for some solitude. I was really burned out—or I don't know if burned out is the word. But it slowly began dawning on me that the easy prescriptions I had been saying from the Bible were not really working for me.

"I questioned whether what I had been taught—and what I was teaching—penetrated as deeply as I was living, things that I was coming up against in my own mind. I began to rebel against this 'ten steps to Christian maturity,' going from one to ten and then you're a mature Christian. There was a lot more to it. There was more to spirituality than pat answers."

While she explored the inner terrain of her spirit, Diana also explored the mountains around her. She bought a Suzuki dirt bike and, after the autumn leaves fell, toured the many logging trails that couldn't be seen in the summer.

"That was one of my best years," she told me wistfully. "Very peaceful and lots of solitude." But her mountain retreat couldn't last forever. She had to decide on her next step. As in her senior year of high school, she knew the kind of life she wanted to avoid; but what should she pursue?

Like many people who lack clear direction, she decided to go back to school. Two factors led her to seminary. One was a sense that she wanted to go into counseling; two counselors she knew had gone to seminary before training in psychology.

The other was a conviction that before she could help others, she needed to "nail things down" for herself. She'd grown up hearing Christian jargon; in seminary she would have a chance to find out what the jargon was all about. In addition to an in-depth study of theology, she expected to learn how the Christian life works.

"*How* does one do this? *How* does Christ save us? *How* does spirituality work? I wanted to find these things out because it wasn't happening for me. I was looking for meaning and a depth of experience. I'd heard these wonderful things, but I, along with a few other people I knew, was not experiencing it. I wanted to know what makes this *work*?"

The questions seemed reasonable enough. Some might wonder whether seminary is the best place to go to answer them. But then, if one can't find out how the Christian life works at a seminary, that would seem to raise questions about the purpose of a seminary education.

To be fair, though, while Diana was asking fundamental questions about her faith, she was also asking fundamental questions about herself: Who was Diana? Who was this person God had created? How was she going to relate to Him? She looked for answers in the places that everyone said they ought to be found—the home and the church, including its various expressions such as seminars, camps, and now seminary. Yet the answer to those questions eluded her.

"In fact, it was even more elusive when I got to seminary," she explained. "I seemed heretical there. Profs would grade my papers and say, 'How did you sign the doctrinal statement?' 'Why are you here?' And I would write on my papers, 'Who's asking this question?' 'Why are we even spending any time on this?' In one classroom it was like a fight. Toward the end I always had my hand up, saying, 'Wait a minute here!' I don't know, they have a right to think what they think. I was the one who was out of place there, probably. But I felt it was good to challenge."

In what way? What sorts of questions was she fighting over?

"Some of them were really theological questions, like inerrancy. Because I've struggled with the issue of authority, of course inerrancy would be something I would bristle at. To me, it seems to be a manmade word that has to do with power. Whoever can gather the most degrees and be the most startling about what they can say, they hold the power. And it just so happens that women can't do this. So men have a lot of power. Boy, I have lots of counterarguments, but those are important questions to me about how I live my life and who I allow to say what I can and can't do in my life.

"Or someone saying the Bible is objective truth. I'm not so sure. It really takes a step of faith to believe the Scriptures are *objective* truth. You can't prove that they are; you believe that they are. And then there are a number of different ways of believing *how* they are true. Karl Barth had an interesting way of talking about that. So did Schleiermacher.[3] Why don't we hear about these ways that these very articulate men were trying to find the truth themselves? They had some really interesting ways of talking about how the Bible is true.

"There are other questions about spirituality and how God brings you along and nurtures you. There is theology proper and then there's the relational aspect of God meeting you."

I agreed that these were honest questions. But what was deficient in the answers she was given?

"They weren't well thought out—and they weren't well *felt* out. I remember a woman from England who didn't care either way for this issue of what women can or can't do in the church. That wasn't an issue for her. But she began getting really angry in one class we both had because, as she said, 'the image of God was being abused in her soul.' I thought that was so articulate, because God made male and female, and the professor was so restrictive with the female role that it tightened my chest almost." At this point Diana looked at me and smiled, saying, "Being a man, I don't know that you'll ever quite know how that feels."

Probably not. But I liked what she said about answers not being "felt out" as well as thought out. The implications of truth and our response to truth are as much an emotional issue as an intellectual one. Even if the intellectual side of an answer is sound, that does not go far enough because truth without love is dogma and lacks humanity.

Much of Diana's frustration during this period, both at seminary and at most of the churches she tried, was that she wasn't feeling respected as a woman and as a person. She didn't feel that her emotions mattered, that her doubts mattered, or that any alternative points of view might be considered as having anything to offer. Things were just a little bit too neatly buttoned down to be realistic.

I wanted to know more about her participation in church. For whatever reason, seminary was not providing the spiritual encouragement or community that she needed. Why didn't she seek out a church to feed and nurture her soul?

Apparently she tried. For a while she attended a Presbyterian church with a large singles ministry, but ended up resenting that way of grouping the congregation. "I hated being herded along like I was some kind of . . . I don't have any needs that anybody else doesn't have. I mean I do, but I like married people as well as singles. I don't have to be herded along with other singles."

She also disliked the homogeneity of the upper-middle-class congregation. There were too many "beautiful people" there for her taste.

So she switched to a small Methodist church with a more diverse group of families, ethnic minorities, elderly, hurting people, and "not a big singles group." "It took some getting used to, the kinds of people that would come in there," but it turned out be "one of the neatest churches I've seen."

The congregation was led by two pastors, a man and a woman. "I just loved them. They were probably more liberal on some issues than I would have been. But he gave a Mother's Day sermon that included every possible scenario that a woman could find herself in: some women might have a hard time with their mothers, some women might wish they were mothers and were not, some might be mothers and wish they were not, some might have their mothers, some might not. The sensitivity! When he talked about women, I was bathed in his intuitiveness and sensitivity toward where people actually were in their lives."

It would seem that Diana had at last found a workable situation. But the pastor moved to another Methodist church. Moreover, she found it difficult to get past the issues of education and class. "The people there weren't very beautiful, but they also weren't very sophisticated. I found myself wanting more sophistication, because I can be that way. I want this and the other, too. I want to grapple with the deep issues of humanity, but I also want intellectual stimulation. It's hard to find both. If you find a really intellectually stimulating church, everyone's got on a pinpoint cotton shirt!" I wondered, could Diana envision *any* kind of church that would meet the needs she had and continues to have? Or is it even possible?

"I remember reading about Elizabeth O'Connor's church in Washington, D.C. called Church of the Saviour. It was so refreshing because it wasn't perfect. People were bumping into their humanity all over the place, trying to learn how to serve the community. To me, it was such a beautiful picture because it affirmed that we have a shadow; a dark, passionate, difficult side to deal with in our humanity. From what I've seen in the church, we never let that out of the bag. By prescribing how we're to behave and what's the right thing to do, we never grapple in the community with our full selves. So we remain cut off from the humanity that's really all around us.

"Mainly, I guess, I want to have a church where people are more real. Of course, it's really kind of scary when people start talking about who they really are in a group. I'm uncomfortable when people do that. But I think if you could draw appropriate boundaries, that if the church were more real and addressed people in a more real way, then that's the kind of church I'd like to be involved in."

It was interesting that one place Diana found that level of authenticity was at a Unitarian church she briefly visited. "I encountered a lot of anger and frustration at the Unitarian church, a lot of people who were so angry at the traditional church. I found people from all walks saying, 'These are the real questions I'm living. These are the struggles, and I can't find any other place to go that I want to go to church.'

"Bill, in the Unitarian Church you'd find a lot of people for your book. There are people there who are dealing openly with homosexuality, dealing openly with having been told when they were little that they were going to hell if they didn't ask Jesus into their heart, or that only Catholics were going to heaven, dealing openly with the problems that face the community."

It was a troubling statement. Where do people go when they walk out the back door of the church? Here was at least one answer, along with some insight into why. Diana herself was troubled by it all. "Is there a way to bring more fabric of the world into the church?" she wondered. The question reminded me of something I once heard about how Christians relate to the culture: at first Christ needs to save us out of the world, but eventually, He needs to save us back into it. Otherwise we lose touch with reality.

By this point in her life, Diana was thoroughly disillusioned. Nevertheless, the camp still wanted her. "The director, who was very dogmatic, very stern, said, 'God will use you here. You've got a year of seminary under your belt. Just be an instrument.' And I just wanted to say, 'Uh-uh. In fact, I don't even know what I think is true anymore!' But I couldn't get her to hear me. She had no idea how unfit I was to be some sort of spiritual guidance counselor for anyone at that point. She was trying to put me in charge because I had been there six summers before, and now I had a year of seminary; now I should even be more ready to share these 'pearls of wisdom' with the counselors on the staff."

For twenty years Diana had been in the faith. For ten years she had been on a search to find out "what it really meant" to be a Christian. Yet now she had more questions than ever—and more frustration. She was angry at a system that seemed to offer so much, but also seemed so elusive in its experience.

Seminary had been a major disappointment. She had enrolled in order to settle basic issues of the faith. Now she decided on a different strategy: to settle basic issues about herself. She sought the help of a psychotherapist.

It was a choice that many of those who leave churches end up making (as well as many who stay in churches). Carl Jung described the situation like this: People who seek insight and self-knowledge start out in a valley, as it were, between two mountains. The one mountain is religion. It offers truth that many find to be the light that reveals their soul.

However, not everyone has that experience. Some do not look for it, and others do not want it. But some, who both seek it and want it, nevertheless fail to find it. They climb and climb the peaks of religion, but they never come to the understanding of themselves that set them on their journey in the first place. So eventually they turn and cross the valley to try the other mountain—the ascent of therapy.[4]

This was Diana's way. I did not press her for the details of the process, as that had little to do with the purpose of our conversation. But I was curious to know the effect of therapy on her spiritual life. "Oh, it has profoundly affected it," she said with firm conviction. For one thing, she felt it had helped her realize how she had used God as a defense against discovering who she really is.

"My therapist has come alongside me as I've stripped away all the parts of me that wanted to be a Christian because maybe it was a good way to fit in, because I was respected, because it gave me a place, a sense of belonging, a community. It gave me all these things I could surround myself with and feel comfortable in. I would be insulated with all that. That was insulation to having just the experience of God Himself."

Earlier, Diana had alluded to Elizabeth O'Connor's *Journey Inward, Journey Outward*. "Therapy has been a sanctuary for me where I could go inward, which was where I needed to go, and see all about my particular soul apart from all the prescribed ways of how it should be. I was finding myself.

"Some people are really critical of that, but I'm so pleased to have had the opportunity of seeing what's there and how God meets with that, of finding the stillness in the very still, still place that I've been able to go to, of self-knowledge—and then offer that to God and let Him transform that so that I'm more effective when I go back out into the world. A lot had to happen *inside* me for me to be truly effective on the *outside* with whatever it is I'm going to do vocationally."

She sounded very convincing. But I knew that it was not a path that everyone would choose. Moreover, I couldn't imagine that she had many people walking along beside her. Indeed, some would probably write her off as a lost cause. "Things have been tough. I've had some people beside me, but not a lot. I've been very sad and very alone and sacrificed a lot of money when I did not have it. I've learned a whole lot about loneliness and aloneness, and solitude as opposed to loneliness.

"Some people don't ever feel these ways; they don't have a need to. They don't feel the unrest and are just there. OK. And then there are people who have a lot of unrest and they just give up and say, 'This isn't for me.' Or they just sit in quiet desperation in their churches, not having any vital aspect of the actual power of God. I never want to become a snob about how far I'm going with my therapy, because I think it's the grace of God that I've been helped and moved along and cared for. But it has been a long haul."

Her talk of the grace of God had a suspicious feel of jargon. But later she said something that showed she had indeed tasted of that grace. "The ironic thing is that the grief and aching and meeting yourself stark naked, with nothing to hold onto and no props, no church, no community—in my case no vocation—to make you look like you're anything neat, not a thing, to be really, literally, kind of stripped naked— ironically, that's the point out of which has grown an incredible sense of God's reality, His presence, His love. Suffering breaks the lives of believers, the dark and the light, the crucifixion, understanding the profundity of the crucifixion in the light of the struggle, of reaching down into the depths—"

Suddenly she stopped and remarked, "Bill, I don't know you that well, and I've been pretty vulnerable here."

Pretty vulnerable indeed! Yet I felt certain that I was only scratching the surface of what God had been doing in her life. It was a privilege to have seen a glimpse of that personal, private "sanctuary" she had described, that inward journey in which she had started to discover herself and, through that, rediscover God.

One question lingered, however. What would she do with the church? Did she feel much motivation to start attending and participating again? "I do. I really do," she affirmed, "—eventually. I feel that more and more." But when she finally reconnects with a body of believers, she anticipates more than just sitting through a worship service. "To me, in the church you enter a group of people with messy lives, and not everything is just fine. Not every sermon is going to be great, and the choir's not always going to sing in tune. You can't have everything at your ideal church, and I recognize that. But I feel like I am a part of the church and that it is an integral part of the Christian life to meet regularly with a group of people."

But right now? "Right now my life, my time is so important to me. I'd rather sit with a book or sit quietly in my home instead of getting all dressed up and spending two hours where I'm not really fed. I don't feel a need right now. I did for a long time and was real uneasy about not going to church because I felt I needed to be giving of myself—and receiving—there. Finally, I just said, 'No, that's OK. Right now I'm not going to church.'

"Sunday mornings are what I have to meditate and pray and read. In the wintertime I might stay in my room, and in the spring I go outside to a place where hardly anyone ever comes by and have a time out there. I felt that was the most wonderful sanctuary I could be in. I'm actually fed by that time. So I've given myself permission not to go to church for a while until I feel like it is time to enter back in. I feel that coming on. It's probably not too far away."

Always one to play devil's advocate, I pointed out that some people would say, "Diana, you're never going to find the perfect church, but you need to be somewhere." That woke up the fighter in her.

"Why do they think they know what anyone needs? How do they know? How can you presume what is going on in the very heart or soul of an individual? *I* know. *I'm* responsible. I may find when I get up there that God would have preferred me to be in church right now, and I'll stand corrected. But He's the only one that's going to correct me. I've learned to trust my sense that it may not be the case that someone needs to be in a church. That may not be where they 'need' to be. I think I'll run the risk of trying it."

I came away from my conversation with Diana with a host of impressions. One that stood out was: I was glad I was not her pastor. She could not be the easiest person to have in one's congregation.

Yet why is that? Is there some flaw in Diana and people like her that makes them unfit for the body of Christ? Some would say yes: they are just too stubborn, too lacking in submission. But if that is true, then aren't we conceding that Christianity is a religion for weak-willed, compliant personalities? That seems unsatisfactory to me.

The fact is, Diana and people like her challenge our understanding of spiritual authority: Who is in charge? Where is the power? Who determines God's will? Who interprets Scripture? Who speaks for God? Who decides what is important?

Only decades ago, answers to these questions were not only well known but faithfully observed. Today, people resist virtually every claim to authority—not so much to be stubborn but to be safe.

If I were a pastor, which would I rather have in my congregation: the early Diana who, as she put it, was "living a life of duplicity," following a script, doing all the right things yet hiding her real self from others; or the "new" Diana, who seems to wrestle with God until one or the other prevails? It would be a tough call. But my answer would say a lot about my perception of spiritual authority. It would also tell me what sort of people I could expect to find in my church.

NOTES

1. According to Leonard Sweet (*Quantum Spirituality: A Postmodern Apologetic*, Whale-prints, 1991, 230), the president of United Theological Seminary in Dayton, Ohio, psychologist Carl Jung had this motto carved over the doorway of his villa in Küsnacht, Switzerland. "In a letter dated 19 November 1960, Jung explained why this inscription meant so much to him, both personally and professionally, that he embossed it on his bookplate and engraved it over his doorway (it was also etched into the family tombstone):

   > I have put the inscription there to remind my neighbors and myself: *Timor dei initium sapientiae* [The fear of the Lord is the beginning of wisdom]. Here another not less important road begins, not the approach to 'Christianity,' but to God himself and this seems to be the ultimate question."

2. Galatians 6:9 (italics added).

3. German theologian and philosopher Friedrich Schleiermacher (1768–1834) rejected the idea of Christian doctrine as a revealed, objective, absolute system communicated by God to humanity through His chosen instruments. Rather, he believed that God's revelation is a more subjective expression of His consciousness onto the self-consciousness of an individual.

   Swiss theologian Karl Barth (1886–1968) believed God to be utterly transcendent or "wholly other." He remains unknown unless and until He reveals Himself. Thus the Bible is but a witness to revelation, not a revelation itself. It remains the word of man until one experiences its message; then it becomes the Word of God.

4. Many Christians will be quick to point out that psychology and religion are not to be treated as equivalent. I would agree. They are not the same. However, neither are they necessarily incompatible. Being neither a theologian nor a psychologist, I refrain from saying precisely where the two overlap. But I would point out that Diana used psychotherapy as a means to gain insight into her emotional life, not as a means of knowing God. Yet ironically, by coming to know her inner life, she was better able to respond to God.

3

Elaine

So send I you to labor unrewarded,
To serve unpaid, unloved, unsought, unknown,
To bear rebuke, to suffer scorn and scoffing,
So send I you, to toil for Me alone.
                                    E. Margaret Clarkson[1]

Elaine had three desires: "To get married and have children, to be a missionary in China, and to be a singer," she announced before I had asked her a single question. Then she added, "I got two out of the three—which ain't bad!"

Not bad at all, I thought. Some people want but one of those three, yet they never even get that one. Of the three, "missionary in China" sounded like the most intriguing request. It turned out to be the earliest.

"I always wanted to be a missionary in China, ever since I heard a missionary from China at my church. I was about four years old. I can remember I was sitting in the front pew when she talked about China. And she said something like, 'Everybody who wants to dedicate themselves to be missionaries in China, come up to the platform.' I was the first one up there. Everybody thought that was cute, because I was only four. So they didn't make much of it, but I was serious."

Serious and sincere—but not quite ready for the mission field. First Elaine needed to cultivate a faith of her own. "I grew up at our family's church. I mean, my family went there since before I was born. And I think at an early age you become kind of sucked into whatever is going on. Not that it was bad. It was good, but I never became a real Christian until I was in high school."

I asked her how that came about. "I was dating this jerk," she began (which reminded me that God works in all kinds of ways). "I had just graduated from high school, and this fellow broke up with me. We were supposed to get married. He just dropped me, and it was devastating, I'll tell you. I went through this period where I didn't eat. I was nothing but skin and bones. And my roommate was a nurse, and she had these pills that I would take to help me sleep. I was a wreck, really. I never slept. I mean I would feign sleep and then get up and walk around the apartment.

"And I was walking around the apartment one night. I was just sitting there—and I really can't explain it to people—but it was like sitting there having a conversation with someone else. I was talking with God. It was like He was right there.

"I was real angry. I was just real angry about everything that had happened. And finally I said, 'I can't do this anymore. I just can't do any of this anymore, and I just really need some peace.' That's what I wanted—peace. I said, 'God, I don't know if You're real. I don't know if You're true. I don't know if You'll take care of me. But if You will and You are, then You better do something fast, because otherwise I'm not going to be here.' That's how bad I was.

"I can remember sitting there, and the room was dark, really dark. And it was just like a light came on. Really! I never felt so peaceful in my whole life. I went to bed and went to sleep, and that was the first sleep that I had gotten in months. I laid down in the bed and I was asleep.

"Got up the next day—felt like I had slept for a year! I was at work by nine o'clock. I was fresh as a daisy. Really! I mean, just a whole new attitude. And it was not something that I could conjure up. I mean, I told God, 'If you're gonna have anybody that fights You, it's gonna be me!' So I said, 'You'd better be very, very strong and do something that I can see—something tangible, just for me.' And I think that was it. I mean, it was like night and day."

It was interesting to me that Elaine had gotten as old as she had without anyone from her church checking on her spiritual condition. Apparently her pastors, teachers, and friends just assumed that she was a believer. In fact, the church had enlisted her in a number of leadership positions, yet no one had ever talked in depth with her about her relationship with God.

So it came as a "shock," as she put it, to her church family when, shortly after her conversion, she decided to join the summer staff of a youth ministry in another part of the country. They were glad that she was going to be involved in a Christian ministry, but they were sad to be losing such a dedicated worker in the congregation.

"There were about thirty-five people at the airport when I left," she told me. "They didn't think I'd go! But I knew. I knew that I had to go. There was no doubt in my mind. None."

As it turned out, that send-off was to be the start of Elaine's career as a missionary. During the summer, she began praying about joining a particular mission organization. "Everything started saying yes, yes, yes. But the biggest hurdle was the money part. I had to raise my own financial support. And I thought, there's no way I can do this. I cannot get up and speak. I can't ask people for money. I can't do anything.

"And then it was just like that night in my living room. I had had a very difficult day. And I can remember walking, and at the end it was a sense like, 'You're going to join that mission, and the money is the least of your worries.' So then I wasn't worried about it. And whenever I made a decision after that, there was always a real peace. Once it was made, that was it. I had no qualms, no misgivings, nothing. It was just go ahead and keep going and you'd get there. And that's how I got on board."

Elaine's first stop was a training center where she and other prospective workers were evaluated in terms of their capacity for cross-cultural ministry. Part of the program involved exercises in teamwork. Teams would play a crucial role in Elaine's work overseas, for two reasons.

First, the work itself would demand it. Modern mission agencies have found that success on the mission field is far more likely to occur through a team effort rather than a solo performance. The literature and lore of the church may have popularized such solitary figures as David Brainerd, Hudson Taylor, or Amy Carmichael. But many of the greatest long-term impacts have come from *teams* of gospel workers, as there is strength and diversity in numbers.

In addition, Elaine's situation especially would demand teamwork as she was to be part of an evangelistic musical group touring the Orient. Not only would the ensemble need to relate well with each other on the road, they would need to blend together as performers.

To her surprise, Elaine found that she was the ideal team player, as determined both through the testing of the organization and by the opinion of her fellow recruits. "That really shocked me, I'll tell you. At

the end of the time, we were all sitting there and everybody was looking at their scores. Then the instructor said, 'Well, if you were going
overseas, who would you want to go with?' They asked one girl and she
said, 'Elaine!' because she said I was the best team player. I almost fell
through the floor."

I wondered what made Elaine such a good team player, and she
revealed an interesting part of herself. "I think I was the kind of person
that never liked to be alone. Never. I always wanted to be with somebody. If I was doing something it had to be with someone. I could not
function alone. That was one of the things I learned in the Orient—to
function alone, to be independent and OK with myself. That was a very
hard lesson."

Once she arrived overseas, however, "I didn't have any trouble
fitting in. I always felt I was home. I can remember the first day I was
there, I hadn't even been there an hour, and there was a knock on the
door. This girl who was a Chinese staff worker was there and she said,
'Would you like to go get something to drink?' And I said, 'Sure!' And
for the next two hours, she just talked to me. She was upset about so
much, and I just listened to her for a couple of hours. I didn't know this
girl. And this would happen to me all the time. All the time.

"I mean, it was nothing for there to be a knock on the door. Like
once it was this Filipino teenager that I had met, and she said to me,
'Can I come in?' I said, 'Sure.' She comes in, she talks, and she says,
'My friends and I want to know what it's like to be able to cook something.' I said, 'Bring them over.' So I had about ten girls in, and I made
an apple pie. They were astounded because most of them didn't even
have ovens, and apples were expensive.

"I'd do something like that and then I'd sit down and have an opportunity to talk to these girls. I mean, it was always like that. I was
never the kind to get into the gospel first. If people needed help, I'd
probably help them first and then give them the gospel.

"I can remember people coming to me with problems, and I'd listen to them. I'd try to help them or whatever. Sometimes all I could do
was listen. And then if I had the opportunity to witness, they were avid
listeners at that point, because they knew I really cared."

Elaine's approachable personality and sensitive witness carried
over into a winsome stage presence. "Everybody [in the group] not
only sang but played an instrument, too. I played the piano, the electric
piano, the flute, and the drums, believe it or not. I had a wonderful time
doing that.

"And then we had puppets. We had these huge, huge puppets, really big ones. And we had a great puppet stage. I usually worked with the puppets because I just interacted with them. I mean it was like they were my friends, and I could really communicate with anybody with them. And I loved it."

I was aware that puppetry and drama were likely to attract enthusiastic audiences in many Oriental cultures. "The Chinese loved it," Elaine affirmed, "and a lot of times I would learn my lines in the language of the audience, and they loved it.

"I started introducing myself in the language of whatever country we were in, and then everybody followed suit. My director told me, 'When you talk, whether it's in English or whatever, you really communicate warmth. You're just very simple.' And I was. I didn't use a lot of clichés. I was just very simple in what I said. I always said the same thing, but it was very, very simple."

Elaine and the rest of the troupe traveled throughout Asia, performing and presenting an evangelistic message in a wide variety of settings: schools, churches, military installations, prisons, and street crusades. But although she felt good about her own performance and her work with individuals, she was deeply disappointed by problems that developed among the group.

"When I went overseas," she explained, "I went with this idealistic thing that, 'I'm on this team and it's gonna be great'—and it just didn't happen! My whole time over there, I tried to bring the others together in doing stuff, and it just never happened."

Several factors contributed to the lack of cohesion. In the first place, life on the road is hard, as any seasoned traveler knows. Living out of a suitcase, rushing to make connections, unexpected delays, a constant barrage of cultural differences—all of these and more can exact a profound emotional and physical toll on the person whose job requires travel.

Traveling as a team only complicates matters. It's one thing if a traveler has only herself to worry about. It's another if she has to look out for others. Given the stress of the road, the fabric of relationships can begin to fray, and whatever unhealth is in a person will tend to spill out onto others.

This is especially true for performers. In an occupation where ego and image count for so much, the contrast between what the public sees on-stage and what performers and their entourage experience off-stage can be extreme—sometimes even pathological. It's no secret, for example, that divorce is a virtual occupational hazard of touring musicians—Christian musicians included.

Elaine's group was no different. As they trekked around the Orient on their missionary journeys, petty conflicts and minute jealousies smoldered. For instance: Romantic crushes created rivalries. Flirting, perceived or real, generated mistrust. Relational dynamics were examined in the most miniscule detail. Friendships developed into cliques. Simple comments were misinterpreted. Envy boiled up over on-stage performances. Assignments were felt as rewards or punishments. Hurts were carefully nursed and kept alive for future reference.

Occasionally these embers of conflict flared into arguments. But as a group, Elaine and her teammates suffered from a serious weakness: they were afraid to confront each other about problems. "I hate to confront people," Elaine admitted.

Then, as if measuring the implications of that comment, she cautiously added, "But I've learned that there are times to do it and times not to do it. Just because you don't like somebody doesn't mean you go and you confront them. You really have to be careful. You have to know that this is something you should do. And then you have to be sure of what you want to say and not hurt the person, but do it in such a way that it's more building up than tearing down. Because of what I went through, that's what I try to do."

She described several occasions on which she tried to address problems as best she could, sometimes with success, sometimes not. For example, "We had one girl who would go through boyfriends like water. And none of the girls liked her. I can remember us saying, 'Somebody has got to talk to this girl! She's young and she needs guidance, she needs direction.' But nobody would talk to her.

"I finally went to the director and said, 'Look, nobody really likes her and nobody wants to confront her.' He told me I should take care of it. So I said, 'OK, I'll pray about it.'"

Eventually Elaine worked up the nerve to speak openly to the woman and was amazed at the result: "You're the first person who's ever come to me and really talked to me about this," she told Elaine.

On another occasion, Elaine went to one of the women leaders of the group after a series of spats with her roommates. "I said, 'You've got to do something. You've got to talk to them. I mean, I just can't keep trying and having blocks put up.'

"She didn't and she didn't, and finally I went to her and said, 'If you're not going to do it, I'm going to do it. And you know what's going to happen: they're going to totally turn me off. But that's what I'm going to do if you don't do something.' And she wouldn't. She would not confront those women. I can remember her saying, 'I'm really sorry. I'm sorry that this is happening. But I can't do anything.'"

All of this may sound petty, but it was the kind of relational dynamic that is all too common among touring groups. It was almost to be expected. What was unexpected—and to Elaine, inexcusable—was the leadership void on the team.

"One time I went to our director about a problem that had been going on and on, and finally he just said to me, 'You know what? I'm not a leader and I don't intend to lead. So if you have any problems, don't come to me because I'm not going to help you.' That's what he said to me! He wasn't a leader. He was just in the position."

Later, Elaine spoke about this conversation with someone who coordinated personnel for the mission. "That person said, 'I know the problem and you're right. I don't know why we have him as a director. But he is. I can't do anything about that.' And I thought, oh my!"

I thought the same, because Elaine was describing not merely problems with a handful of individuals, but a systemic problem of the mission itself. Apparently the organization was willing to tolerate a lack of quality among key personnel.

And yet for Elaine, the real tragedy of it all was that the team's disunity ultimately affected its performance and therefore its ministry from the stage. "I was extremely disappointed," she said, "because I so much wanted to be a part of a group and part of a team, and it just didn't happen. And consequently, the music never came together. Musically we were terrible. I was very disappointed to be part of something that was that mediocre.

"And I can remember praying, 'OK, Lord, if I have to do stuff alone, that's fine. Musically, I don't care what they ask me to do. I'm just gonna do it and do the best that I can. And hopefully whatever I have to say gets out there so it can help somebody.'"

In fact, the message that Elaine and her teammates delivered—however problematic their own relationships may have been—did help numerous people. Large crowds of Asians responded enthusiastically to their performances and hundreds indicated a desire to follow Christ.

Yet apparently that was not good enough for those overseeing the troupe. Elaine told me a chilling anecdote that showed how tainted the team was, and especially its leaders, by the inability to handle confrontation. "My director had a supervisor over him, and my director never objected to him. Even if something was done that was wrong, he never objected. Never. For example, say we had a hundred people pray to receive Christ. They'd put down five hundred. They didn't object to that.

"I don't think our headquarters ever really knew what was going on," Elaine surmised. "And even if they did, they would say that we were probably wrong and not the director or his boss. That was the feeling I got because that's basically what happened. But it was wrong."

Elaine related other incidents about the group and its leadership that were likewise distressing. Some of what went on sounded like immaturity, but some of it bordered on outright sin and abuse. But having listened to the dark side of Elaine's experience as a missionary, I wondered why she stayed with the musical group and its sponsoring agency. The reason, she told me, was that in spite of everything she had a sense that she was doing the work that God had sent her there to do.

Furthermore, she said, "I don't abandon anything. I go to the very last. And if I get pushed out, that's another story. But I felt like I really needed to do everything that I could do." It was the sort of loyalty that some might admire, but in the end it left her wide open to being exploited.

As she told me the circumstances that eventually led to her return to the States, a picture emerged of an overworked, overstressed, and probably overcommitted missionary who didn't know where or how to draw boundaries between the demands of the task and her own needs. Finally, her health broke down.

"I only weighed ninety pounds," she recalled. "I was very, very thin at the time, and very, very sick. My intestines were enlarged, my liver was enlarged. There were tons of food I couldn't eat because it was very hard for me to digest it. I couldn't eat vegetables, no salad. I could eat chicken. My doctor was telling me I had to eat yogurt every day.

"And because of my condition, I had these attacks that were extremely painful. Extremely painful. Worse than stomach cramps."

So bad, in fact that she was forced to come home—perhaps the only way she would have done so, I suspected. In any case, her arrival in the States was a complete contrast to her send-off years before. There were no cheering friends to greet her at the airport, no "Welcome Home, Elaine!" signs, no banquet to honor her service. Her church had relocated while she was gone, and its membership had turned over dramatically. Most of her old friends had drifted away.

But by far the greatest and most unexpected disappointment of her return was the way the mission agency treated her. So eager to recruit her years before, now the organization virtually ignored her. She recounted a number of odd experiences that occurred when she finally was well enough to visit the mission's headquarters.

"The first couple of days I bumped into people that I had known, and they were happy to see me and I was happy to see them, and we chit-chatted. But the third day, things started to change. I would see people coming and stop to say hello, but they'd sort of hurry past with, 'Oh, I can't talk right now.' By the fourth day, I thought, 'Something is going on!'

"I met one of the top leaders one day, and this person asked, 'How are you, Elaine?' and I said, 'Oh, I'm fine.' I said, 'You know, I've been sick,' and I told him about that. He asked me, 'What are you going to do?' and I said, 'Well, I'm not really sure, but I'm really interested in some of your new ministries that you're starting. I'd really like to talk to you about it.' He said, 'That would be great. I want you to. You come and see me tomorrow afternoon. I'll be in the office.' I said OK.

"So the next day I went to the office, but his secretary wouldn't let me in. I said, 'Tell _____ it's me, Elaine. We talked yesterday, and I was supposed to come. She said, 'Sorry, _____ can't see you.' I said, 'Why not?' She said, 'We don't know. Things are real busy.'"

The same thing happened on several other occasions. "There were several people at the headquarters who I had known over the years, and I made appointments to see them. And when I went to the appointments, they had been canceled. Nobody ever told me. They just canceled them. There would be no reason except that, 'He's too busy. He can't see you.' 'Well, can I see him later?' 'No.'"

The whole thing sounded bizarre. I asked her whether she could think of any reason to account for it. Was there a story circulating about her, for example? Or had something she'd done overseas come back to haunt her? "I don't know," she said, shaking her head. "I never found out."

I had my own hunches, based on an incident Elaine had mentioned earlier in our conversation. One time while she was in the Orient, the head of the mission and his wife scheduled a visit to the team. "I wanted to talk to [the wife] about some issues I thought were very, very important. And about two weeks before they were going to come, my director and his supervisor came to me and told me that while the two of them were there, I was not to speak to them."

This sort of "gag order" struck me as incredible. Yet it fit with some of the deception that apparently was going on. Equally disturbing was what happened just prior to the concert the team gave when the mission head and his spouse arrived.

"My director took me aside and told me that I was the most unspiritual thing he had ever met, that I probably hadn't been spiritual the whole time that I had been there, and that I had caused more trouble than anybody he had ever met. I felt like screaming at him and telling him that *he* was part of the problem, and *he* didn't help things any. But I didn't say a word to him."

Perhaps things might have gone differently if she had. Perhaps not. I asked her what he found so "unspiritual" in her? "Because I confronted him over some things," she replied, "and they didn't want confrontation."

No conflict. No confrontation. No honesty. Just one big, happy family. I wondered: could that have anything to do with the relational Twilight Zone that Elaine ran into back at the organization's headquarters?

Whatever accounted for it, her virtual ostracism by the leaders of the mission deeply affected her emotional well-being and even began to test her sanity. "I was feeling totally dejected—and *re*jected. And I was angry! I was angry that no one would even bother to talk to me. Whether I was right or wrong wasn't the issue. But nobody wanted to talk to me. I stayed by myself. I didn't know what to do. And I ended up getting migraines. I had terrible migraines. They would start about eight in the morning.

"Then they told me I had to go debrief. I went to my appointment several times with this person who was supposed to debrief me. The first time I went, he said, 'Well, you're here to debrief.' I said 'Yeah.' He said, 'Well, that's it.' I said, 'I beg your pardon?' 'That's it.' He didn't talk to me. He never asked me any questions. I never debriefed. I guess the fact that I'd shown up for the interview was enough. But there wasn't a debriefing. Nobody wanted to see me, nobody wanted to talk to me."

I suppose a valid question to raise at this point would be, how much of what happened to Elaine at the mission's headquarters actually happened, and how much was merely Elaine's *perception* of what happened? Isn't it altogether possible, for example, that people actually were too busy to see her, but that she interpreted their hectic schedules as an attempt to avoid her?

This issue of perception is important, not only in regard to Elaine, but for every other person interviewed in this book. For the truth is, none of us knows all the facts. We're only hearing one side of the story. Indeed, for virtually every statement recorded in these interviews, someone somewhere could probably give an alternative version of what "really happened."

But that's just the point: everyone has his or her version of what happened. However, in this book I'm less interested in what "really happened" than in the *impact* of whatever happened on the people with whom I spoke. Because regardless of what happened, these people have decided to back out of churches and organizations to which they once felt great allegiance, and some have even backed out of the faith, or at least come close.

"But why should you believe them?" someone might ask. "They're only giving their perception." To which I reply: of course it's their perception! That's exactly what I asked them to give me. This book is not concerned with nailing down "the facts," even less with determining who was "right" or "wrong." It has to do with why people are leaving churches and ministries.

By this measure, the only way we could be cheated of the truth we need to know is if the interviewee lied about what he or she was really thinking and feeling. The mission team of which Elaine was a part serves as a perfect example of how that operates. No one wanted to be honest. Team members avoided confrontation.

For example, Elaine said nothing when her director berated her for her "unspirituality." "I felt like screaming at him," she told me. Yet she didn't. So she did not reveal what was really inside her. I do not believe that she felt the same need to hide her true reactions from me. By contrast, she was remarkably forthcoming. I don't mean to imply that I have no use for objective truth and reality.

Of course I do. But people's perceptions and emotional reactions are just as real, just as "true" as the external "facts" that give rise to those perceptions and reactions. And if you want answers for why people leave churches, you are far more likely to find them in the truth that is inside the people than the truth outside them in the situation.

In Elaine's case, there were plenty of external facts to validate her account. One of the most sobering was that not long after she came home, the mission was forced to remove her former director from his

BETHEL SEMINARY WEST
LIBRARY
6116 Arosa Street
San Diego, CA 92115-3902

position because of homosexuality. Actually, his supervisors had known for years that he was gay but had not taken action until circumstances threatened to expose the matter publicly.

So that was a significant vindication for Elaine. Yet even apart from that, I took her statements very seriously. She certainly did. Whatever happened at that mission headquarters, it left an insult and an injustice that she still feels. Not that she lies awake at night in obsessive bitterness at her former colleagues. But there is a wound in her that has not healed. Perhaps it never will this side of heaven.

"I kept a journal," she told me, "and I was so hurt and so angry when I came home that I ripped it up. I had to divorce myself of that organization. But I never should have ripped it up. I came across my journal and I read it, and I cried so hard. I couldn't even bear to finish it. I didn't want anything around me to remind me of this group that I basically gave my life for that didn't care for me.

"Looking back, it was a good notebook, because a lot of it was how I really talked to God. You know, I would say anything and everything in that notebook. And I'm sorry I ripped it up, but I did. I just couldn't . . . I couldn't look at it anymore."

When she left the mission, Elaine had no job, no leads to a job, no health insurance, and no savings other than $1,000 she had elected to remove from the agency's retirement fund. (She told me about being audited by the Internal Revenue Service. "The IRS guy couldn't figure out why they wanted to audit me. He looked at all my records and he said, 'You don't make anything!'")

She also experienced significant culture shock as she re-entered an American society that had changed dramatically during the years she had been stationed overseas. "You had electric typewriters and computers. I didn't know what a computer was. I didn't even know how to get money out of a bank. I had never seen an electronic teller machine. I didn't know how to use it. It was very difficult when I got back. Americans would speak so quickly. And I didn't understand their jokes and their little things that they would say. Even getting on a bus was difficult."

Then she added a very telling comment: "I was more at home in Asia than I . . . in my first year, that was a big thing. I wanted to go home to Asia."

In other words, Elaine had become a stranger to her homeland. Yet her medical condition dictated that she stay in the United States. She made a slow recovery, but it was hard. Her friends did not always

R. BERRIEN WEST
LIBRARY
6116 Arosa Street
San Diego, CA 92115-3902

understand when she lacked the energy to do things with them. She took a part-time position at a church, but after just a few weeks was forced to quit because she could not stand even that much strain.

Nor did she have much energy to find a suitable church. Her old church was full of strangers and much farther away. She tried several churches closer to home, but nothing appealed to her. She was much older now and had little in common with young singles who tended to be looking for mates. "There were times I'd be standing right there in the singles group and they'd all make plans to do something, and they would never invite me," she said.

"So I ended up doing things with the married couples. And I thought, 'This is so unhealthy it's pathetic!' Finally I said, 'I'm not doing this anymore.'"

I asked her how she nourishes her spiritual life now. "That's a good question," she replied, framing a response in her mind. "The biggest thing is that sometimes I do a lot of reflecting on how God has really taken care of me. He's never really disappointed me in that area. He's always taken care of me.

"I think I have probably neglected a lot. I don't do as much Bible reading. I'm not in a Bible study. I think more than anything I need to get back in with my own family. I haven't really had a lot of energy. This is the first year that I'm almost back to normal. I mean, I can stay up till nine. 'Big deal.' It *is* a big deal! But the people who were there for me were my family."

She talked in a very touching way about her family—her parents in their senior years, her siblings, her nieces and nephews. They have become far more significant than before she went overseas. In many ways they've become the focus of her "ministry" now and the primary recipients of whatever energy she has to give.

"I take my weekends very seriously and I'll go to [nearby areas where my friends and family live], and to me that is more important than going to church. My mother doesn't understand that, but I've said to her, 'You know, for years I gave everything to the church. I gave up everything for the ministry I was in. And right now I need time for myself.'

"And whether it's ten years, five years, fifteen years . . . who's to say? I'm not really worried about it, because I think when the time comes for me to be there, I'll be there. And I can't let that rule my life. Especially where I only have . . . I only have so much energy to give, and I'm going to put it where I really feel, 'This is going to be better for me right now.' And that's being with my family, being with my friends."

Elaine had three desires for what she wanted out of life: marriage, missions, and music. She spent herself for two out of three. Whether she got what she wanted is hard to say.

NOTE

1. From "So Send I You" by E. Margaret Clarkson, copyright 1954, 1966 by Singspiration Music, Inc. All rights reserved. Used by permission of the Benson Music Group, Inc., Nashville, Tenn.

4

Robert

It is an item of faith that we are children of God;
there is plenty of experience in us against it.
P. T. Forsyth[1]

Robert assured me that I couldn't miss his building—an Internal Revenue Service center. He was right about that. As I coasted through a suburban valley of neatly trimmed lawns and upscale townhouses, I came upon a massive complex that towered over its neighbors like a monument airlifted from Washington, D.C.

The sheer size of this overscale behemoth proved humbling. But as I made my ascent to its entryway, the thought occurred to me that while the federal government may waste taxpayers' money on things like Alpine slides in Puerto Rico and $900 toilet seat covers for airplanes, no one will ever accuse it of squandering public funds on taste.

Or clarity. Given a choice between filling out tax forms and finding my way around that IRS building, I think I would have taken the forms. Fifteen minutes after walking in the door (I hesitate to say the "front" door, as there was no indication whether the building had a "front"), I was still wandering a labyrinth of unmarked corridors, most of which were empty and eerily silent, despite a jam-packed parking lot of hundreds, perhaps even thousands, of cars.

Just as I was about to give myself up for lost, a voice called out my name: "Bill Hendricks!" In a different setting, such recognition probably would have brought a great deal of comfort; here, I found it somewhat unnerving—to be identified by a complete stranger in the halls of the Internal Revenue Service.

It was Robert. As a tax auditor, he was no doubt used to tracking down lost visitors in the building. He looked me over with a practiced eye, and even though I was there for a different purpose, I was glad I had my accountant's number handy.

However, he quickly put me at ease by suggesting that we sit outside and have lunch. It was a spectacularly beautiful day, but no one else seemed to care for the sun. So we sat by ourselves, and Robert began to describe his ambivalent relationship with the church.

"I've not been going to church for about two years, since we moved here," he explained. "We left our previous church and thought, we're going to move away and I don't want to get involved superficially. And when we came here we didn't want to go for a while because we had a new baby and our experience with leaving him at the nursery was horrible. Now I want to move again. I don't want to be here. So I don't want to get involved again because we might be gone in six months. When we settle down, my goal is to get involved in a church, with no doubt."

What kind of church will that be? "I don't know," he mused, "I'll pick the best." Pressed to describe his ideal congregation, he recalled the church where he grew up, which he described as "a Bible-believing, fundamentalist church. I think it was a very good church. My father built the church and we were all very, very active, which was a very good rounding. It was experiential and fundamental."

But immediately he added, "I like the worship of the charismatic church. I don't like the way church services are set up. They're sort of a monarchy. A guy gets up and tells you how to live for forty-five minutes, and there's nothing wrong with that—especially if he's good in the Bible. But if he's not, I don't know. I'm not sure I like the whole way it's set up. I'll do it. I'll sit there. But I like the charismatic approach where they'll sing for twenty or thirty minutes. I'd rather be in that."

Robert's mingling of Bible-church orthodoxy and a charismatic style of worship recalled an early and perhaps formative period in his relationship to the church. Looking back on his family's congregation, he said, "It was a great church, but it changed when we got a new pastor. Things changed there a lot. It was a different ministry. A lot of people liked him; the old people liked him. And he was certainly a decent man. But there was reason for me not to respect him or trust him.

"I was in a band and we would play at the church and do concerts, and they would get on our case. We would bring in a lot of kids, and they would get upset because the kids would be drunk or rowdy, or it would be too loud. Something would tick them off."

It sounded like a classic case of generational conflict, the sort of cultural clash that occurred in countless congregations during the '60s and '70s. But then Robert commented, "I think the bottom line is that if people analyze why they go to church, they have to believe that the pastor is spiritual. Probably not many members of the church are going to go sit under a guy that they don't respect as a spiritual man."

Which means? "People define that differently, but by my definition, that pastor didn't fit. A friend of mine critiqued him best when he said that his—the pastor's—idea of Christianity was a code of behavior that we are responsible to follow, and that if we do, we will fulfill God's commission for us.

"Certainly there's an element of that that I would accept. But I've done some reading recently in a book called *Heresies.* There have been different movements, apparently, through the history of the church. One was the Huguenots and another was the Pietists, and I think I adhere more to that. I went to a more charismatic church after my old church, and I think both of them are out of balance. The one lacks experience and the other emphasizes it too much. Maybe in some way there's a weird balance and it's good, but I never knew what the balance was."

The word "balance" proved to be the touchstone for understanding Robert's faith. For some, balance involves placing in proper perspective the various emphases of Christian teaching. For Robert, however, balance involved something beyond and far more difficult than that—trying to reconcile what are actually opposing views of the Christian life. "My own disillusionment has to do with working out the balance between what God does in your life day-to-day, how personally involved He really gets. The question that's common for people in their thirties is, Is God really that involved? You can see maybe on a macroscale a difference, but on a microscale—

"Some people would define Christianity as that God cares about every little thing: What time do you brush your teeth, what clothes you wear, da da, da da, da da? Another perspective is obviously deism, where He has no concern. I don't know what the balance is. In different churches you see different interpretations. One is that we've been given a code to live by and you do that, and the other is that every minute you're on your knees. In my perspective, there's some balance and it's hard to strike."

Hard indeed. As Robert realized, the church in the United States is far from a monolithic institution. Different traditions offer different perspectives. As a result, instead of speaking with a single, unified voice, the church speaks with countless voices that offer mixed and sometimes conflicting messages.

The burden of sorting it all out falls to the individual. "As I got older I realized that more and more I had to make up my own mind and make decisions. As you mature, there's more and more things that you have to learn to do."

One of those things is to find a job. Prior to working for the government, Robert had tried his hand at two careers, music and investments. Both put his spiritual convictions to the test and raised troubling questions of how involved God is in one's day-to-day experience. "I took on some risky careers, I think, out of faith. Maybe not purely out of faith. But I don't think my nature's that gutsy, and I think my faith in God made me a lot more gutsy, because I wasn't afraid of failure. In those careers I experienced a lot of failure. Then it was like, what happened? Where was God? It's still hard to resolve."

We talked about the music business and how extraordinarily tough it is on people—the travel, the meager pay, the disappointments, the uncertainty. "In that whole thing it was hard, like, where's God? I thought God was in this and I don't see Him in this! I remember I used to pray that I would give it up, or that God would take away the desire for it. I'd be trying to give it up, and a year would go by and I'd get a call from somebody who'd heard a tape and thought it was great and wanted to meet me. Then they'd meet me and say, 'We think we can do something with this,' and want us to record. So I'd put my band together again—and it would fall apart down the road."

Did he ever feel that God had let him down? At one time he might have, but now he takes the view that "that's the way life is, and to try to spiritualize it to the point where you'll be insulated as a Christian is not very realistic. You can't constantly go through life holding God's hand so tightly that you sort of remain a child, so to speak.

"But then, how far do you go with that?" he suddenly asked, as if an inner voice was warning him that he was in danger of promoting an extreme. "I don't know, it's a balance question, and obviously I'm still trying to resolve that.

"I don't know if I have any regrets with music. I mean it was a great time in my life and I had a moderate degree of success. I wanted to live off of it and couldn't. But I was able to do it for several years, and I had people who enjoyed what I was doing. I think what was hard was that I felt I had a message, and that was my ministry, or I hoped it would be. It probably was, to a point, but on a much smaller scale than I had anticipated.

"I actually got into investing because I thought that was God's provision for me to make enough money to record my own album. But that didn't pan out either! Then again, I can look back and think, I was really blessed that I was able and had the time to do a dream, to do what I wanted to do. A lot of people never get to pursue their dreams. I probably accomplished about three-quarters of what I set out to do."

After deciding that his career as a musician could not support him and his family, Robert began investing in commodities futures. Unlike many in that high-risk field, he has done fairly well. But I wondered how his faith affected that work. "I didn't see much of God's hand," he admitted. "I saw it more in music than I did in investments." Then he laughed, "I don't know to this day that I've seen God's hand at all in investments! Many hours I spent on my knees, praying about this investment and that investment. And then after years I stopped doing that and just sort of prayed for wisdom.

"Of course, years later I look back and wonder—did I ever get wisdom? I think I have at this point. But it probably has more to do with being in it for a while and being willing to pay the cost."

I was not surprised by the dichotomy that he felt between Christianity and his day-to-day work. Most Christians live in two worlds—the privatized world of their personal religious convictions, and the rough and tumble "real world" of the workplace. Few make any relevant connection between the two. In fact, as I have written elsewhere, most people are unaware how much their everyday work matters to God. [2]

I was therefore curious whether Robert ever talked with others about applying his faith to his work. "I remember asking people some of my dilemmas when I was facing them more, and I didn't know anybody who'd experienced the things I had. But I know it's common.

"I would talk to a minister friend of mine and I'd say, 'You always have a validation that you're doing God's will.' You don't have that when you're in investments. You just don't. You can't spiritualize it, really. I'm sure people in the ministry have doubts all the time about whether they're doing the right thing. But they have a validation that they're doing the good work of the gospel that I don't have, because I'm not doing it. Sometimes it makes me think there are different dispensations for people in ministry."

In other words, ministers have a higher calling. Again, I was not surprised to hear Robert say this, given his assumption of a dichotomy between the sacred and the secular. But I thoroughly disagreed, and I told him so later. Yet I could hardly fault him for coming to that conclusion. Precious few resources exist to help believers think intelligently about what difference biblical truth makes in the marketplace.

However, he had come across one book on the subject. "I read in this book about a guy who went to the trading floor in Chicago, and he was very spiritual-oriented—you know, the idea that God would lead him into what to do. There was a Christian who was sort of mentoring him and kind of laughed at the guy because it wasn't very long until he wiped himself out and he was gone.

"So there's this sort of practical element that's a difficult thing to resolve. What I saw [among many Christians] was the conservative, stiff upper lip, a lack of vulnerability, the idea of being God's man by never showing any weaknesses—which I don't buy at all. I think that's a lack of spirituality for a guy not to be able to be honest. I don't believe it when somebody acts like that. I think there's dishonesty. And the other extreme is the guy who says, 'God spoke to me last night, and this is what He told me to tell you.' So you kind of have this thing going back and forth."

As I listened, I was struck with the irony of a futures trader now working as an auditor for the IRS. "My goal has always been to work for myself, so it's just a little bit against my nature," he said, motioning toward the imposing structure behind him. "But you do what you have to do! I like to think it's perfect symmetry—being a rock 'n' roll guitar player in my twenties and working for the IRS in my thirties. In some ways they're complete opposites!"

Yes, we were back to a collision of opposites. Wherever he turned, Robert seemed to have run into competing extremes. So I was not surprised when he described leaving some of the churches he had attended because of conflicts over how the faith works itself out in practice. For example, "I used to go to a charismatic church where the preacher was very good, but I'd go home ticked off. I taught for about five years. I spent extensive time reading and studying, and after a point where I could intellectually discuss some of these issues with them and challenge them, sitting there I just couldn't receive it all. I wanted to debate or fight or investigate or challenge them.

"After about a year of that, I couldn't take it anymore. It became negative going to church. I'd come home and wrestle with and disagree with some of his presuppositions or premises that would subtly come out. Fatalistic Christianity, passive Christianity, is taught a lot. 'Let go and let God.' I do accept that principle, but there's a balance. I don't know where it is, but I know it's there."

Somehow Robert seemed to be finding something of that balance. But he knew of others for whom it remained elusive. "I've seen younger Christians fall from disillusionment. I was in the hospital one time and a girl came in and laid hands on me and believed God had told her the night before that I was going to be healed from her ministry. It didn't happen, and she became very angry at me, which was a funny response. I mean, that's part of life. Christians get divorced; Christians have a lot of things that don't work out for them. I don't know how you reconcile all that. You can blame it on yourself and say you didn't have enough faith. Or you can say that's the way life is, we're in a fallen world. I think that part of maturity is that it's kind of a paradox, and you have to learn to live with both truths in some respect."

Robert rejects as "magical thinking" the sort of fatalistic, passive spirituality that he observes among many believers. He feels that "letting go and letting God" might be a stage along the way to spiritual maturity, and admits that a lot of Christian beliefs appear to support that attitude. But he decries the habit of some who try to use God as a sort of magic genie to get what they want.

"The culture in America is very materialistic and self-fulfilling, self-actualizing, an orientation to get the most out of life. I think a lot of those concepts have crept into the church. I don't hold the church totally responsible because there are close parallels in the Bible that God will meet your needs and fulfill you and be there to guide you every step of the way. There are many verses you can read with a little twist and interpret them as, 'This is God's will for your life—to have everything you want.'

"But I got to a point where I realized that wasn't happening in my life, and I knew I had sought God. It was like, what happened, what went wrong? I have a different perspective now. Things just aren't that simple. Now I think it's really close to heresy, or is heresy. In the old days, I would have thought all that prosperity stuff was just a weird interpretation. But now it offends me more."

It offends many others as well. The scandals of several prominent televangelists in the late eighties along with recent exposés of several health-and-wealth preachers have had a profoundly negative effect on the public's perception of religion in general and fundamentalism in particular. Yet despite his disappointment with prosperity teaching, Robert did not abandon his faith. Rather, he seemed to gain a new perspective on the issue of success.

"It's a common human instinct to want to have success. But I think the promises of God are based more on needs than on lavishness. In our culture, a high percentage of people have their needs met. So it becomes competing on a different level. The Israelites were talking about basic provisions, of having a home where they were not in danger of enemies and an environment where they could have their basic needs met. From that perspective, if that's [the kind of society to which] some of those promises were written, it's very different from living in America in the twentieth century.

"There's a choice, too, on some of these things. It's just a choice to choose to complain about something that didn't work out. I tell my wife, I probably have nine out of ten things in my life I wanted, but I'm a perfectionist and a little obsessive, and I want it all. If Jesus was talking to me, He'd probably say, 'Be thankful!' It's true, happiness is a choice. I'm trying to work on that a little bit right now, to realize that God's been good to me in so many areas of my life. I could spend the rest of my life saying, 'I didn't get this and this and this so I'm angry,' but that's a childish reaction, really."

The more I spoke with Robert, the more I admired his perseverance in wrestling with the mysteries of the faith, particularly when they lead to such vastly different practical implications. Many people, faced with the same challenge, either end up in dangerous extremes or else quit in frustration, rejecting Christianity as nothing but a confusing set of contradictions. Robert seemed committed to finding a middle ground.

"There are a lot of questions, a lot of paradoxes in Christianity," he observed. "I'm reading a book for the second time by Hugh Ross called *Fingerprint of God*. He makes a comment that there are paradoxes in Scripture, that that's a verification of a higher intelligence. You don't get that in any other world religion. That's interesting. It shows a depth of thinking that is beyond human experience."

Thus, despite the paradoxes—perhaps even because of them—Robert remains loyal to the basic conviction that the Bible is true and has authority. Even so, he has a hard time with how to work out his faith in practice. For instance, "What does being filled with the Holy Spirit mean? Being controlled? I can be controlled in my experience for maybe a minute or an hour. But you spend all your time worrying and working on that."

He seemed daunted by the thought of it. "Some of these things . . . I don't know, realistically, if you can live that way. Then I wonder if some of those interpretations are even a hundred percent correct—that every time you sin you have to confess your sins, and on and on. But then, I know it kind of works if you're willing to make the effort. But it can be self-deprecating, sort of, to be constantly on guard. It can be interpreted legalistically. I don't know.

"Where I am is that I'm resolving these things in my mind in the last few months. I'm in my late thirties and trying to get to a point where I don't get mad at God because things don't make sense. People say to me, 'Well, you shouldn't get mad at God if these things don't work out,' and I say, 'Well, I always give Him the credit when things do!' It doesn't seem balanced."

Is there a point to the struggle? Or is he just an obstinate child of God? "There's a principle, and C. S. Lewis has an example,[3] that he felt many times—I don't know if it was after the death of his wife—that God let go of his hand in a moment he might have needed Him most. And he said he would fall, whatever that meant to him in his experience. But he described it as if he felt God just—even though he couldn't walk on his own—just wanted him to develop the will to try to get up. Some of the things we do in life, I think God's hand in some ways is removed and I have to learn how to do it."

Was Robert satisfied with learning how to "do it" apart from a local congregation of believers? I reminded him that a lot of folks would think he was seriously wrong not to attend church. "That's an easy call to make. I would agree that it's not scriptural. You're supposed to be in fellowship. I don't want to justify myself."

But though he himself seems reluctant, Robert's family situation will probably determine how quickly he returns to a fellowship. "Our boy's getting old enough where it's about time he needs to have that exposure. We may start doing that. I'll have to go once or twice and see if it works out. I'm kind of tossing that around. We have a neighbor who's going to a certain church near our place where we may start going. If not, there's a lot of good churches around here."

I knew that there were. Somehow, though, I had my doubts whether any of them would spell the difference in Robert's spiritual pilgrimage. "I think my own relationship with God has to be resolved," he told me, "and the church can't do that for me." I couldn't have agreed more. Frankly, I wish that more people could come to such an awareness of personal responsibility for their spiritual lives.

NOTES

1. *Christian Perfection* (New York: Dodd, Mead, and Co., 1899), 9.

2. See Doug Sherman and William Hendricks, *Your Work Matters to God* (Colorado Springs: NavPress, 1987).

3. Perhaps Robert had in mind Lewis's comments in *A Grief Observed* (New York: Bantam, 1976), 4–5, or 53–54: "Meanwhile, where is God? This is one of the most disquieting symptoms. When you are happy, so happy that you have no sense of needing Him, so happy that you are tempted to feel His claims upon you as an interruption, if you remember yourself and turn to Him with gratitude and praise, you will be—or so it feels—welcomed with open arms. But go to Him when your need is desperate, when all other help is vain, and what do you find? A door slammed in your face, and a sound of bolting and double bolting on the inside. After that, silence. You may as well turn away. The longer you wait, the more emphatic the silence will become. There are no lights in the windows. It might be an empty house. Was it ever inhabited? It seemed so once. And that seeming was as strong as this. What can this mean? Why is He so present a commander in our time of prosperity and so very absent a help in time of trouble?

"I tried to put some of these thoughts to C. this afternoon. He reminded me that the same thing seems to have happened to Christ: 'Why hast thou forsaken me?' I know. Does that make it easier to understand?

". . . I have gradually been coming to feel that the door is no longer shut and bolted. Was it my own frantic need that slammed it in my face?" The time when there is nothing at all in your soul except a cry for help may be just the time when God can't give it: you are like the drowning man who can't be helped because he clutches and grabs. Perhaps your own reiterated cries deafen you to the voice you hoped to hear.

"On the other hand, 'Knock and it shall be opened.' But does knocking mean hammering and kicking the door like a maniac? And there's also 'To him that hath shall be given.' After all, you must have a capacity to receive, or even omnipotence can't give. Perhaps your own passion temporarily destroys the capacity."

5

Jennifer

I came here to study hard things—rock mountain and
salt sea—and to temper my spirit on their edges.
'Teach me thy ways, O Lord' is, like all prayers,
a rash one, and one I cannot but recommend.

Annie Dillard[1]

One of the common plots in modern literature is the naive young person from the country who is lured to the bright lights of the big city, only to be corrupted by the evils of urban life. There is probably some truth in such tales. Nevertheless, the scenario rests on a dubious premise—that the home of evil is the city, while the country is the haven of good.

The real world is not so simple. In fact, a good case can be made for the idea that rural communities are at least as harsh and vicious as any of their urban cousins. And why not? Removed from the prying eyes of neighbors and the restraining arm of authorities, who knows what hideous forms human nature, fallen as it is, may take? As urbanologist Ray Bakke puts it, evil began in a garden; heaven will come down in a city.[2]

Jennifer grew up in a large Midwestern city. Her decision to leave began with the simple choice to marry a minister. "David was in his next to last year of seminary," she recalled. "We were talking a lot about where were we going to go, what were David's strengths, what were his gifts? He didn't feel a leaning to be a pastor. That wasn't where his heart was. But he's had a lot of experience in back-country wilderness, taking groups into the wild country as a teaching ground. He knows the back country. It's his back yard.

"So he said, 'Let's go do what I'm good at.' We brainstormed a lot, dreamed a lot, talked a lot, and the idea of a Christian training center in the mountains came on paper, and we put it into action."

That sounded rather novel to me. Did she find it exciting? "No! I had never been away from my family, and that was a hard move to make. I mean, we're in the heart of the Rockies here. I went from flat, flat, flat country to the mountains. I cried all the way. I did! But, you know, I'm committed to my husband and I'm committed to what he believes, and my heart's for wherever the Lord wants us. Now, as I look back, I'm glad we moved. It's been the hardest ten years of my life, but I'm thankful for it, because I've really grown a lot."

David and Jennifer worked hard to establish their unique program of Christian leadership training in a wilderness setting. Within a few seasons, the concept had proved itself viable. Meanwhile, they began to meet their "neighbors" in the isolated region they now called home. Actually, most of these new acquaintances lived miles away in secluded cabins. Few were particularly friendly. Indeed, most had moved to the area to get away from people, equating freedom with solitude.

Yet they could never escape their spiritual needs. Gradually word spread that a preacher (of sorts) had come to the area, and soon David found himself acting as a chaplain to the locals.

"Finally we started a church, and things went quite well for about three years. The church was growing. It was doing great. There had never been a successful church around here. They'd always come and gone, come and gone. And the fact that this church was growing spiritually, numbers weren't a big issue—although the numbers were growing. But the *people* were growing, and that was the exciting part. We could see changes in people's lives. Marriages were being saved. There were people turning away from drug and alcohol abuse. There were great things happening. There were definitely victories in God's kingdom."

She related this account of apparently successful church planting with confidence and conviction. But there was a texture of hesitation to her voice, as if her memory was reluctant to dwell on details and eager to be free of some great weight or weariness. Finally, having committed herself, she explained that about three and a half years into the church, she and David experienced what she called "personality problems" with a number of the members. What she went on to describe, however, sounded far more serious than mere personality conflicts: "Attacking David, attacking us as a family"—here her voice broke—

"accusing us of child abuse, calling David, um . . . that there was only evil in him, Christ was no longer in him."

I found it easy to imagine the situation. I've known quite a few people who have started a church, only to have it blow up in their face after three or four years. In many cases they have sown the seeds of their own destruction. Maybe it was the way they organized the church or the values they instilled in the people. Maybe their particular style has worn thin: the people tolerated it when things were new and exciting, but no more. In other cases, the pastor has done nothing wrong; the people simply have chosen to forsake the unity of the body.

Whatever the cause, major conflict in a start-up can be devastating to a pastor and his family—the accusations, the threats, the lies. "And this was from who we *thought* were our best friends!" Jennifer exclaimed. "People we had really poured a lot of ourselves into. So that was quite a shocker! I had never, ever encountered anything like that in my life. Neither had David. It was like someone had smacked us in the face and we were reeling from the blow. Just the shock over it. We're still feeling the shocks of that to this day."

In what way? I wondered. What was the lingering feeling? "Betrayal. I'd trusted these people and then they abused me. So there's no longer any trust there. And I still don't trust them. I'd be friendly with them, and I would help them if they needed help—and I have helped them since then, helped watch their kids or whatever. But I don't trust them." Her tone of voice backed up her statements.

To what extent did the church members use the faith as a tool of abuse? Did they spiritualize feelings or use Bible verses to make accusations? "Oh yes! All the way! You know, they've got the truth now and David doesn't. Actually, the way we see it, there was a lot of envy there on their part because David is trained and these people were not."

I knew by experience that that can be one of the perils of working among a rural population. Regardless of one's specialization—the professional ministry, medicine, veterinary medicine, teaching, whatever —uneducated people, which rural areas often have, feel distrustful of trained and degreed professionals, for a variety of reasons.

At the same time, "we made some mistakes," Jennifer admitted. "We've looked at it and we can see, OK, we were wrong here, we messed up there. We've also wondered whether God really wants us up here. Maybe we made a mistake. Maybe we missed the signals. We've wondered is it time to move on. 'Do You want us somewhere else, God?' I think we've covered the whole gamut of questions and doubts, and always come back to, is it us?"

Those kinds of questions are hard enough to answer, let alone to try to answer them in an isolated area. At least in a city a pastor has access to other pastors, counselors, advisers, seminaries, libraries, and other resources. But in a community with the nearest grocery store twenty miles away, David and Jennifer were on their own. They were a lot like missionaries in a remote setting. "There may not be a language barrier," Jennifer pointed out, "but the culture is different, the people are different, it's a whole different way of life.

"But you know what? It was the beginning of learning a lot. Out of that betrayal we started reading some books. The first one was *Love Is a Choice,* by Frank Minirth and Paul Meier. When we read it, our mouths just dropped open. We had never heard about codependent people before.[3] When we read about that, I pulled out our church mailing list, and David and I went through it. Every single family in that church was on its second marriage, except for David and me. Every one of them! And they all were children of alcoholic parents or they came from alcoholic, drug-abuse backgrounds themselves. Every single one of them!

"And it started explaining a lot that we felt but didn't know what to call it or say about it. Just a lot of questions that we had and things that were going on in the church, and that a lot of the pretending, performance, legalism—Man! Was it strong in that church! Because they were comfortable with that. I mean, we look back and see all that and understand it now, but we didn't at the time.

"We kept thinking, 'Maybe the problem is with us.' We still do that! Not as much as we did then. But I mean, we were really asking, 'What is wrong with us? Are we deluded or something?' Because we're terribly isolated up here. Not just physically isolated, but we're isolated from healthy believers. They don't exist up here. And of course, David and I, every time we say that, we look at ourselves and go, 'Then why are *we* here? Are *we* unhealthy and just part of the clan here?'"

Fortunately, David had at least one outside group that could lend some perspective, the board of his training center. "We bounce everything off our board members," Jennifer explained. "There are ten of us on the board, most of whom live outside this area.

"And David would call different pastors. He'd call his former pastor from a church where he used to work. We'd call other pastors all over the country, because we didn't want it to be localized. We wanted to bounce it off all the different cultures. We asked, 'What are we doing wrong here? Is it us? What do we need to change? What do we learn from this? What does God say about this? Can you help us, give us direction?' I mean, we really fought to be open, to be totally honest, to be totally vulnerable before these people."

In the end, David and Jennifer decided to stay. The center was doing well, and that was their main purpose for coming to the area. The problems in the church were not enough to make them give up that effort. Jennifer continued a program she had started for the children. "There was a great need in the church for teaching the children. We had no program for them whatsoever, so I fell into that slot. I was the Christian education department. I have a lot of creative talents, so I threw those abilities into teaching. I somewhat enjoyed it, other than being totally burned out after a while."

Burnout was a distinct possibility, because David and Jennifer were wearing many hats—running the center, pastoring the church, teaching classes, working in the community, being parents. "We were up to our eyeballs with involvement," Jennifer recalled, "especially in this church. Even though the hurt and the pain were still there—you know, 'I'm afraid to trust you, but I'll still do the work of the Lord'— that was my attitude."

Two incidents, however, led to a painful outcome. The first had to do with Jennifer's attempts to help a woman whose marriage was in trouble. "She and her husband were breaking up. They were both weaning themselves off drugs. She had come to Christ through another church that had started here for a couple of years but folded up like all the others. It was very guilt-inducing—guilt and shame, guilt and shame. She gave up. She said, 'I can't live up to these expectations.' She gave up.

"In the meantime, our church started. So she and I spent time together. We'd walk together four or five times every week, a couple of miles each time—a lot of talking time and a lot of discipling time, and just accepting her, loving her: 'I don't care that you're still smoking pot. I don't care that you and your husband aren't getting along. Let's just work at loving you, accepting you.'

"This went on for two and a half years. She'd call every day: 'I've got this problem, what do I do?' It was a high-maintenance relationship, and it was very draining. But, nonetheless she was growing. It was so neat to take a simple principle from God's Word and trust it and put it into practice and, you know, use it by faith. It worked for her. It was so exciting."

But then Jennifer's friend attended a religious retreat where the emphasis was on an emotional style of spirituality and ecstatic experiences. "My friend totally bought into it." Jennifer sighed. "Swaying in the Spirit, holy laughters, personal prayer language, the whole gamut. And after that, she came over with her husband and sat David and me down and put conditions on our relationship! She said, 'I can't handle what you talk to me about,' meaning the times when I would voice my own frustrations.

"I thought that two and a half years into the relationship, she was someone I could pour my heart out to, to vent my frustrations. I thought it was a mutual relationship. Wrong! She says, 'I can't handle that.' There was a lot of rejection in it, the way she put it, and how she put controls on the relationship. So that was one more added to the list of rejections from the folks in the church.

"I can't tell you the grief I felt that she was embracing these extra-biblical experiences. She would justify things. Like, she always struggled with respecting her husband. Always. Now she was justifying it, because God 'told' her: 'It's OK, you can go ahead and go to this meeting even though your husband says he doesn't want you to.' It was a personal hotline to God! 'God says this and God told me that.' It was obnoxious, Bill. It was repulsive. I didn't want to even be around her. She was like the old person, the way she used to be years ago. So that was another relationship down the tubes."

The loss was a crushing blow to Jennifer. But the knockout punch came when her husband's teaching provoked a showdown with one of the other elders. "David started teaching an adult Sunday school class on Galatians, and he came to chapter 5. He was really trying to point out how ticked off Paul was, and he used the vernacular language of our day.[4] That offended this one elder in the church. So this elder went around to other people asking, 'Were you offended with that choice of words?'"

As one might guess, the elder polled everybody else before bothering to talk about the issue with David. Finally, though, "he called up David and there was a lot of heavy discussion. They brought in a third party, a pastor from forty miles away. They laid everything out on the table. We had this big meeting. The wives were there, too. And what it came down to was, this elder didn't trust David. He was very legalistic. He had this list of do's and don'ts that he was comfortable in, and so of course he thought those should apply to everyone in the church. David and I didn't exactly fit that mold. We were quite laid-back by comparison."

Laid-back, maybe, but not willing to be completely passive. For months and even years, Jennifer had held her tongue about the abuses she had endured. In fact, while "getting totally cut down day after day after day," she had gone to others in the congregation "to ask forgiveness in areas where we knew we were wrong. 'Have I ever done anything or said anything to offend you?'" she asked the other women. "I wanted to make sure that there was a completely clean record."

But no one wanted to own up to the existence of conflict. "There was only denial—tons of denial."

Anne Wilson Schaef has described the "addictive organization,"[5] in which emotionally damaged group members live out their unhealth through the organization's structure. The dysfunctional patterns become so ingrained, accepted, and even institutionalized that the only way to restore health is for someone to break the system, to violate the status quo. But when someone does, he or she is bound to face the full onslaught of the group's well-fortified defenses.

Jennifer broke the system. "At this meeting I said, 'Look, we're all coming to church and we're performing. We're putting on a big show. We're pretending every Sunday. I can't do this anymore!'

"I was in tears about it. 'I can't do it anymore! I'm just putting on a big show every week!' And I put most of it on myself, though I did point out that we were all doing it. But I put the responsibility on myself: 'I'm not going to do it anymore.'

"And with David's permission, I chose to not go there anymore. I couldn't take the abuse anymore. I couldn't take phone calls from people in the church every week. It was always one hot potato after another. I couldn't take it anymore. I was emotionally wiped out. That meeting was it. I was going to go off the deep end if we didn't stop.

"Anyway, out of that meeting, David and this elder agreed to disagree. They agreed to work together, to continue to work together at church. The very next Sunday, David apologized to his Sunday school class. 'I apologize if my words were too crude and they were offensive,' he said, "but I will not apologize for the Word of God.' Well, one other deacon, a deacon who had *attacked* us before—and I use that word strongly—called up David that night and said, 'I don't think your apology was sincere.' And David said, 'Wait a minute, brother, are you saying you're judging the motive of my apology, whether it was sincere or not? You're judging my heart?' He said, 'You bet I am!'

"That was it. David typed up his letter of resignation. And then the very legalistic elder censored David's letter. 'You can't say this and you can't say that.' So we just quietly pulled out and didn't say anything to anybody."

No one knows how many other people across the country have followed a similar pattern to that of David and Jennifer: enthusiastic involvement in a fellowship of believers, followed by a period of conflicts that are never quite resolved, leading to a crisis in which the decision is made to leave, and finally a quiet exit—sometimes to another church, as often as not to no other church. I would put the number in the hundreds of thousands, if not in the millions. Whatever the total, I believe it is growing.

But what fascinated me about David and Jennifer's story was that as I interviewed people for the book, I found many who had left a church or parachurch organization because of an abusive *leader*. Ironically, here were a minister and his wife leaving a church because of an abusive *congregation*.

I don't mean to exonerate David and Jennifer, as though they contributed nothing to the situation. They admit having made mistakes. I don't know all the facts. But neither is it my purpose to assess blame. I can only guess that their gravest failure in starting the church was probably naïveté. In that case, they are no worse than millions of others in the faith who have hoped for the best but, in the end, experienced the worst.

So is that what we can expect from Christianity—the worst? Is God committed to dashing our hopes? Actually, God is committed to destroying whatever is unworthy of Himself, and therefore unworthy of us. That may mean dashing our hopes if our hopes are misplaced.

That is what Jennifer discovered. Her expectations for her life were based on a faulty premise. "I had always wanted to marry someone in the ministry," she explained. "You know why? Because I saw the pastor's wife at the church where I grew up, who was so loved and so accepted, and I wanted to be loved and accepted. And I thought the only place where I would be loved and accepted—unconditionally loved and accepted—would be in the ministry."

She recalled a statement I had made about the nature of disillusionment. I had said that before one can become *dis*illusioned, one had to have an illusion to lose. "My illusion was to be unconditionally loved and accepted in the church," she told me. "The ironic thing is, I have never had so much hurt and pain as I have from the church. But, the good thing out of all this garbage has been finding the unconditional love and acceptance of my heavenly Father, that I never experienced before. When all these relationships around me were falling down and being torn apart, and there was nothing but hurt and pain and heartache, where else was there to go?

"I can't say there was any one specific moment when that happened. It was probably over two or three months. I started to grasp, 'You love me, God, even though I mess up. You still love me and accept me.' That has been my lifeline here."

I was glad that she had finally found in God the security for which she longed. But I wondered, did she ever feel angry at God, that somehow He had betrayed her or let her down? "I'm pretty sure I did subconsciously. I wouldn't say it to His face, 'I'm angry at You, God, because You let this happen!' When the intense part of the pain was taking place, my relationship with Him was not strong enough for me to say that, even if I felt it. I thought that would have been disrespectful. You don't talk to someone like that.

"But a lot of the anger was vented toward the people, toward our relationships. 'How could you do this to us? We trusted you!' Over and over again, that lack of trust came out. That was a big issue. Then it finally hit me, 'God, I'm afraid to even trust You! I'm afraid to trust anybody! I'm afraid that You're going to zap me with more heartache and more pain.' So I confessed that and said, 'I don't want be in that position. I don't want to have those feelings toward You. I want to trust You. Help me to trust You with just a very simple thing today, and let's start from there and grow from that.' And He has. He's been so faithful to that."

Jennifer had been close to burnout when she left the church. Now, without the responsibilities of teaching and acting as a pastor's wife, she had much more time and energy for herself and her family. "During this healing time, it's been time to take care of myself—and it's been wonderful! I use my creative abilities around the home. I quilt and I haven't felt guilty that I wasn't studying for Sunday school or being at this party or getting ready for that meeting or studying or, you know, on and on and on. I've been able to thoroughly enjoy it.

"I've learned to play chess with my kids; they've taught me how to do that. They're going to teach me how to downhill ski. Just spending time and being relaxed. I've never been a relaxed person. I've always been an uptight person. So it's been nice in that respect.

"It's also been nice to feel relaxed in my quiet time—to just sit down and be still. I've never felt that before. I actually enjoy reading my Bible now! I've never felt that before. It has always been an obligation, a responsibility. 'This is what I'm supposed to do.' This is what I've been taught my whole life. I look forward to it now, and I've never done that before."

Then she added a telling comment: "I was talking to someone a couple of weeks ago, and he was saying how much more he has grown spiritually since he has pulled out of the church. And I thought, what a sad commentary on our churches!"

Sad, indeed. But what does Jennifer plan to do about church? Her options might be limited right now. But has she completely given up on the body of Christ? She grew up in the church; how does it feel not to be attending anymore? "I've just not allowed myself to feel guilty about not being involved," she said. "I just look at this as a healing time. Our board of directors told us to take time off from the church and just take care of ourselves. We have their blessing on that. It's not like we're off on a limb by ourselves."

Actually, the loss of a fellowship is a tender spot for her. With tears in her eyes she told me, "I dream about being able to just go into the back of a church, to just slip in to worship and be fed, and slip back out. I'm not anxious to be involved—although someday I do plan to be again, because I enjoy that. I do have gifts of teaching. I know I have creative abilities."

She also longs for her children to have a church home. "Our kids have a very bad taste about church. They recognize what happened, and they are well aware of our love for God. We haven't chucked God out the window by any means. If anything, our relationships with God have grown stronger, even here in the family. And we talk and we dream about someday being in a neat church, a big church with a wonderful youth program for our kids."

But for now she is content to nurture their spiritual development at home. She would rather have them attend no church than to place them in an abusive church. "People have criticized us, 'Why aren't your children at church with you every Sunday? As a spiritual leader, it looks bad if your children aren't in church every Sunday.' There are all kinds of expectations.

"Yes, it is important that our children be in church; but don't put the expectations on me just because that is what you feel is right for your family. If my kids aren't learning anything from church because there's no Sunday school program or whatever, I'm not going to cram God down their throats! David and I feel very strongly about that. We've seen so many people in the ministry where they've forced their kids to embrace God and everything about church, and they cram God down their throats, and the kids just vomit it all up as soon as they can. They don't own it. There's no personal ownership."

By now I had ample evidence that Jennifer had not been glib when she told me that the last ten years had been "the hardest ten years of my life, but I'm thankful for it, because I've really grown a lot." I had no doubt that she had grown a lot. Living in the mountains had cost her a lifetime of illusions about being a pastor's wife. But in the process she found herself—and God.

My only concern was that she recover some hopefulness about the people of God. "I recently heard a preacher talk about the body of Christ functioning in the Spirit. We all have our different gifts in how to minister to each other. He brought up an illustration of one member of the family hurting, and how the person with the grace of mercy comes in, the person with the grace of helps, and so forth. And I'm thinking, 'You've got to be kidding! I've *never* seen this in action! I mean, I've read it in God's word, but that's not reality in my world.'

"And when I look back over these years, the hurt and the pain, do you know where it's come from? It's come from the family of God. It hasn't been from unbelievers.

"I've had such a strong dose of abusive members in the family of God that I have a hard time believing that there *are* healthy members in the family of God—that there *are* people with the gift of mercy who exercise it to hurting family members, that there are people with the gift of grace and the gift of giving and so on, who do exercise them in the way God intended. I have a hard time believing that that exists."

NOTES

1. *Holy the Firm* (New York: Bantam Books, 1977), 13–14.
2. Dr. Raymond J. Bakke is head of International Urban Associates, based in Chicago. IUA's mission is to help the "whole church take the whole gospel to the whole city." Ray knows more about the world's cities than anyone else I've ever met. He has shown me that the Bible is actually far more *urban* than it is rural. He also has taught me to quit thinking of the countryside as a utopian enclave of peace and harmony, and, conversely, of the city as the breeding ground of evil.

3. Codependency means many things to many people. Melody Beattie probably has as good a definition as any: "A codependent person is one who has let another person's behavior affect him or her, and who is obsessed with controlling that person's behavior" (*Codependent No More*, Harper/Hazelden, 1987, 31).

4. See Galatians 5:12. Paul was "ticked off" at a group known as the Judaizers, teachers who insisted that belief in Jesus was not enough for salvation. They said that one had to keep the law of Moses as well. Paul countered by arguing that Christ *alone* is sufficient for salvation—nothing more and nothing less.

5. See Anne Wilson Schaef and Diane Fassel, *The Addictive Organization* (San Francisco: Harper & Row, 1988).

6

Julia

*"But what if you were to choose the profession of looking
at things to see their beauty, to see what they meant, to
find in the world as much of the truth as you could find?"
"For that you need to be independently wealthy."
"What about a professorship?"
"Of what?"
"Aesthetics."
"Aesthetics?" the father asked. "That's ridiculous.
You'll live like a slave for twenty-five years.
Better to go into the Church."*
Mark Helprin[1]

If you've sat in a movie theater at any time during the past five years, chances are you've been exposed to Julia's work. You never would have found her name in the credits, however. Julia is a foot soldier in the unheralded army of session musicians who perform musical scores for the film industry in Los Angeles.

The job has absolutely no glamor (as is the case with most work associated with filmmaking). You show up to a recording studio. You look over the part. You run through it. You record. You leave. You go home and practice. You check your answering machine, hoping another gig is waiting. If not, you work at a second (or third) job.

As one can imagine, only the strong survive. Julia is a survivor. She's cobbled together an impressive career in a field where success is measured less in financial terms than in reputation. That is to say, in credits: *With whom have you worked? What films have you done?* Julia has worked with the biggest and the best.

Even so, the life of a studio musician must be a somewhat tortured existence. Your work is heard by literally hundreds of millions of viewers worldwide, yet you labor in obscurity. Trained as an artist, you earn your keep in entertainment. Yet what alternatives do you have, really? There are only so many symphony orchestras in the world, and too many cabs.

One consolation for Julia is that she knows there is more to life—and art—than filmscores. "My family was part of the cultured class," she explained as she named off a string of her elders who had excelled in the arts, succeeded in business, served generals, and befriended presidents. "There was a premium placed on intellectual curiosity and artistic achievements."

In high school, while other kids spent lazy summers hanging out by the pool or cruising in their cars, Julia toured Berlin and other European cities as a member of a youth orchestra. "I derived a lot of identity and satisfaction from that," she said, looking back. "It gave my life a lot of meaning."

Another stream of cultural identity was her father's background as a Jew. "It was a cultural heritage that was passed down to me. I remember the family, especially my father's family, giving me books and photos and other things to remind me of where they had come from and where I had come from. It was something to be proud of, to be a Jew, to have a Jewish heritage."

It was a thoroughly secular heritage, however. "God was a nonissue in my household. I have no memory of us ever really talking about religion much. It was never discussed." Even though her forebears were Jewish? "No, no one in my family—no one for generations—has been significantly religious. It wasn't that they were opposed to it, it was just . . . their thought processes didn't lie in that direction. Actually, my ancestors were pretty left-wing, some of them—pretty radical. I guess that's been a real influence on me."

As for Julia's mother, she was nominally Protestant: "baptized as a Lutheran, went to Sunday school as a Presbyterian, confirmed as an Episcopalian—and then she dropped out!"

Did any of that carry over into Julia's upbringing? Only indirectly. "I had these friends who used to get dressed up for Easter, and I was jealous of their Easter clothes. I always thought that was so great. So I ended up going to the Lutheran church as a kid on Easter. I wanted to get dressed up and be in the Easter pageants."

I found that easy to believe. For people in the church where I grew up, the buying of a new "Easter outfit" was an annual rite of spring. Indeed, in countless churches of the '50s and '60s, Easter Sunday was as much a fashion show as a religious celebration. The occasion must have held irresistible aesthetic appeal to someone of Julia's temperament.

Even so, really, "I was raised with no religion at all."

Perhaps as a result, Julia never asked what she calls the "big questions" in high school—the meaning of life, why are we here, is there a God. She was quite satisfied as a person. She had her family, her position in the youth orchestra, and a fairly well adjusted personality.

Her first encounter with what she termed born-again Christians took place at college. "I was *astonished* that such people existed," she recalled. "I couldn't believe that so many people were into it, and also that they were so serious about it.

"I went to some event that was billed as a social. I think it was a cookout. We all sort of stood around, you know, talking and eating, and finally this person stood up and gave a religious pitch." Her reaction to this unexpected gospel presentation was singularly negative. "I felt shafted! I felt like the whole thing had been set up under completely false pretenses, and I resented it.

"That was my first encounter. My second encounter was when this sweet, naive woman came up to me one day while I was studying and pulled out this booklet on how to become a Christian. I listened to her for a few minutes, and then I said, 'Excuse me, I'm going to have to interrupt. You're making assumptions that I believe in God, or that I even care. You don't know anything about me!' I'm sure I must have scared her to death, but she really was being insensitive in the approach she was using."

Actually, Julia was by no means resistant to the gospel. "In my dorm there was this guy and his roommate who were Christians—I mean serious, born-again Christians. I remember they would invite me to go to church, and we talked a lot about God. I was impressed with their sincerity and their sense of certainty. They seemed to know what they were talking about."

Those two young men made a far more positive impression on Julia than the more confrontational believers she had met previously. Still, religion held only passing interest for her until she transferred to another college. It was then that she fell in love with a boy who was "really strong in his faith," as she put it. That made her take a much harder look at Christianity.

I have often heard people joke about "evangelistic dating." But the truth of the matter is that romantic love plays a far more powerful role than most of us realize in why unbelievers end up in the faith and join churches.[2]

And why not? Teenagers and young adults are, on the whole, keenly interested in the opposite sex. So if a non-Christian young person finds someone attractive and discovers that Christianity plays a major part in that person's life, it is quite likely that the non-Christian will start paying attention to religion. I know a number of people who have entered the faith (and also left it) through that process. I also know of youth ministries that actually count on that phenomenon as a recruitment factor in their programming.

In any case, romance played an important role in Julia's eventual conversion to Christianity. It was not her main motivation, but it gave her reason to examine the faith more seriously. "He went to church, so I went to church," she explained. "Then he began to proselytize.[3] The problem was, he was pretty new to the faith himself, and he couldn't answer my questions—especially my questions about some of the awful things that the church has done to Jews down through the years.

"One thing he did do, which was a good thing, was give me some C. S. Lewis books, which I read. They were pretty interesting."

Books had been one of the primary means by which Julia's relatives had passed down their Jewish heritage to her. Therefore, it only made sense that books would be unusually helpful to her as she investigated Christianity.

"Still, all I agreed to do was to go to church," she pointed out. "I made it clear to my boyfriend that I wasn't going to convert just to please him."

But by going to church she met Valerie, who also came from a Jewish background. "Valerie seemed like she was really rooted in her faith and at the same time was pretty down-to-earth about it." That relationship was probably as important a factor as any in Julia's decision to become a Christian. With her boyfriend, romantic infatuation was always mixed up in whatever thoughts she had about Christ. But with Valerie she was able to talk about the faith without that emotional "clutter."

Furthermore, she and Valerie shared a common bond in their Jewish heritage. Valerie could speak firsthand about the possibilities—and problems—of a Jew accepting Jesus as the Messiah.

"The turning point for me came one day when I was alone in my dorm room, cleaning out my desk. I found a copy of that evangelistic booklet that the girl had given me as a freshman. I have no idea why I kept the thing. But I read it through again, only now I understood a lot more. And finally I prayed and said, 'I have all these questions that aren't being answered, and I can continue to ask from this side, from an antagonistic side, or I can exercise what faith I do have, and keep asking.'

"So that was the start. Since then I've had various periods when I've been up and when I've been down. But God has been there."

Julia's description of her conversion reminded me of the experience that many intellectuals have had in choosing to follow Christ. They have exercised faith not because all their questions were answered, but because they concluded it would be easier to answer them from inside the faith rather than outside it.[4] Fortunately, God accepts them with their questions and doubts.

But do other Christians? Can we accept people who have placed faith in the gospel of Christ and yet differ radically from us on issues of all kinds—philosophical, theological, moral, political? Can we tolerate people's search for answers *after* conversion as well as before? In fact, is intellectual inquiry not merely tolerated but *encouraged*? What if someone comes to different conclusions? Is she still welcome in our church? In many cases, no. In many cases, Christians act as though there were a single, monolithic "Christian position" on every question to which any "true believer" must hold.

Julia was fortunate in that the church she was attending was open to curious seekers and new believers with lots of questions. She participated in a women's Bible study and other programs and began to grow in both her knowledge and experience of Christ. "I respected the leadership of that church," she recalled. "The people were intellectually honest, and they seemed pretty smart."

Those relationships became especially important when Julia encountered the first major test of her faith: "My boyfriend dumped me. Then he pulled out of everything. He quit going to church. He said he didn't want to be a Christian anymore. I was devastated. I mean, here was this guy who, if anybody was going to be a Christian, it was him. And now he didn't want to have anything more to do with it. During that time it was Valerie and my other friends at church who kept me going."

Julia continued in that church until she finished her program and moved to Los Angeles. Before going, she talked with one of the pastors about churches in the L.A. area. He suggested one, and as soon as she arrived she showed up on Sunday morning. "It was OK, but there was no place for my age group, no class for people like me."

By coincidence, her friend Valerie also moved to California. Valerie became involved in a large charismatic church. One day as the two were talking, Valerie invited Julia to visit her church. "All you do is come home and complain every Sunday about this and about that," Valerie told her, "so why not go somewhere else?"

Julia agreed and began attending with Valerie. This time the demographics fit. There were lots of people of Julia's age with similar needs and issues. "I went to that church for two years," Julia recalled. "There were a lot of good things about it, and a lot of great people. I was even playing [my instrument] in the worship service."

Nevertheless, Julia encountered a fundamental problem. "I tried to be charismatic and I just couldn't. One time I even had people praying over me, trying to get me to speak in tongues. But it didn't happen.

"And then it started to get really weird. I don't have anything against charismatics. I mean, in some ways I think they have a lot [more to offer than] the more conservative types of Christianity. But the problem with this group was, they just got too pushy. I felt less and less comfortable, and eventually I quit going."

Then she added: "I also knew that I could never take my family there." It was an unexpected remark, but very revealing. It showed that she had a growing concern for the spiritual life of her family. She wanted them to experience some of the faith that was growing inside her. But the comment also showed that she still identified with her family. She had not cut them off, nor had they cut her off—unlike many Jews who convert to Christianity.

I pressed to know more. Why would she not have invited them to that church? "*I* wasn't comfortable," she said. "It was an OK church, but it wasn't me." By extension, she was saying it wasn't for her family, either.

The comment fascinated me. It has long been assumed by many in the American church that people come to faith as individuals, that they leave their pasts behind, including their families, and become members of a new family, the household of faith, the people of God. Theologically that is true.[5]

But the experience of the church throughout history and in many places around the world today suggests that people in fact do not follow

Christ merely as individuals, but as members of a family, a clan, a tribe. Consider the case of the woman at the well.[6] Once the woman realized who Jesus was, she returned to the city to find the men (4:28–29). Remember that she had been married to at least five of them and been intimate with who knows how many more (4:16–18); so she was a connection to the entire village. Note that the city as a whole, or at least a major portion of it, believed in Jesus (4:39–42). It was a group decision.

The point is, every believer is from a group. We in the church may regard the person purely as an individual; I believe God also sees him or her as part of a larger family. Indeed, it is difficult to imagine otherwise in light of His promise to Abraham: "In you all the *families* of the earth will be blessed."[7] "Families" are *mishpachah*, "clans," "kinds," "relatives," "tribes." A similar idea occurs in the so-called Great Commission: "Go therefore and make disciples of all the *nations*."[8] The "nations" are the *ethné*, the Gentiles (as distinct from Israel), or the "people-groups" of the world. God intends to make disciples of all the people-groups of the earth.

My point is not to take away from individual relationships with or personal accountability before God; rather to reclaim a sense of people's roots. We all come from a long line of predecessors. We all have a family story, whether we know that story or not. God takes our genealogical histories seriously. So should we.[9]

In Julia's case, for example, the church was not dealing merely with a single woman who happened to be a musician. It was also touching a representative from a much larger Jewish family of highly intelligent, artistically talented people who traditionally have been skeptical of religious claims in general and contrary to Christianity in particular. Julia was unusual in that she was willing to give the faith a chance. She had indeed found some personal benefit to her spiritual life as a result. But she had not yet found anything that could speak convincingly to her family. To that extent, the church was touching only the surface. It had yet to penetrate to that deep part of her that connects her to generations past and generations yet to come.

After working in California for a while, Julia landed a job in Europe, playing in orchestras in Germany and Austria. "It was a lot of fun living there. I loved the work. I toured the Continent. That really helped me improve my German."

Asked about the impact of the European tour on her spiritual life, she replied, "After the Lutheran churches and the Catholic churches, which were pretty dead, I was left with two kinds of Protestant churches—ones that were older and more conservative and pretty boring, or ones that were newer and charismatic but also very dogmatic. So it was a real struggle.

"In Austria I went to this Pentecostal church one time. They had a layman preaching. He was preaching in this tone that really bothered me. It seemed somewhat anti-Semitic. I really wasn't sure what I was hearing, so I went up to him afterwards. He seemed pleased with that.

"But as he began to figure out the line my questioning was taking, he asked if I was Jewish. I replied that my answer shouldn't determine the content of his sermons. At that point he basically came out and said, 'If I had known you were here, I wouldn't have said what I said.'

"That's when I just lost it. I said, 'It's shameful that you use this Book to promote your own racism! I'll never set foot in here again!'

"After that I went to some other churches. But they were pretty boring, and after a while I just stopped going. It was too much effort to get up and go on Sunday mornings after my Saturday night performances."

However, even though most of her experiences with churches in Europe turned out to be disappointing, Julia did encounter one small fellowship of Pentecostals "who were really living out their faith. It was like the way the church is supposed to be. It was multi-generational and they had this worship with this great music. In fact, that's how I found the church. I heard their music and figured out it was a group of Christians."

In addition, she met a missionary couple who became good friends. "They were not the kind of people I'd normally choose as friends," Julia told me, "but I liked them. I liked their kids. She had a Bible study going with English-speaking and German-speaking women, and I used to go to that. It was great. All these German women would make a fuss over me because I was an American and I was the youngest in the group.

"And through that I met Therése and her husband—who are still good friends." A sudden sparkle in Julia's eye indicated that the couple had made a profoundly positive impression on her. "They *live* their faith," she stated with great conviction. "They live this very simple life. I think they're in business for themselves now. Anyway, I just remember Therése being so down-to-earth about Christianity.

"She couldn't stand it when Christians, especially from the United States, would say, 'Praise the Lord!' when things were really bleak. 'So many of these American Christian people!'" Julia said, imitating Thérése's voice. "'It's all so Pollyanna—"The Lord does everything for a reason!" They're out of their minds!'"

I was struck by Julia's attraction to the realism she found in this woman's perspective. It seemed to be what Julia had been searching for among the various churches she had tried. As Julia described her, Therése was not anti-faith; she was merely advocating an *informed* faith, for a trust in God based on the Bible and common sense rather than wishful thinking.

Eventually the European tour came to an end, and Julia returned to Southern California. "After I got back I felt I needed to go to church. I decided to go back to the church I first visited. I ended up in this weird adult class of misfits, people who didn't have anyplace else in the church to go. We were all mostly singles who were trying to figure out where we all fit in."

She insisted that there was actually a bond among the members of the group. "I stayed with it because it met my needs."

Maybe so, but elsewhere in our conversation Julia made several disparaging remarks about classes designated for "singles." Nor was she alone in her disapproval. A number of unmarried people with whom I spoke voiced similar dissatisfaction—if not outright anger—with the segregation of "singles" in their churches. They seemed to be wondering: who determined that the Lord's appointed way of carving up Sunday school classes should be by marital status?

Or by age, for that matter? Several felt that churches could benefit enormously by structuring at least some educational programs to include people of varying ages, so that children interact with the elderly, for example, or retirees learn alongside of young adults. [10]

In any case, Julia made the class of "misfits" work for her, but the camaraderie was short-lived. While she went on tour again, "the singles group disintegrated. The personalities, pathologies, and conflicts finally brought it down. I don't know what happened. Anyway, that was pretty much 'the church' for me. So when I came back, it was like the ship had sunk and the driftwood was floating. I wasn't interested in going with the 'remnant.'

"I attempted to find another Sunday school class, but I didn't like any of them. They were all married people or people looking for marriage, or things like single moms or divorcées. Nothing that I was looking for."

What was she looking for? "Well, I think in a church you're looking for friends. Except that sometimes in church there's no reason to be friends with these people, except that you're in church. Also, all the Christians I've really liked have been married or not someone I could have a romantic or friendship relationship with. Anyway, after that Sunday school class disintegrated, I just drifted off."

She paused and then said, "The funny thing is, my mother was amazed that I was no longer going to church. She was wondering, 'What's happened? What's going on with Julia?' It was like she really wanted me to find a place that would work. I think she was sad that I wasn't going anymore."

It has been more than two years since Julia stopped attending church regularly. I asked her where she sees her spiritual life going. "I don't know where I'm going with it. Sometimes I think about going to the Unitarian church. But I don't know."

What would she *like* to see happen? "I'd like to find a group of people I could relate to intellectually, artistically, spiritually, and so on."

I left my conversation with Julia feeling profoundly troubled. Here was a remarkably bright, gifted person who, despite fifteen or more years in the faith, found herself grouped with the "misfits," the people "who were trying to figure out where we all fit in." That comment, more than any other, neatly summarizes Julia's life as a Christian: an intelligent, single woman—a professional musician from a Jewish background—comes into the church and wonders, *Where do I fit here? Is there a place for me?*

I was troubled that someone such as Julia should even have to ask such questions. I was even more troubled that I could not be certain of the answers. For this was not the first time I had had occasion to consider how the church handles the best and the brightest. How often over the years have I been reminded by spiritual leaders of Paul's words to the Corinthians: "Brothers, think of what you were when you were called. Not many of you were wise by human standards; not many were influential; not many were of noble birth. But God chose the foolish things of the world to shame the wise; God chose the weak things of the world to shame the strong. He chose the lowly things of this world and the despised things—and the things that are not—to nullify the things that are, so that no one may boast before him."[11]

In other words (so the argument goes), the church's bias ought to be for the little people. If you happen to be wise, influential, of noble birth, and so on, don't expect special treatment. It's as if Paul were encouraging Christians to practice a form of reverse discrimination.

As one might guess, I hold to a sharply different interpretation.[12] What I find ironic is that while Christian leaders line up to decry the decline of our culture, someone like Julia slips through the system. I do not mean to absolve her of personal responsibility for her spiritual life. But it does seem to me tragic that a person with the ability to interpret Bach, Bartók, Mozart, or Mahler should struggle to find her place among God's people. In Julia's family "there was a premium placed on intellectual curiosity and artistic achievements." After hearing her story I had to wonder: how much are these valued by the church?

NOTES

1. *A Soldier of the Great War* (New York: Harcourt, Brace, Jovanovich, 1991), 110.

2. Actually, studies have been done that bear this out. For example, Reginald W. Bibby and Merlin B. Brinkerhoff looked at growth rates among twenty evangelical congregations over a five-year period. They found that "some 32 percent (42) of the 132 proselytes were either engaged or married to evangelicals at the time of their conversion." (See "The Circulation of the Saints: A Study of People Who Join Conservative Churches," *Journal of the Scientific Study of Religion*, 1973, 12:273–83.)

   Similarly, sociologist Dean R. Hoge has published a study titled *Converts, Dropouts, Returnees: A Study of Religious Change Among Catholics* (New York: The Pilgrim Press, 1981), in which he interviewed 200 people in three categories: recent Catholic converts, dropouts from Mass attendance, and former inactives who have returned to Mass attendance. Among his key findings: "Intermarriage represents the greatest single source of conversion to Catholicism—and, conversely, the greatest source of disidentification with the faith."

3. Julia's term. I find it interesting that (in my experience) Jews almost always speak of evangelism as "proselytizing," which may say something about how they regard Christians' outreach.

4. Countless examples could be cited. Here is how Sheldon Vanauken eloquently expressed it: "I *choose* to believe in the Father, Son, and Holy Ghost—in Christ, my lord and my God. Christianity has the ring, the *feel*, of unique truth. Of *essential* truth. By it, life is made full instead of empty, meaningful instead of meaningless. Cosmos becomes beautiful at the *Centre*, instead of chillingly ugly beneath the lovely pathos of spring. But the emptiness, the meaninglessness, and the ugliness can only be seen, I think, when one has glimpsed the fullness, the meaning, and the beauty. It is when heaven and hell have *both* been glimpsed that going back is

impossible. But to go on seemed impossible, also. A glimpse is not a vision. A choice was necessary: and there is no certainty. One can only choose a side. So I—I now choose my side: I choose beauty; I choose what I love. But choosing to believe *is* believing. It's all I can do: choose. I confess my doubts and ask my Lord Christ to enter my life. I do not know God is, I do but say: Be it unto me according to Thy will. I do not affirm that I am without doubt, I do but ask for help, having chosen, to overcome it. I do but say: Lord, I believe—help Thou mine unbelief" *(A Severe Mercy,* Harper & Row, 1977, 99).

5. For example, see Matthew 19:27–29 and Ephesians 2:19.

6. John 4:1–42.

7. Genesis 12:3, NASB, italics added.

8. Matthew 28:19, NASB, italics added.

9. Along the same lines, look at how many times the New Testament speaks of entire *households* following Christ. For example: a royal official with a dying son (John 4:53); Cornelius (Acts 10:2; 11:14); Lydia (16:15); the Philippian jailor (16:31–34); Crispus of Corinth (18:8); and many others.

10. The real issue behind these comments is not marital status—although unquestionably that is involved—but what best helps people learn and grow in the faith? To be sure, marital status may be an ideal classification system for certain obvious needs and topics. But there are any number of other ways that adult learners could conceivably be grouped. What matters is, what's the best way to help people learn and grow in the faith?

11. 1 Corinthians 1:26–29.

12. In the first place, Paul wrote, "Not *many* of you were wise"; he did not write, "Not *any.*" As a point of fact, the Corinthian church included several prominent citizens, including Titius Justus who lived next door to the synagogue; Crispus, the ruler of the synagogue, and Erastus, the city treasurer (Acts 18:7–8; Romans 16:23).

   Furthermore, Paul's words were directed at divisions in the Corinthian church—divisions caused by believers who tended to think more highly of themselves than they ought to have. Paul was pointing out that most of them had little of which to boast. He makes a similar point in 1 Corinthians 6:9–11.

7

L. J.

*A thousand mini-popes were strutting around telling
their followers what to believe, how to behave,
whom to marry, with whom not to associate.*

Os Guiness[1]

L. J. lives with about as much job security as a man could want.
Two-thirds of the population of California lives in Southern California. Two-thirds of the water supply comes from Northern
California. California is running out of water. L. J. works in water management in Northern California.

"We're almost at 8,000 feet here," he said, describing his location
high on the eastern slopes of the Sierra Nevadas. "We're at the top of
the water source. It doesn't get any better. The water's better than
bottled water.

"We take care of it from the snow pack all the way to the faucet.
We do all the water treatment and the transmission lines. We do
stream management and work on the dams, and then all the way to the
treatment plant—and then all the way, actually, to the property line.
We take care of all that, so we're pretty busy."

Pretty busy and pretty remote. "When it snows it comes real
heavy. *Real* heavy! We can be closed in for two, three days. We've had
the road avalanched a couple of times. Then you're stuck here until
they open the road, and sometimes it's been up to about three days."

The irony is that L. J. grew up in Orange County, the epicenter of
Southern California's population explosion. Only he lived there in the
1950s. "Oh, it was beautiful," he recalled. "In the Orange County area
it was just miles and miles of orange groves, citrus groves. It was pret-

ty in those days." Today, of course, Orange County is all highways and houses. "And malls," L. J. added with a certain scorn.

And churches. Thanks to booming suburbs and rapid population growth since the '60s, the Jesus movement in the '70s, the church growth movement in the '80s, and now the megachurch movement in the '90s, Southern California may have a greater concentration of churches—especially large churches—than any other region of the country.

"I started going to church with my mother and father," L. J. said, looking back. "I'd say pretty young—as early as I can remember. First it was Presbyterian. Then we went to another church that was fire-and-brimstone-type stuff. They were pretty legalistic, and it really turned my whole family off. I mean, we quit going to church for years."

His parents' decision to leave that congregation suggested that he came from a family that valued its moral freedom, one that was not about to be cowed by rigid rules and regulations. His parents' choice also set a pattern for L. J. to follow. It legitimized choices that he was to make later on in life.

Rather than look for another church, the family "just kind of backed off for many years. You know, my faith was always there, but I never fellowshiped."

Furthermore, he explained, "I was a pretty heavy surfer, and that took up most of my time. In fact, that's what I did professionally for a while—surfing. So that took up a lot of time. I did a lot of traveling. But I still had my faith."

It was not until six or seven years ago, after L. J. had taken the job in water management, that he returned to regular participation in a congregation. I asked him what it was that ultimately brought him back. "A failing marriage," he said matter-of-factly. "Our lifestyle at the time was pretty wild. We were falling away from the faith, and . . . our marriage was right on the brink. There was a lot of conflict. We were seeing a Christian counselor, and he counseled us and then supported it all by the Bible. And not being *real* stupid, you know, I could see black and white here, and I decided, 'Well, something's got to change.' So I got real active in the church. My wife had been going for a while."

L. J.'s concern to save his troubled marriage reminded me of the many reports I had read about why Baby Boomers are returning to religion today. Many left the church in the '60s, '70s, and '80s with the assumption that life would be a lot more fun outside the church than in it. But after being ravaged by divorce, debt, and dysfunctions of every kind, many of those wanderers are giving organized religion a second chance. The church has reemerged as a source of healing and hope.

For L. J. and his wife, their congregation also became a source of friendships in the community. "Our church is probably about thirty people that show up the majority of the time. It's a real small church" in a really small town where everybody knows everybody else. "Oh, yeah. You get tired going down the street 'cause your hand's waving all the time!"

Many people who live in major cities, where the sense of community often dwindles behind fences and police locks, speak longingly of that kind of neighborliness. But L. J. found a downside to knowing folks that well.

"The church started to get pretty legalistic. They were putting pressure on you. You know, if you didn't do a certain thing, then, well, 'Hey, you're not quite measuring up!'

"We'd let our children leave after Sunday school sometimes. We'd say, 'OK, you guys have gone to Sunday school. You don't have to stay for church. You can go home.' And I was called on the carpet for that a couple of times. There were a few other things like that. My wife and I, we talked to people and said, 'It's really none of your business.'

"But they said it was. 'We're your elders. We're your spiritual parents. Biblically it says we are.'

"And myself, being a little bit redneck, I said, 'It's none of your business!' in no uncertain terms. We had three people pull us to the side and talk to us about that, and that's where it really started turning me off. I felt like I wasn't quite up to par. And finally it got to the point where I just said, 'If I'm not up to par, then I'm sorry! It's not *you* that I have to answer to, it's somebody else much higher.'

"So I've really shied away from there. It's been less than a year, but I haven't been attending church that much lately."

Sometimes legalism is a result of bad doctrine. In the case of L. J.'s church, it was probably more a result of familiarity breeding contempt. Such a small congregation in such a close-knit town can function much like an extended family or clan. Absent the privacy and anonymity of the large church, members of a tiny body of believers can often turn on each other with nitpicking criticisms and self-righteous condemnation. Minor concerns can become magnified into supposedly major sins. It's no accident that many of the New Testament letters, which probably were sent to relatively small groups of believers, warn against exactly that kind of destructive behavior—rumor, gossip, legalistic judgments, and the like.[2]

Moreover, in the small congregation members may find it easier to inflict on others whatever unhealth they bring with them into the faith. Long-term problems in relating to people, deep-seated feelings of fear or hostility, counterproductive ways of handling conflict, chronic needs for control or attention—patterns like these can get out of control very quickly, as the small church often lacks a strong system of checks and balances. And in a group of thirty, one unhealthy person can have a far more pronounced effect than in a group of 300 or 3,000.

It would be one thing if the kinds of problems L. J. and his wife ran into were the exceptional case of a tiny church dominated by a handful of strong and even overbearing personalities. Unfortunately, their experience is probably not that uncommon. There are about 350,000 Protestant congregations in the United States, with an average attendance of 75. Statistically, then, the small church is the norm. The odds are high that many of them face problems of legalism and infighting.

For L. J., the decision to leave was especially tough because there were no other churches for miles around. "But when I make a decision, it's right or it's wrong. But I make it, so I live with it. I stick to my guns. Unless somebody can thump me between the eyes and say, 'You're wrong,' then I will accept that. But it's going to have to be *very* convincing."

One would have thought that because of the history of L. J.'s parents leaving a legalistic church, he would have quit for good this time. Had he lived in a large city, he might well have. But living in such a small community probably worked to his spiritual advantage: day after day he had to face neighbors who were also church members. That motivated him to seek reconciliation with some of them.

"You know, I have gone to some of the people and I've made some amends with them. Told them that I was a little overly sensitive here, and I could have been a little wrong there. Of course, then I also pointed out that I still stand by my guns. But I really think there has been some healing."

If I had any reason to doubt the sincerity of what I was hearing, L. J. dispelled it with his next comment. "Our first Sunday of the month is Communion, and I shy away from that like the plague because I've still got some ill feelings and I won't take Communion until I am completely over that," meaning over the unresolved relationships. "Because, you know, you're not supposed to [take Communion] if you have some problems with your brother or your sister."

L. J. seemed to be referring to passages in the New Testament that challenge Christians to seek peace and purity in their relationships before coming to worship God.³ I was struck with his fear of the Lord in this regard. He did not seem the type to need to invent a pious excuse for refraining from taking Communion. His reasoning seemed straight-forward—and dead serious.

He went on to add, "My wife and I are still going to marriage counseling right now, and we're still having some problems ourselves." In other words, for L. J. the importance of mending broken relation-ships begins right at home. "I feel no shame at all that we're having problems. It's just . . . marriage is work!"

It was an incredibly responsible statement. And the fact that he and his wife were sticking with their counseling indicated they were serious about doing the work of marriage. "Yeah, we are," he affirmed. "We're both committed to our marriage. The vows that we said weren't hollow. We're working [our problems] out.

"And then some Sundays I'll get a little bit irked at her, and I just say, 'Forget it! I'm *not* going to church to be a phony and act like I'm happy. That's one of the reasons why I've kind of shied away from the church. I mean the phony bit. We were fighting up to the door of the church and then—*woop!*—'OK! Here we are—the perfect couple!' That wasn't working. That finally got real old."

L. J.'s passion for integrity was refreshing. I found it easy to imag-ine that he would not be especially welcome among a covey of legalists, people interested in control based on external standards rather than internal character. For that matter, L. J. would not be the easiest per-son to have in anyone's congregation: his bent seemed to be to speak his mind boldly and hold his opinions tenaciously.

For example: "I felt the church just had their priorities wrong. I've got a real soft spot for the homeless and children, and in this day and age in this country, nobody should be going hungry. But you see, we don't have a church building ourselves, and I don't see how we could ever afford one, because we're a pretty small congregation. But yet we've still got several thousand dollars sitting in the bank doing noth-ing—but that's our building fund.

"I've been saying that's not our money, that's the Lord's money. We need to get that out and start feeding some people, looking around, making the money work—because it's not our money, it's the Lord's money. So let's do something! Let's do some projects. Let's sponsor a kid. Let's have a monthly donation to Feed the Children or something like that.

"But I got a lot of opposition on that. I've made that known, that this is what I feel. To them it's more important to save that money and get interest. And I've said I don't agree with that."

It was hardly the first time I had heard about Christians disagreeing on how a church should spend its money. But even though L. J. had taken a strong—and contrary—stand on the point, I learned that he had not completely given up on his fellow believers. In fact, he told me that he could foresee the time when he might return to active participation in the fellowship. He was by no means down on the church as such. "Not at all. In fact, like I've said, there's healing going on now between me and the church and in the church in general.

"In fact, one person that I was having a pretty hard time with, we went and lived with his family for about three days recently due to certain circumstances with our house. We'd been good friends for years, and then we kind of had differences of opinion and some strained times, but we did some healing during that weekend. And, you know, it was the Lord's way of putting us together.

"This friend and I, we used to talk about coincidence and just kind of smile at each other. For instance, it was a 'coincidence' that I was having trouble in an area, and then I go to church and that's exactly what the pastor was talking on! And he says, 'Yeah! Just coincidence, huh?' And we'd smile at each other like the pastor was speaking directly to me.

"So I really do think that was one of the things where the Lord brought us together that way. Because we were definitely having a tough time with each other."

Even so, I knew that L. J. had not been attending church regularly for about a year. So I wondered how he was nurturing himself spiritually. "A friend I work with is a brand new Christian. We speak quite a bit about the Bible." I understood that to indicate that L. J. read the Bible quite a bit. "Not as frequently as I should. It's kind of a guilt thing I put on myself, but it's just something I haven't. . . . I love to read. But I just haven't been cracking the Bible like I should, like I feel I should."

There seemed to be a lot of "shoulds" surrounding L. J.'s Bible reading. I wondered whether he felt the same way about prayer, so I asked whether he prayed much. "Not publicly. I don't feel comfortable praying out loud in church. I don't pray with my wife as often as I should. In fact, very seldom.

"But my silent prayers, my prayers . . . you know, I'm out in the woods a lot." His tone changed noticeably, and I felt as though I had entered a very private and holy place. "You know I . . . it's kind of like a running conversation I try to keep up. It's not a real formal prayer, but I try to keep a running conversation: 'You know, Lord, I'm having problems here,' or, 'Hey, what about this?' You know, you're supposed to pray unceasingly, and I think most of the time I do. I try to keep Him in my thoughts as much as possible."

I felt certain that L. J. talked to God the same way he talked to everybody else—with simple, straightforward, heartfelt words. Many of the great sinners in the Bible prayed that way; for that reason, many of them are remembered as great saints.

L. J.'s mention of prayer on the job intrigued me. I'm always curious how people integrate their faith into their day-to-day work. So I asked him about it. "You know, people look at me sometimes and go, 'Boy you're a fool!' Because I try to be just as honest as I possibly can. You know, it's a cliché, *you gotta walk your talk*. And if you're going to be a professing Christian, you can't be a sneak or say, 'Well, I'll kind of pull some strings here.' You can't do that! You gotta be that light out there. You gotta be, 'Hey, I'm an example here!'

"We just had our taxes done, and people are wondering, 'Wow! You're claiming only that much?' And we say untaxed money is not right. You know, pay Caesar his due. And if we get shorted, that's tough! That's the way it's supposed to be."

A light in the midst of darkness. As I soon found out, that metaphor from Jesus' Sermon on the Mount[4] was more than an overworked platitude for L. J. It spoke directly to the spiritual life of his community. "This town used to be a dark little town," he explained. "There was a real high percentage of drug abuse, a lot of alcohol use. And my wife and I were just saying the other day that we could really feel the Lord's presence in this town. It used to be dark.

"I mean, there's one little bar here in town, and that place is just . . . you walk into it and it's *evil*! You just *feel* the evil in there. And it seems like a lot of people who used to frequent that thing—There's fewer and fewer of them, and more and more of them are speaking the "B" word—you know, *Bible*.

"It just seems like there's more people. . . . They aren't outward. They aren't going to church. But they're not following the darker
life. It seems like things are kind of lightening up."

It almost seemed contrary to all the messages about Christian unity and love as the ultimate apologetic.[5] Somehow, L. J.'s church, with
all of its problems, all of its legalism, all of its disunity, had had some
sort of impact for God in that "dark little town." Dim though its light
may have been, it nevertheless had shown the truth that Christ is the
light of the world. The group of believers there may not have been
exactly a lighthouse, as one might have wanted. But in pitch blackness,
even the flicker of a match can help.

NOTES

1. *The Gravedigger File: Papers on the Subversion of the Modern Church* (Downers
   Grove, Ill.: InterVarsity, 1983), 138.
2. For example, 2 Corinthians 12:20; Galatians 5:16; Ephesians 4:29, 31–32; Colossians 3:9; and Titus 3:2.`
3. For example, Matthew 5:23–24 and 1 Corinthians 11:17–30.
4. Matthew 5:14–16.
5. See John 17:21.

8

"Chris"

*He was not bitter, just disillusioned. All he wanted now
was to . . . leave Washington forever. He was looking for
a job in industry, a management position, but it was
difficult. His name had been in the papers often. He would
not work for the White House again even if asked to come
back. He . . . wished he could write. Maybe then he could
express what had been going through his mind. Not the
cold, hard facts of Watergate, necessarily—that wasn't
really what was important. But what it was like for young
men and women to come to Washington because they
believed in something and then to be inside and see how
things worked and watch their own ideals disintegrate.*
Carl Bernstein and Bob Woodward[1]

*E*xit Interviews is a collection of people's real-life stories. But
had I written it as a novel, I might well have developed a character and a plot to match the interview in this chapter. In fact,
that would have been easier in many ways and perhaps more
effective.

For one thing, I could have avoided the problem that I created for
myself when I promised anonymity to my interviewees to protect their
privacy. In this chapter, I am choosing to go so far as to identify the
person only as "Chris" (not the person's real name). I will not say
whether Chris is a man or a woman; however, I will write as though
Chris were a man. Nor will I say whether the incidents that led to
Chris's disillusionment took place through a church, a seminary, a denomination, or a parachurch ministry; let's just call it an organization.

Of all the interviews I conducted, the one with Chris was by far the most disturbing. Most of the others described individual cases of disappointment with a particular faith community, or else a more general and abstract history of mounting disillusionment with the church. But Chris's story had the dark feel of a Watergate.

What troubled Americans about Watergate was not simply the facts of that sorry incident; people have committed far worse crimes. Rather, it was the cover-up by the highest leaders in the land, people who obviously knew better. Yet far worse even than that was what the scandal implied about our system and the people running it.

Millions of Americans became convinced that, in the end, they cannot trust their government, that at best they are being told half-truths. Indeed, only through some reporter's aggressive digging will they be lucky to learn even that half of the truth. Thus, the most damaging and far-reaching impact of Watergate was to permanently poison our nation's public discourse with cynicism.

However, I am not prepared to turn Chris's story into a Watergate. My purpose in this book is not to expose secrets but to explore the spiritual pilgrimage of people who are leaving the church. For that reason, I offer Chris as a case study in what happens when a bright, eager person rises higher and higher in a system, only to learn that sin and scandal have been covered up at the highest levels, and that the spiritual cause to which one has devoted one's life is led by people who play by a different set of rules than the ones they hold over underlings or proclaim to the public.

To meet Chris was to meet a person who looked, as they say, like someone who had been through the wars. Only Chris's battles seemed to be as internal as they were external. He appeared to be trying to hold together vast contradictions, trying to make sense out of nonsense, as though every other word in the language had changed meaning. I had met young kids whose naive illusions had been shattered by sudden crises. Here was a middle-aged veteran of the faith sifting through a lifetime of wisdom, trying to piece his world back together.

There was little in his family background to fall back on. "I came to the faith as a small child," he began. "I grew up in a Christian church, a very fundamentalist church in a small town. That's all I knew my whole life, basically. It was my mother who took me to church and introduced me to Christ, although the Christianity was definitely more cultural than anything else."

It was a Christianity based on fear and authoritarian control. "My pastor preached *against* everything—against long hair, against music, against Elvis Presley, against short skirts—you name it. He was always against something, you know. He didn't preach *for* anything.

"Then he had an affair with my mother. It lasted a number of years. She was the church secretary."

Hypocrisy. Scandal. Shame. Betrayal. Pain. All of it linked to a church. I couldn't think of a better program to drive someone away from the faith: to show him the worst side of so-called Christianity, to show him some of the worst people, to put him as a child through some of the worst emotional experiences. No wonder Jesus uttered those scathing words "Whoever causes one of these little ones who believe in Me to stumble, it is better for him that a heavy millstone be hung around his neck, and that he be drowned in the depth of the sea."[2]

Chris himself came close to drowning in a tide of bitterness and cynicism. "You know, in a lot of ways, it really colored me," he admitted. "To this day I have trouble with church. Absolutely. I know it goes back to that. That touches on it."

Did no one step in to put a stop to the situation—the men in the church, for example? Did they do nothing about it?

"I don't know. I don't know. See, as a kid I didn't know what the governing, political side of it was. I was completely out of that. The only thing I remember is my dad physically beating up the pastor and leaving him lying in the driveway of his house.

"My dad was Archie Bunker. That was his style. You know, redneck. So I grew up with that kind of hypocrisy. Christianity was more oriented around don'ts than do's, more around negatives than positives, more around prohibitions. It was ugly, really."

Terribly ugly. It was a Christianity that made God out to be a vindictive tyrant, someone who almost delighted in catching people in sin and punishing them.

Not surprisingly, Chris began looking for a way to escape. He ran away from home at sixteen but returned after getting into trouble. Later, though, he made a permanent break by enrolling in a Christian college several hundred miles away.

"Why I even went there, I have no idea," he said, looking back. "I think it was one of the few schools I was even aware of, because I kind of lived a cloistered life. But it was away from home. That was probably the biggest attraction. It was hundreds of miles from home. And then, probably more importantly, it was hundreds of miles from that church."

Ironically, "the church looked down on the school to some extent, because to them it was liberal." Chris laughed just thinking about that, because the school was actually quite conservative. "But it was OK. They didn't expect me to amount to that much, anyway. So that was good."

Was college a liberating experience after the confining legalism of his youth? "Actually, it was more of the same. My theology teacher ran off with his secretary. Another teacher walked into class one day and kind of forgot himself and started out his lecture by making reference to a movie. He had broken a rule because we weren't supposed to go the movies, and he had gone to one. It just clicked in my head: *They're playing games again.*

"Of course, you have to understand, I was young at the time, a rebellious teenager looking for reasons to kick something. In all fairness, you have to look at that some, too. It was how it was hitting me emotionally, I think. I got into a lot of trouble at school—a *lot* of trouble! I was breaking the rules. I never really did anything immoral. But you didn't have to go very far to break a rule. If you couldn't walk a straight line, you'd bump a wall. So it kind of became a sport to see what I could get away with. I don't know, it was my way of just screaming at the rules.

"One guy in the school kind of saved my emotional life, a dean. Two deans, actually. They cut me some slack. For example, you weren't supposed to hold your girlfriend's hand. So I'd wait until I was in the presence of a dean and then reach over and get my girlfriend's hand—making sure he saw it. I did things like that which were rebellious to get turned in.

"And then this particular dean would have me sit in his office long enough to make it seem to the other dean like I had been chewed out. In fact, he disagreed with the rules himself, but he was caught in the system. He was good to me. You know, I wrestle with the implications morally of what he was doing. But he sure went a long way to help me.

"I remember one time he showed me this picture hanging on a wall. It looked like one of these pieces of abstract art. I couldn't figure out what it was by looking at it. A couple of right angles, some circles and things like that. I said, 'What is this?'

"And he said, 'This is the corner of something we couldn't have in here. I tried to get it in here, but we couldn't have it. It would have made one of the donors quit giving money or something.'

"I looked and looked and looked and still couldn't make out what it was. Finally he said. 'It's the corner pocket of a pool table.'

He said, 'They didn't know what it was, either. But I got this in here, at least.' That was his only way of rebelling, I guess."

I was amazed, in light of all that Chris had told me to this point that he had not taken the first chance he could get to run as far away as possible from anything with the label "Christian" on it. "You know what?" he said reflectively. "It seems kind of a strange thing—I've always been kind of a thinker—but one of the things that kept me hanging on is that I was aware enough of the early church to know that all the disciples, with the exception of one, died terrible deaths for what they believed. It wouldn't make statistical sense to think that they'd all been nuts.

"So I kept having this nagging feeling that I was missing something. But I didn't know exactly what it was. I think that kind of kept me hanging on, like I wasn't being told the whole story or something. It was a simple little thought in a way, but I keep coming back to that as what kept me hanging on. And you know, even though my pastor was a jerk and so many of the people in the church were jerks and everything else, I still . . . something just kept me hanging on."

No doubt the grace of God. In any case, Chris held on until one day he met someone who talked to him about the Christian life in a completely different way than he'd ever heard about it before. "They put it to me that you want God not just to be a resident in your life, but you want Him to be president."

I thought it ironic that such an authoritarian description of Christ would have any appeal for Chris, but it did. "I had never really heard of that before from that angle. I'm not sure what it was—maybe it was the way [the gospel] was packaged or something. But I think when I was nineteen, when I was at college, that's when it could be that I actually became a believer. That's when it really made personal sense to me."

It helped a lot that the person to whom Chris spoke was one of a group of believers who were "the first Christians I had ever run into in my entire life who seemed normal. You see, the church where I grew up was viewed by the town as some sort of a cloistered group that wouldn't let their kids dance or do other normal things. Kind of an odd bunch of birds. But within the church, that was viewed as a positive because 'we are a peculiar people.'" Sarcasm dripped from Chris's voice as he quoted this King James phraseology, now often understood with other than its original meaning.[3]

"I've heard that verse a million times: 'We are a peculiar people.' And the more peculiar, the better! So if the town was for something, our church needed to be against it.

"But this group of kids I met during college were people. They weren't 'peculiarities.' They were just normal, laughing, having a good time. They didn't abstain from some of the social things I abstained from or was told to. It was attractive. I was drawn to the lifestyle, to the lives. Watching the lives. That's what did it. It just appealed to me. It was a 'brand' of Christianity that was extremely refreshing, if I can put it in those terms. I'd never run into it before.

"Some of the more narrow people at my college didn't like them. So I thought, 'Hey, if *those* people don't like them, I'm going to check them out!' It's funny, I look back and think the Lord guided me in my rebellion!"

Some Christians might be scandalized by the notion of God "guiding" someone in rebellion. But what other hope is there when the truth of God has been exchanged for a lie—grace, for example, transposed to mean rules and regulations? Under those conditions, the fight for truth looks and feels like, indeed is, rebellion—a good kind of rebellion, against error.

The irony is that many of the people who would scoff at the idea of God's sponsoring such behavior stand in a tradition that is itself a rebellion—*Protest*antism—and whose founder was a young man faced with circumstances not dissimilar to Chris's. They actually celebrate the fact that God led him in his rebellion. And what were his words? "Fear God and sin boldly."[4]

Chris needed little encouragement to follow either side of that dictum. "Sure enough, I started dating a person at the school who was involved in a group that a lot of the kids didn't like, because it was kind of a socially dangerous group—because they sang music and did things that were sort of not acceptable. The thing that attracted me to those kids was that they tended to be a little sharper group of kids. Socially more apt, more extroverted, and so on. They sort of stood out in a way.

"And there was this person who kind of hung with that group in a social sense. And there was an attraction there, and I ended up marrying that person."

So, despite its limitations, college was a net gain for Chris. His suspicions that there must be more to life and the faith than what he had grown up with had been confirmed. He had met one or two authority figures who extended grace and freedom to him rather than rules and condemnation. He had made friends with a group of attractive, "normal" kids. And he had found a mate who shared his hopes for a healthier way of living. Most important, he had come to know Christ as a Person who could be trusted—and as a Person one *needed* to trust.

The key to these developments was the group of kids. They opened the windows for Chris. Indeed, they probably saved his life. "I shudder to think what direction I might have gone if I had kept finding no answers, no answers, and no answers," he said grimly.

Instead, after graduating from college, Chris was invited to join the organization[5] where he would make his career. He had met some of the leaders of the group while in college, and as before was attracted to their cause through the relationship that developed and the winsomeness of their lives.

"I think why I went to work with them was very simply that. It wasn't an issue of being called to the ministry, even though that kind of went with the package. It was basically a 'brand' of Christianity. As I look back, maybe it had something to do with that thought I had earlier, that there must be something more to this.

"But it was the relationship with one or two people that tended to draw me initially to it. With that relationship came the other things that I was aware of just by being around the group—their cause and so on. If the cause hadn't been there, would I still have gone with them? I don't know. If it were just a commune or something, probably not. But for me, it was definitely more heavily weighted in the area of the relationship and the family, the sense of atmosphere, of family."

An extraordinarily powerful dynamic was operating here. The organization that Chris joined in effect replaced the church in which he had grown up. Whereas the old church had been narrow-minded, negative, and "peculiar," the new group seemed open, appealing, and "normal." Where the old tolerated hypocritical, authoritarian leaders, the new offered attractive, positive role models intent on inspiring people to their best. The old preached *against* everything; the new spoke of vision, of mission, of making an impact on people. Most important, where the old controlled its people through fear and shame, the new group inspired intense loyalty by fostering close relationships among its members.

In fact, not only was the organization a replacement for Chris's church, it became a replacement for his family as well. To be sure,

Chris and his spouse were creating a home of their own. But they were doing so within the context of the organization.

The group was like many communities where the work calls people out of the larger society and brings them together in close association—start-up ministries, mission outposts, military bases, certain companies, small colleges, diplomatic communities. In these settings, friends and colleagues are not merely neighbors, they are all part of the same "corporate family." In fact, many organizations describe themselves with precisely that term.

There can be real advantages to that sort of group bonding. But there are also inherent perils. In the case of someone with Chris's background, the organization can become a surrogate family. But whatever unhealth one has brought from his or her family of origin is almost guaranteed to be transferred onto the corporate family. Thus there is all the likelihood in the world that the person will expect more from the group than the group can (or should) deliver.

Likewise, the person may extend more loyalty to the group than the group deserves. That, in turn, invites the danger that the organization will abuse the person's commitment—through unrealistic demands, for example, or by justifying what is actually unfair treatment with excuses like, "He's a trooper," "It's his duty," or, "He owes us; think of all we've done for him."

I cannot say to what extent these factors played into Chris's situation. But he made it plain that the organization had enough idealism associated with it that it smoothed over many a potential or actual conflict with words about the priority of the vision and the need to sacrifice personal interests for the good of the cause. "Oh, absolutely," Chris affirmed. "There were always enough goals to reach and ideals to pursue to keep you enamored with the situation."

Chris remained content and busy for a number of years, handling a variety of important but relatively low-level assignments during a period when the organization was growing rapidly. He was excited about the group's progress. He also felt that he and his associates were making a difference for Christ through their cause. "We were riding a crest and doing things in ministry that no one had done before."

After several years in the trenches, Chris began receiving upper level assignments. "And that's kind of where my troubles began," he explained. The higher he went, the more "dirt" he learned about people —below him, on his level, and even above him. The organization was becoming complex. It was broadening. As a result, there were more opportunities for people to get away with things that went against the ministry's principles. The more abuses Chris uncovered, the more troubled he felt.

"It was not so much an issue of running into people who wanted to do things differently than I did. It was more issues of integrity and morality—or immorality. That bothered me more. Maybe things were going on all along and I just didn't know it until I got up there in that level of management to see it. I don't know." Then, as an afterthought, he added, "I've never really made a connection before between that and my past. I don't know; it's an interesting connection. Could be something there."

I thought so, but based on other things that he had told me, I was certain that Chris was mature enough not to be rocked by the moral failures of others. He had been in the system too long and was too realistic about people for that to happen. He had his eyes wide open to the nature of sin and to human nature, so that he accepted people's lapses as a part of life. Indeed, he spoke of his dealings with various offenders in a way that I felt showed remarkable compassion toward the people without minimizing the wrongs they had committed.

Ironically, it was this very maturity and proven stability that brought Chris into the position that ultimately led to his departure from the organization. He took an assignment with one of the top people in the group, a high profile leader who represented the ministry and its cause to the public. So if there was any hint of problems, Chris was in a position to be among the first to detect that something might be wrong. "I was very much that person's shadow," he explained. "Chief-of-staff would be a good analogy."

So when allegations of wrongdoing began coming in from a variety of quarters, "I wasn't far enough removed from that individual to be able to disassociate myself. It cast a shadow across me because I was in that shadow all the time. I was this person's representative. I was to speak the individual's desires to others. When too many situations of integrity arose, and then eventually immorality, I couldn't live with that and be true to myself personally. It was just too much."

I pressed Chris for some detail, to make sure that the "situations of integrity," as he described them, were not mere peccadillos or bad habits or things that simply bothered others. "That wasn't the issue at all," he assured me. "Little stuff like that you can build mechanisms to deal with." No, the recurring allegations against Chris's superior were of a far more serious nature: financial improprieties and marital infidelity, among others. At that point, "It became a basic issue of trust," Chris told me, a feeling that "I cannot trust you."

I have known others who faced similar crises in their organizations. The first thing I always ask is whether anyone has spoken directly with the person about the situation. If so, what were the results? If unsatisfactory, then has anyone spoken with the person's supervisor or board?

Chris had confronted his boss on the facts that had come to light. Unfortunately, the person made no attempt to accept responsibility or make changes. So did Chris go to the top and lay out the issues? "No, I didn't go to the person's supervisor and say this is what I know. I didn't do that initially. Eventually I did. I didn't do it initially because I was afraid of what I knew."

The statement sent a chill down my spine, for two reasons. First, Chris's fear and silence in the face of gross immorality seemed like a repeat of the tragic situation with his childhood church and family. For years, the sin of adultery had been tolerated and no one had done anything about it. Everyone had closed their eyes to it, establishing a pattern of denial and cover-up. Now, years later, Chris was getting sucked into a similar conspiracy of silence.

But there was something else that made me uneasy: Chris had reason to be afraid of what he knew because what he knew had some staggering implications. As in Watergate, it was not the facts themselves that were so arresting, but what the facts pointed to—particularly the people they pointed to. "I knew that the supervisor and my boss were real close friends. They went way back together. And that made me real unsure of myself and what might happen to me.

"So I thought, 'Well, I'll just get out of town. I'll write a letter of resignation and say some nice things. I'd say what I could say. But my boss wouldn't permit it. My leaving somehow cast a poorer light on my boss. So it came to a place where I had to tell my boss's supervisor the fundamental reason why I was leaving. And that's when I discovered that the supervisor already knew about everything—and hadn't done anything. That's when the heat got turned up on me."

I assumed that Chris meant heat from his boss. "No, from my boss's superior! That person's angle was that they knew about that. They were handling that, and somehow it was wrong of me to make an issue of that."

Despite those assurances, Chris remained unconvinced. And knowing what he knew, he was astounded that the supervisor had not dismissed Chris's boss long before. It seemed to be a clear case of collusion between two old friends. Their loyalty to one another apparently superseded their loyalty to the organization—or its spiritual principles. In Chris's opinion, gross sin was being tolerated rather than dealt with. Not by people who were young and inexperienced but by veteran leaders who absolutely knew better.

"This is where it gets real foggy," he went on. "I don't know if they were afraid I was going to make an issue out of it, which would, in effect, take it out of their hands completely, or what. I have no idea. All I was focused on at the time was just getting out and getting away and going on to something else. They were agreeable to that. It was damage control."

So, with the ship on fire and his superiors threatening to make him walk the plank, politically speaking, Chris jumped of his own accord, feeling lucky to have his dignity and reputation more or less intact. But he still had to face the emotional and spiritual aftermath of his ordeal.

In that regard, it's important to remember that although his exit was precipitated by a single, localized problem at the top of the organization, Chris was also directly or indirectly aware of a number of other problems of a similar nature, or at least of a similarly serious nature, within the group. Furthermore, this was a ministry with which he had spent his entire career. These were his life-long colleagues, his friends, virtually his family from whom he was walking away.

"It was more than any one issue or any one thing by itself," he told me, looking rather exhausted. "That one issue all by itself was not that insurmountable. But when you put them all together, the cumulative effect of it all pretty much reached the breaking point."

I asked him to enlarge on what he meant by the breaking point. What conclusions, if any, had he come to? "Sometimes my conclusions are emotionally descriptive more than anything else," he replied.

Well, then, what kind of emotions did the whole affair raise for him? "What in the world am I doing in Christian work? That was one of the emotions I've come to. At least vocationally speaking. There are times when I don't *want* to be in Christian work. I want to be in secular work. I don't *want* to be identified as a Christian.

"You know, I had a good friend who recently checked into a motel and just ended it all. He'd been in Christian work all his life. That was his solution. You know, there were other things involved, certainly. But nevertheless, that was his bottom line. He was extremely disillusioned."

More like ultimately disillusioned. The anecdote disturbed me as I looked at the person I was interviewing. "Yeah, it's made me think," he admitted. "Made me think. I'm not going to check into a motel or anything. But it's made me think *real* hard about the fact that I've got fewer years ahead of me than I have behind me.

"And I'm thinking in terms of living it on purpose and not by default. Living it on purpose. Living it the way I want to live it and not the way some supervisor or somebody else thinks it ought to be lived. You know, in terms of physical chronology, I've given probably the best years of my life [to the ministry]. And yet, in terms of the most productive years of my life, they're probably still ahead of me."

It was a hopeful outlook. "I just have to be careful of that emotional disillusionment—that's probably a good word—to fill that void at times. I have to be careful of that, that it doesn't become a crippling mechanism. I want it to be more a triggering mechanism and trigger me *into* something else. It doesn't have to be crippling."

Nevertheless, Chris *was* somewhat crippled by what he had been through. At the very least, he was limping along. He had lost all enthusiasm to attend church, for example. "When I drive down the highway, maybe on a cross-country trip or something, I look at all these churches and all their signs out along the highway and I think, 'There's not one of them I'd want to go into!'

"Look at the names of these churches. What are these people thinking? It's like they get together and say, 'Let's come up with a name that will chase as many people away as we possibly can!' So they put this idiotic name up that has words in the name that are meaningless! Why? What's the point? They're certainly not doing it for the person who's outside the walls. I wouldn't even want my name associated with that.

"Some of it perhaps is a throwback from my past. I've been a believer all my life. I go to church, that kind of thing. But more often than not, even to this day, church bores me. There are exceptions. But I leave the average church wondering why I went."

So if church was out, how did Chris nurture his spiritual life? "I read a lot. I read two to three books a week, and that's probably a big part of it right there. I'm careful what I read. There's a lot of junk out there in the Christian world as well as the secular. But that's one way.

"And then I try to be with people who will stimulate me. The last few years in particular have been pretty dry. Church attendance has been real sparse—not that that means if it were more regular, it wouldn't be dry.

"So," he finished up, "part of the answer is, I'm not doing enough."

I wondered whether Chris's experience had altered his view of God. In his youth, he was offered a God who was angry at people, a mean old Man cracking a whip. Later he met people who were following a much more benevolent, compassionate God, and he responded to that Person with trust. Now, having served that God all his life and ending up on the losing side of some political fisticuffs, how had his image of God changed?

"Well, that's a good question. It's a question I'm still in process on, but I think it's affected my view of man more than my view of God. Certainly it touches on my view of God. But you realize that we live in a world that's not the world God created. It's a world that's been destroyed and polluted by what we call the Fall. I hope I'm not just intellectualizing here. Much of this [situation] is a product of that reality. And much of what I've witnessed and what I've felt and what I've observed, it doesn't say as much about God as it does about man.

"There are times where I've emotionally asked myself, where is God and when's He going to do something? Or when's He going to give me relief? I'm not even sure what relief means. But I really don't think it's hurt my view of God in any substantive way.

"Even though there are some similarities between nineteen and today, I'm not the same person I was when I was nineteen—thankfully. So maybe the same set of circumstances now mean different things to me than they did when I was nineteen. I guess part of what I'm saying is that it says more about me. Who I am. You know, I think part of where I am is a function of, in some ways, I've grown up. I don't mean that in an arrogant sense, but in some critical ways. I've grown up!"

I was saddened by what "growing up" seemed to imply. At age nineteen he felt he had learned a fundamental truth about God: you could trust God and know Him as a friend. Now, at middle age, he had come to a different truth about people: you could not completely trust people—especially, it seemed, people in the ministry, people who claimed to speak for God.

The comment reminded me of John's sobering words concerning Jesus: "While he was in Jerusalem at the Passover Feast, many people saw the miraculous signs he was doing and believed in his name. But

Jesus would not entrust himself to them, for he knew all men. He did not need man's testimony about man, for he knew what was in a man."[6]

What was in a man, and therefore what is in any institution that a man creates or leads. I wonder if we know what Jesus knows—the true condition of our humanity—and if so, whether we take it seriously enough. Not that we go looking for sin; Chris's hometown church excelled in that. But we can just assume that sin is present in every one of us, and thus in our organizations—even those devoted to "ministry."

The hard question is what to do about that. The church has been rocked in recent years by scandals of various kinds. Several have been well publicized. But it's easy to dismiss most of those as the anomalous excesses of a lunatic fringe. More troubling are the ones tied to organizations such as the one Chris belonged to, ministries at the center of modern-day Christendom. I have no suggestions to offer here on this problem. I'm just thankful that there are people in boardrooms all across this country with heads far wiser than my own who are struggling with the issue—an issue that defies easy answers and demands that each case be treated individually.

However, ministry scandals relate directly to this book by their impact on people like Chris. In my experience, the people affected most severely by the moral failures of spiritual leaders are not their supporters or the constituents that their ministries serve, and certainly not the general public, either Christian or non-Christian. The most seriously affected are the offenders' spouses and children and their staff workers.

Staff workers are the backbone of the industry that Christian ministry has become. Churches, parachurch organizations, mission agencies, Christian publishers, church-related hospitals, Christian schools, seminaries, and dozens of other ministry-related agencies employ thousands upon thousands of these dedicated people. They are the ones who lead the Bible studies, plan the conferences, write the brochures, answer the mail, prepare the reports, edit the tapes, teach in the classrooms, deliver the services, and help raise the money.

Like Chris, these people are "true believers." The vast majority have signed on primarily for the sake of the cause—certainly not for the paycheck. Thus, one overriding quality that ministry staff workers seem to have in common is their tenacious loyalty. Christian ministry today depends as much on that loyalty as on any other factor.

But that asset, if abused enough, can turn into a severe liability. For instance, when leaders *bend* the rules, staff workers may be disturbed and disappointed, but they can usually overlook it. Their loyalty makes them very forgiving. When leaders *break* the rules, the workers may be disillusioned, but even then, most are willing to hang in there, depending on how the situation is handled.

But suppose it comes out that leaders have *blown off* the rules as if their position grants them a special exemption? Then those loyal workers can be devastated. It's no longer an issue of accepting human frailty; it becomes a matter of trust. Here is someone workers have followed, have stood up for, have given their energies and skills to support. The leader has probably had impact on their spiritual lives. He or she *embodies* the ministry. Therefore, whatever workers have done for him or her, they have done *for the ministry.*

So when workers find out that this person has not only broken a moral covenant but has trampled a personal covenant—a covenant of human trust—the reaction is as understandable as it is predictable: "What in the world am I doing in Christian work?" as Chris put it. Such is the cry of formerly loyal workers who have withdrawn belief, not only in untrustworthy leaders, but in ministry itself.

No human system can support itself for very long apart from loyal people. Yet even though I knew that, I was still hesitant to accept Chris's story, given its implications. "Look," I asked him at the end of our conversation, "you're describing what sounds like major structural flaws here. To an outsider, it looks like the organization you were part of is doing God's work. Frankly, they've had a lot of success. So one might ask, if they were really doing something wrong, God certainly wouldn't be blessing them the way He has, would He?"

"That's definitely an accurate characterization," Chris replied, "but to me it is false thinking. That's not really accurate at all. A lot of things look like they've been blessed, but in fact they just do a function, or it's just a good businessperson making a good decision. Otherwise, we have to wonder why the Mafia does so well, and other things that God obviously hasn't blessed."

It was a sobering way to end our discussion. At the same time, I was glad that Chris was leaving the ministry and not the Mafia.

NOTES

1. *All the President's Men* (New York: Touchstone/Simon & Schuster, 1974), 84. The passage cited is part of Carl Bernstein's description of Hugh Sloan, one of the key sources for Woodward and Bernstein's Pulitzer-Prize-winning reporting on the Watergate scandal.

2. Matthew 18:6 NASB.

3. The King James translation renders the first part of 1 Peter 2:9 as, "But ye are a chosen generation, a royal priesthood, an holy nation, a peculiar people." The phrase "a peculiar people" was how the seventeenth century translators rendered λαος εις περιποιησιν (*laos eis peripoiesin*), literally, "a people for possession." In other words, believers belong to God; they are His possession. Peter is recalling language from the Old Testament that describes Israel as God's chosen people (for example, Deuteronomy 14:2; Psalm 135:4). Paul does the same in Titus 2:14.

   As God's people, believers are to pursue moral purity, to "be holy as I am holy." Unfortunately, some groups, such as the one to which Chris belonged, stress the term "peculiar" to the point of bending it from its original meaning of "belonging to oneself alone" or "not being shared with others" (Latin, *peculiaris*, "of private property"; hence "a people for God's own possession," NASB), to the idea of "odd," "eccentric," or "strange." It's a misunderstanding of both the Greek text and the King James translation.

4. Martin Luther. To be accurate to the context of this famous line, Luther was writing in response to his friend Melanchthon, who was complaining about his many sins. Luther pointed out that the things Melanchthon was calling sins were actually minor issues that had more to do with his humanity than his sin nature. Luther advised his friend to pay more attention to God's grace and "worry" only about major (or true) sins, thereby "fearing God." As for the minor issues, he should just live his life and be himself; or, stated in typical Luther hyperbole, "'sin' boldly." He was not advocating that anyone presume upon God's grace.

5. The reader should keep in mind my earlier qualification: to protect Chris's identity, as well as the group of which he was a part, I am using the broad term "organization" rather than indicating a specific church, seminary, denomination, or parachurch ministry for which he worked.

6. John 2:23–25.

9

Vince

I remember sitting day after day at the same table in a dull restaurant where I had to eat my lunch. There was a beautiful red rose in a small vase in the middle of the table. I looked at the rose with sympathy and enjoyed its beauty. Every day I talked with my rose. But then I became suspicious. Because while my mood was changing during the week from happy to sad, from disappointed to angry, from energetic to apathetic, my rose was always the same. And moved by my suspicion I lifted my fingers to the rose and touched it. It was a plastic thing. I was deeply offended and never went back there to eat.

Henri Nouwen[1]

There's a store in the Dallas area that sells nothing but water. I find that remarkable, given that North Texas has so much water that its population probably could quadruple without affecting the supply. Furthermore, its water is relatively pure, at least as pure as that of any other metropolitan area. Yet even though any thirsty person could turn on the tap for a virtually free drink, someone has figured out a way to make money off the sale of water.

The secret may be that the store is not really selling water. It is selling *choice.* As I understand it, you can buy distilled water, purified water, spring water, artesian water, normally filtered water, extra-filtered water, naturally carbonated water, artificially carbonated water, deionized water, mineral water, demineralized water, desalinated water, flavored water, unflavored water, imported water (Texans consider any water from out of state to be "imported"), or local water (water from nearby Arkansas is sometimes allowed as "local"). Oh, and by the way, would you like that already bottled, or would you prefer to bottle your own?

Needless to say, you don't walk into a store like that and ask, "Can I have a glass of water?" You ask, "Can I have a glass of *that kind* of water?" as you point to your selection. A surfeit of choices has changed the equation. It's no longer enough to know that you are thirsty; you have to know *what you are thirsty for!*

A similar situation exists in many churches today, as I discovered through a study I once did for a foundation. I was asked to visit about a dozen large churches around the country to gather certain kinds of information. These were all cutting-edge *megachurches*, enormously large congregations (more than 1,000 people, some many more than that) that offered extremely varied menus of programs.

There were programs based on age groups: nurseries, children's Sunday school classes, youth activities, college classes, singles' groups, young couples' fellowships, middle-age growth groups, activities for retirees, even octogenarian clubs, and more.

There were programs based on particular categories of need: therapy groups, 12-step programs, programs for the engaged, the newly married, the divorced, the single parent, the widowed, and many others.

There were programs built around interests: educational classes, new member classes, seeker classes, Bible studies, discipleship groups, volunteer training classes, evangelistic outreach ministries, social concern ministries, athletic teams, sewing clubs, reading clubs, even computer clubs, among others.

There were even programs organized according to people's weekly schedules: Sunday morning classes and services, Sunday evening meetings, midday activities, weekday evening classes and services, Saturday morning fellowships, and Saturday evening services, not to mention programs and groups operating all day long throughout the week.

Again, as with the water store, that kind of choice sort of redefines what it means to "go to church." You can't just walk in and say, "Here I am!" You have to have some idea of why you're there in the first place, so as to ask, "Where can I find _____?"

In fact, the experience is much like going to a shopping mall. The genius of the shopping mall is that it brings together under one roof a splendid variety of boutiques that specialize in meeting particular customer needs. But unless you're there just to window shop, you have to know what you want to buy to make effective use of the mall. It was no accident, I thought, that all but one of the churches I visited were located near shopping malls.

Now there can be no doubt that churches that have employed a strategy of choice have grown enormously over the last two decades. The strategy works. And many churches have adopted it in order to attract people like Vince and Sharla. They fit the profile. They were perfect "customers" for the megachurch: white, upper-middle-class Baby Boomers, early thirties, educated, two incomes, no kids, already converted, eager to grow, lots of non-Christian friends, looking for a church.

So why has Vince stopped going? One reason, ironically, was an overload of programs. "Don't throw the programs at me!" he told me emphatically. "Don't inundate me with the programs and tell me, 'Hey, it might be good for you to be at this.' I mean, I've got a lot going on. I work fourteen hours a day. I got too much going on to be at these other things."

It might appear that Vince was using one of the most common excuses there is for lack of involvement in a church: "I'm just too busy." But I did not hear it as an excuse so much as an honest statement of frustration. Vince could afford only so many hours a week for church activities, so it mattered little to him how diverse the church's programming was. He was interested only in the one or two offerings that met his needs.

The statement "I'm just too busy" may say as much about the church as it does about the person. In fact, Canadian sociologist Reginald Bibby argues that some churches today may be declining not because they offer too few choices, but *too many*. Churches "have responded to a cultural demand for a specialized contribution. By being so graciously compliant, the groups have essentially served up religion in whatever form consumers want. They have not provided a religion based on what religion is, but a religion based on what the market will bear.

"The result is that service attendance is just another fragment to be drawn on when customers find it convenient to do so. Ironically, religious groups are losing active attenders not because they are failing, but because they are succeeding."[2]

It would be grossly unfair as well as unwise to draw too many parallels between the experience of one person, such as Vince, and the larger population. As we'll see, there were many factors involved in his decision to drop out of church.

Nevertheless, Vince's cry, "Don't throw the programs at me!" recalled a question that Bibby put to inactive church members in Toronto: Was there anything the church could do to bring them back? The most frequent response (30 percent) was no. Why? Because "from the cold standpoint of a 'cost-benefit' analysis, most of [them] were already getting an acceptable . . . return from the church. The question . . . is perhaps analogous to asking people, 'What would it take to get you to eat five meals a day?' and having them answer, 'I don't want to eat any more than three.'"[3]

The metaphor of a cost-to-benefits analysis is particularly appropriate to Vince. As a businessperson, he was used to evaluating his use of time on that basis. Unfortunately, when it came to the church, he felt he was not getting a good return on his investment. I asked him why not. He spoke about the one event of which he made the greatest use, the Sunday morning worship service.

"It was a production. It was an incredibly well orchestrated production—and I didn't like the orchestration. Everything was cut right down to the tenth of a second. You see it on television all the time, and this church was no different from what you'd see on television." (As a matter of fact, the church service was carried on the radio.)

"The preacher was there as part of the show. Part of the show? He was the main act! He basically had a twenty- or twenty-five-minute stint. But he was the main act. I'm slipping out of bed at eight o'clock in the morning to get to church to go through an introduction before he gets up there for twenty minutes. I'm worn out by that time, because I'm so bored with the people and the presentation and . . . I'm worn out! I want outta there! I'd catch about sixty, maybe sixty-five percent of what he was saying. Is that what I'm going to church for? I've got better things to do.

"You know what I would rather do? Sleep, read my Sunday paper. Oh, I love reading my paper on Sunday morning. I hate anything to interrupt that. And I gotta tell you, that church wasn't giving it to me, not to get me away from my paper on Sunday morning."

The irony is that the service at Vince's church was specifically designed to draw people like Vince away from their papers and into the sanctuary. The objective was not simply to keep the congregation awake but to involve it in a sense of participative worship. To accomplish that, the program featured winsome personalities on the platform, a relevant, moving message from the preacher, and lively music performed by a large choir and an ensemble of talented musicians.

Yet despite this minutely planned and extravagantly choreographed event, Vince's reaction was simple and straightforward: "Boredom! Bored me to tears. I mean, the programs? Bored me. The people? Bored me. The approach? Bored me. The services? Bored me. I can't begin to tell you how I spent many a Sunday, an hour and fifteen minutes, just like going through the motions. Going through the motions. For twenty-five minutes—*maybe!*—the preacher had something to tell me. I was there to hear that. But I didn't need the other fanfare."

Perhaps the problem here was one of style. For whatever reason, the style of worship at the church did not resonate with Vince. Rather than attracting him, it repulsed him. It grated. He felt uncomfortable. So I wondered why he hadn't tried a different church, as there were many others in his area. "I started to search for another church. But you know what I was finding, Bill? I was trying more churches, but they were all trying to beat [the church where I'd been]! You know! I felt that they were saying to themselves, 'If we did this and we did that, maybe we would have more people, too.'"

I was familiar with the problem. Of all the pressures pastors feel today, perhaps the most severe is the pressure to put people in the pews on Sunday morning. So when any church appears to have discovered effective ways to do that, other churches that hear about it often wonder, "Would that work here? Maybe we should try it." Before long, countless churches are using the same strategies, with varying degrees of success.

Unfortunately, copycats rarely turn into tigers. There's nothing wrong with learning from the successes of others. But who wants to attend a church that is nothing but a clone of some other congregation? How often we urge people not to compare themselves to others but to rejoice in their own special talents and abilities and personalities as God has designed them. Why not do the same with our churches?

The issue is not how one's congregation can be like some other "successful" (i.e., large) church, but how it can be the unique church that God intends it to be. Do we know what that church is? Do we know what particular purpose and mission God has called it to?[4]

At any rate, one reason that the style of worship at Vince's church may not have appealed to him was that he had come from a Roman Catholic background. He was now attending a low-Protestant church. It was not that he missed what he called the "ritualistic" format from his youth. But there were certain subtleties rooted in his upbringing that influenced his perceptions. For example, he saw the easygoing style that marked many of the Protestant church members' approach to the faith as lacking in sincerity. It was too smooth for him, too slick. There was nothing hard about following Christ, nothing to work at.

"It was easy," Vince explained. "I could fake my way through it so easily. People would turn around and look at me just because I could rattle off a couple of Bible verses better than the average Joe. You know, I had my act together in those days, and I could carry on a very intelligent conversation biblically and joust intellectually with people, which would be a lot more difficult for me to do when you just focus on Scripture." Then he paused and said, "That church was a watered-down version of what had originally attracted me to Christ, the call to the faith."

What was Vince's call to the faith? How had he gotten started? "My conversion was really quite simple. No one had to convince me that Christ died for my sins. A lot of people really have to be pulled along; I believed it all my life. It was no big deal. I mean, really, it was no big deal."

What was a "big deal" for Vince was the implications of his faith: What difference did it make? How did it affect how he lived? So when a friend in college began showing him ways to act on his beliefs, "he had a captive audience, because I was looking for the fundamentals. Give me a couple of fundamentals here. Bring it down to my level.

"I'm not talking about a program. I didn't want to follow a cause. I wanted to buy into faith. There were a lot of people selling causes out there. But the people I was around were helping me buy into a faith. I believe that. I felt that happen to me back there."

One of the most helpful of those people was a pastor at a church Vince began attending. "You know, I continually use the words 'authenticity' and 'authority' to describe him," he said reflectively. "And not a lot of pretense. There wasn't any. I mean he didn't really give a hang whether you walked out and never came back, in the sense of having his own personal worth involved."

Vince drew a sharp contrast between the take-it-or-leave-it style of that pastor's ministry and what he viewed as an almost fawning eagerness to please at the church he and Sharla attended, where "there was more of an emphasis on numbers. How many people are coming? How many people are you bringing? That first pastor was not really concerned if a visitor came and didn't have the Broadway production. He was a guy who would get up there and tell it the way it is.

"You know, the preacher in our second church had so many altar calls that were an embarrassment. They were an embarrassment! Because no one showed up. He held a party and no one came! I'm sitting there whispering to Sharla, asking, 'Why is he doing this? That woman sitting over there in that twenty-thousand-dollar mink coat ain't getting up, Sharla. I guarantee it. I'll lay my life on it. She's not getting up there.' And this guy sitting next to her is this distinguished looking guy who might be chairman of the board of some company. He cannot get into going up there.

"That church was intimidating. It was a very beautiful church. And a very 'nichey' church. If you wanted a program, they had a program for everything. You want a solution? They had a solution for everything. But what I'm looking for is someone to slap me around a little bit."

I understood Vince to be saying that he didn't want a church that catered to everyone. He wanted some authority, some direction, someone to say, "Here's what you need to do," even if it meant that people might walk away from it. "Absolutely! Absolutely!" he affirmed emphatically. "I *want* the authority. I want to hear it. I want someone to make me believe as a little child."

Again, he felt that the pastor in his earlier church had spoken with that kind of authority. "I remember some of his sermons, and I felt, 'Hey, this is the fire and brimstone! This is a prelude to the music that I'm going to face.' Because we're all going to have to face the band sooner or later. This is a prelude to what's going to happen when I'm called on the table to give an account of myself."

Then, with great deliberation, he added, "The one thing that I really like as you read through the Old Testament is those guys really talked a lot about *fear.* Now I know we have salvation through the blood. But those guys . . . it's a common theme throughout the entire Old Testament—the fear of God! You know? I don't hear that today! I don't hear it. I haven't heard it in a long time, and I just think we're too busy saying everything's gonna be OK. What I get down on more than anything is that I don't sense . . . I don't hear that, you know, that shake-me-up, slap-me-up-the-side-of-the-head, saying, 'Hey, I'm just telling you, man! You make the choice."

In other words, he wanted the church to take sin a little more seriously and preach to that. "Right! You're a hundred percent right. Get me away from the life of sin that I can lead. Show me why I had better change. You know, don't pamper me, man! Don't make it easy for me."

Vince could accept that people are sinful and that they fail. But he wanted to hear spiritual leaders call sin sin and failure failure. He wanted them to name sin first and then talk about what God has done and is doing about it. He felt that too many preachers tend to glide over sin as if it were "cool," as if it were just a little problem. "You're nice, you're a sinner, we're gonna forgive you, you're forgiven. . . . Aw man, I've heard it before!"

I was fascinated to hear this perspective. Many churches and Christian leaders have gone to great lengths to distance themselves from the fire-and-brimstone extremism that characterizes some Christian groups. It's a brand of Christianity that can prove embarrassing and infuriating, dwelling as it seems to on sin and hell and condemnation and the worthlessness of people, with comparatively little attention paid to the good news—the grace of God and His provision of Christ for salvation, the forgiveness of sins, and eternal life.

But I wonder: has the pendulum swung to the opposite extreme? Is there such an exclusive emphasis on God's love, on human worth and dignity, on emotional well-being, and on the positive in general that many churchgoers are left to wonder whatever became of sin? This seemed to be Vince's complaint.

He seemed to be looking for a church with teeth to it. But not because he had a weak ego that needed an authoritarian moralist to tell him how to live. Rather, because he knew what a lot of churches seem to have forgotten—that people like him still struggle with sin. Whether or not preachers call it sin or speak to it with any authority, people have to confront their own sinfulness and the sinfulness of others. Traditionally, they have looked to the church for insight and help in dealing with that.

So has the church lost sight of its "core business," the business of bringing sinful people to maturity in Christ?[5] For Vince, apparently it had. Jesus spoke of hungering and thirsting for righteousness.[6] Vince was a thirsty man. He didn't just want to feel good, he wanted to actually *become good*—which is what righteousness is all about. But like the

customer in the water store, he discovered that his church was no longer in the business of providing just a plain old drink of water.

Vince was a terribly thirsty man. Three major incidents in his spiritual life help to explain why. The first was that his friend from college,
the person who had been a catalyst in helping Vince nail down what he
called "the fundamentals" of the faith, informed him that he was gay.
"He came to me," Vince recalled, "he laid it on me. I remember embracing him when he left. But I was consciously hiding my shock and
disbelief. It was a shock to me."

It was still a painful relationship for Vince to talk about. I asked
him whether he felt betrayed. "I have felt that," he told me. "I have felt
it. Because I believe that that guy—more than the church, more than
any Bible study, more than anybody—that guy had more of an impact
on how I approached people with the Word than anyone else. So yes, to
an extent I felt that."

But he added, "My anger is not because he's gay. For me to articulate the type of anger is difficult. I felt that he did not deceive me, but
he deceived himself all those years. He deceived himself. He was gay
back then [when I was in college]. How would I have reacted had I
known he was gay? That's what I ask myself. And how would I have
treated my Christian roots, my born-again Christian roots, had I known
he was gay? Suppose someone said to me, 'Vince, I want you to meet
this guy. He's gay. Listen to him.' How would I have reacted?

"But you know, that guy's done a lot worse than becoming gay. I
think he made poor decisions on how he approached people with his
gayness. But what angers me now is that he doesn't think he's doing
anything wrong! It would have been a lot easier if he had just come to
me and said, "You know, I'm pretty messed up right now. My whole
life is messed up. I need help. I want you to know this and how it
happened.

"Instead, it was more like, 'Everything's cool. Let me tell you
why it's cool.'" Vince described how his friend had used Bible passages
to justify an actively gay lifestyle. That, more than anything else, outraged Vince. Choosing his words with great care, he said, "See, something's wrong here. That type of experience with that has created in me
a really standoff . . . calculated . . . judgmental . . . real hard view of
the church and whom I choose to get involved with." Clearly, a bond of
trust had been violated.

Yet even with that, Vince spoke with a certain compassion about
his friend and the situation. "It could have been me. It could have been

anyone. It happened to be him. Now if God used him [in my life] in the midst of him struggling with homosexuality back when he knew me—and I'm convinced that He did—I really feel, today, that I'm a much better person for it. I believe that. I would not have the relationship with Christ that I have today had it not been for that guy."

I wondered whether Vince held a similar attitude toward the pastor in the church that he and Sharla had attended, especially after it came out that the man had been cheating on his wife. "Well, I gotta tell you," he said reflectively, "I would love to be able to use that as an excuse: 'Hey, Bill, how do you expect me to be involved in a church? The guy who disciples me turns out to be gay. The one pastor who finally has a little bit of an effect on me, to bring me back to the church, ends up having an extramarital affair.'" He shook his head. "But I can tell you that it didn't set me back. It really didn't set me back."

Why not? "Because it's like what I said before, that somehow God used my homosexual friend. Well, I know that pastor reached a lot of people. OK, he did something he shouldn't have done. So do I have to hold that over his head and say, 'Man, what the . . . !' Hey, maybe back then I would have. Maybe I would have burned him at the stake." But not today.

Apparently many in the church had wanted to burn their pastor at the stake. "It was unbelievable!" Vince exclaimed with a mixture of surprise and irritation. "I mean, for cryin' out loud! The guy had an affair. It's been happening since the beginning of time! It just so happens that he's a real man of God, and it's a sin. And why we look at adultery as the sin of sins, you know. . . . I really could never get over that."

Such a statement of tolerance might seem surprising to some in light of Vince's earlier remarks about the church's soft-pedaling sin. But a third incident in Vince's life helps explain his accepting attitude: "No one ever thought that I would get divorced, you know. Everyone always put me on a pedestal as far my relationship with Sharla was concerned, because of the way we approached life together. But I went through [what the pastor went through] to an extent. A divorce was the sin of sins."

The breakup was not caused by adultery. Vince and Sharla grew apart and eventually separated. "We were amicable. We were friends. There was nothing hostile about our divorce," he explained.

Nevertheless, "I was humiliated by the thought of it. See, to me, the end of the marriage was like as close as you could come to the term 'condemnation.' I'm not talking so much by the Lord but by the public that witnessed the ceremony. My family and friends. I think it was like, I became human. See, I think some people thought I was something other than human in the way I led my life.

"Sharla and I attracted a lot of people to us. We had a lot of friends. But we always professed our faith to people. We never gave up on that, which attracted more people to us. We were good at it. We were good at it as a team. Which saddens me the most, because we were so good at it. That was probably the only way I can ever recall God using us as a married couple. We were really good at telling people about our faith and bringing people to understand Jesus.

"So I probably felt the humiliation of our breakup because of what we professed. It was probably very similar to what my gay friend would have felt at another time coming out of the closet, which is what kept him in the closet. I didn't tell my mom that I was separated. I didn't tell my business partner. I was humiliated. I mean, it was unbelievable."

It didn't take a psychologist to see as much self-condemnation in Vince's statement as any condemnation he may have felt from others. Perhaps the source of that dated to his college days, when, like many young believers, he took a rather strident if not arrogant approach toward explaining his newfound Protestant faith to his Catholic family.

"The posture I took with my family was devastating. Because when I went home, I didn't just read the Bible, I started memorizing it all, verse by verse. When I went back after my freshman year, I was well known in my town, and word spread really quickly that I had gone off the deep end, like I was in some sort of cult.

"And I gotta tell you, it really destroyed my relationship with my whole family. And it carries over to this day, because I got married outside of the [Catholic] church. I came from such a ritualistic Catholic background, and I got married outside the church. We tried to soften the wedding some. But that was one of the hardest things in my life."

So when Vince's marriage came apart, he felt doubly humiliated. Not only had his marriage to a non-Catholic failed, but the memory of his self-assured attitude in college came back to haunt him.

On the other hand, the experience had its positive side: it made Vince far more compassionate. "I think it's hard for certain people to accept the fact that I was married as a Christian. I got married in a real Christian ceremony. I led life as a Christian. But I got divorced. And a lot of times I feel like I want to work with those types of people who have had similar things, because there are a lot of people who are like me, who care much more than I do about what people think of them within the church. Me, based on what I've seen, I really don't care. I mean, it really doesn't bother me that much. A divorce was the sin of sins. Did it keep me away? No, it didn't keep me away from the church."

A spiritual advisor who turned out to be gay. A pastor who had committed adultery. A failed marriage. The three situations cast an entirely different light on Vince's adamant statement: "I *want* the authority. I want to hear it. We're too busy saying everything's gonna be OK."

Things were not OK, and Vince would not go back to any church that seemed to suggest they were. Not that he had given up on the faith: "I believe that I would be lost without Christ in my life," he said. "But for the grace of God, truly, I would be hanging out there somewhere, way different from wherever someone perceives me to be today.

"Do I feel that I'm in a bad position today as far as my Christianity is involved? Right or wrong, I don't feel like I'm in a bad position at all. I know what's right, and I know what's wrong. I know when I mess up, and I know how I should be living my life as how Christ would want me to walk the life. Do I really do it? No, obviously I don't always do it. Do I feel like I've lost that much of my faith because I'm not going to church? Because I'm divorced? No, not at all.

"But I ain't going back," he added with definite conviction. "I'll never be back. You know, I try to convince myself sometimes that it's only a matter of time. But I know myself. I know what it's going to take to get me off the dime, to really convince me that I need it."

Then, as if the thought had suddenly popped into his head, he said, "The guy who has had the biggest influence on my life over the past few years is a fellow named John [a business acquaintance in another city]. He's had a profound influence on me, because he's dealt with me like that. He takes *nothing* from me, you know? He takes absolutely nothing from me! And I need that. Maybe everybody doesn't respond well to that, but I do.

"He has incredible integrity. I mean, I talk to him once or twice a week. I don't buy into everything he says, because he takes an approach that is too archaic for me sometimes. But if we're going to talk about some hard things, that's what I want to talk about with John, because I pay attention to him, because he doesn't color it. He's the guy I turn to today. And if I'm spiritually nurtured in any way, shape, or form over the past few years, it's from him. Not a church. Not a preacher."

I was glad to hear that Vince had at least one source for spiritual guidance and accountability. I could see he was unlikely to return to a church anytime soon. Still, I asked him directly whether he would like to find a church that preached a message along the lines he described.

"Would it please me to find a church?" he asked himself, seeming to turn the question over in his mind. Finally he answered, "It would please me like you wouldn't believe!" Then he added, "Of course, that church probably wouldn't have much sex appeal. But to be honest, I'm just a little tired of trying to get there."

NOTES

1. *Creative Ministry* (New York: Image Books, 1971), 105.

2. Reginald W. Bibby, *Fragmented Gods: The Poverty and Potential of Religion in Canada* (Toronto: Irwin Publishing, 1987), 134. I should point out that Bibby was specifically referring to Canadian churches. However, his research has application to the church in the United States, as he points out.

   Bibby's comment that "service attendance is just another fragment to be drawn on when customers find it convenient" echoes reports from the Barna Research Group that Baby Boomers demonstrate a "lack of felt commitment to any single congregation" and therefore prefer to attend several different churches on an "as-needed" basis rather than establish a more traditional "church home" (*National and International Religion Report*, Sept. 25, 1989), as well as George Gallup's insight that "believers" are not the same as "belongers" (Interview, Reformed Theological Seminary newsletter, 10–11, date unknown).

3. Bibby, 134–35. An "acceptable return" means that people expect so little from church that all it takes is an occasional visit or even a lingering psychological or cultural connection with a religious body to satisfy the person's needs. It does not imply that everything is just fine, with churches doing a splendid job and people thoroughly satisfied and engaged in the program. Otherwise, the 30 percent that Bibby is talking about would not be classified as "inactive."

4. Rick Warren of Saddleback Church in Mission Viejo, California, describes this as a "purpose-driven church." One way to start finding out what a church's purpose is (or ought to be) is by asking the three fundamental questions that Peter Drucker says every organization needs to ask itself: Who is the customer? What is "value" to the customer? And what is the nature of our business?

5. Ephesians 4:12–13.

6. Matthew 5:6.

10

The Baby Busters

All I want is reality. Show me God. Tell me what
He is really like. . . . I want the real thing.
And I'll go wherever I find that truth system.
                              "Baby Buster" Lisa Baker[1]

One way to tell the difference between Baby Boomers and Baby Busters is that Boomers can tell you exactly where they were when they heard that John F. Kennedy had been assassinated; Busters are liable to ask, "Who was John F. Kennedy?"

Baby Busters are the roughly 68 million Americans born between about 1960 and 1980—so-called because their lot was to follow the birth "boom" of the post-World War II era. "Their earliest memories include gas lines in 1973 and the fall of Saigon in 1975. . . . They watched Ronald Reagan's first inaugural address. Today they are in their [teens to early thirties], and their lives as workers, householders, and consumers are just beginning."[2]

In contrast to Baby Boomers—an idealistic generation if ever there was one—Baby Busters tend to feel disillusioned and abandoned, demographers say. In fact, they view Boomers as selfish and materialistic and even "blame the Boomers for having ruined the world for them," says researcher George Barna.[3]

Does that include the ruination of the church? It very well may. "If you were to chart the spiritual commitment levels of successive generations this century, it would be like skiing down the side of a mountain," Barna reports. For example, weekly church attendance among "older adults" stands at about 49 percent; among Busters it stands at 34 percent.[4]

I began to understand why this might be the case after spending an evening among several dozen Baby Busters during the course of my travels for this book. A friend of mine happened to be hosting a party in his home while I was visiting his area. By coincidence, a majority of the attendees were probably in their early twenties.

I was not surprised when people at the party began to ask me about my book project. Nor was I surprised when they began to relate incidents from their own experiences.[5] But looking back on that evening, I was amazed at the correlation between the research I had read and the statements I was hearing. Barna and the others seemed to be right: Baby Busters are "probably the most pessimistic generation we've ever seen."[6] The ones I spoke with were especially cynical about the church.

Now obviously it would be foolish to extrapolate from one evening of random conversation to an entire generation. Baby Busters are as unique and varied as any other group, and the ones I met at this gathering were anything but a representative sample. Still, it was interesting to compare notes with my other "exit interviews," so many of whom were Baby Boomers. Whatever else I might make of what I heard, it certainly confirmed that "disillusioned Christians" are by no means limited to the Woodstock Generation.

Here, then, are a half-dozen of the many stories I heard that night, personal anecdotes of why individuals had left churches or ministries—and why some of them had not yet made it back.

JEFF

Jeff told me that he had grown up in a church that concentrated on personal holiness to the point of teaching that sinless perfection is possible this side of heaven. "So everything was real legalistic," he explained. "They worried about every little thing. We had these impossible standards about what you should do, what you should think, how you should spend your time. Nobody could live up to them."

In fact, no one did. The church's obsession with sinlessness only managed to drive sin underground. People put on an outward show of morality, but meanwhile "everyone was sinning in secret," Jeff recalled.

Then, during his teen years, Jeff began reading books that talked about the biblical concept of grace. He felt a theological breath of fresh air as he learned about God's provision for sin and the freedom from guilt and shame that grace could bring. He also was amazed to find out that grace—rather than law—held the power to motivate believers toward righteousness and holiness. All of this was completely new information to him. But the book backed up its claims by verse after verse of Scripture.

Eventually Jeff asked his pastor why he wasn't preaching grace to the congregation. "He told me, 'Jeff, if we preached that, people would start living any way they pleased.'

"But I already saw people living any way they pleased—only they were hiding their sin! So when I graduated from high school, I was gone. He was preaching the Bible, but he sure wasn't preaching all of the Bible."

LEON

"I heard you're writing a book on why people leave the church," Leon said as he shook my hand. I told him that I was.

In a very direct manner, as though he had been thinking on the topic for years, he told me, "I think the reason people leave churches is not really hypocrisy. Even though they may say that. But it's not really hypocrisy. See, everyone fails. Everyone sins. So people may say, 'Look at all the hypocrisy in the church.' But then, they have to admit that there's hypocrisy outside the church, too."

He paused and then went on. "And another thing. It's not the teaching either, so much. People can take bad teaching, you know. Like where the preacher's messed up in his theology and stuff. People can handle that. The people I've met, anyway.

"The main reason I've seen that people leave churches is if the leaders don't pay attention to them as people. I mean, we're all made in God's image. So we have to treat each other that way. And as human beings we all have certain needs. So we have to meet each other's needs. I mean, it's little things like remembering their names. Or like, have you ever asked a pastor to pray for you? You know, we tell people to share their prayer requests. Well, how many times does a pastor come back and ask you how it came out? 'What happened, man? How did God work? What can I be thankful for?'

"I just think churches have to start taking people seriously. Treating them with just a little human decency. If not . . . "

I suddenly remembered that I had met Leon earlier in the day. I began to wonder: had I remembered his name?

MEGHAN

"I'm twenty-two years old," Meghan told me up front. "My parents are in their mid-forties. They've always been real into their careers—*real* into their careers! Which is kind of sad, because now they're both about to get laid off and it's like—*bam!*—everything's gone. It's over."

The conversation eventually came around to the topic of her faith. "My folks are heavy into New Age kinds of thinking. I mean, it's funny because *I'm* the straight one! *I'm* the Christian!"

So how did that happen, given her background? "That's what's so weird about it," she explained. "Even though they were off in their own beliefs, they wanted me to get exposed to Christianity. I mean, it sounds odd, but that's what it was. So they sent me to this private Christian school. And that's where I found the Lord."

"How did they feel about that?" I asked. "I assume they were happy. After all, that's why they sent you there, wasn't it?"

"Actually, they weren't real happy at all. See, what happened was, first I became a believer, and then I got involved in this ministry that works with high school kids. They didn't like that. It was too much. They wanted me to get an exposure to Christianity. But I sort of 're-belled' by really getting into this group, and becoming a leader and all."

Meghan explained that the group was led by a young man with a dynamic, charismatic personality. He was not trained in theology. In fact, he had no college education. Nevertheless, the sponsoring organization had put him in a teaching position, and he was very effective. He had an especially strong influence on Meghan. The way she described the situation, it sounded as if he and the group were providing her with the kind of attention that her career-focused parents were not.

As high school came to a close, the leader encouraged Meghan to join his organization for the summer. "It sounded like a really neat thing at the time, and they told me that all my needs would be taken care of." That sounded like a recipe for disaster, but somehow Meghan survived relatively unscathed as she worked the summer and stayed on into the fall. "It was a lot of fun, really, and I probably learned a lot. But I'll tell you, they didn't follow through on their promise. At end of a year, I had been paid a total of fifty dollars! So I quit."

Had that been the end of Meghan's troubles, she probably could have chalked it up to experience and moved on relatively unimpeded in her spiritual development. However, she walked smack into another negative experience when she applied to a nearby Christian college.

It was hard to understand exactly what happened, but she described a lengthy ordeal of red tape, miscommunication, missed deadlines, and obstacles in connection with some scholarship money to which she was entitled. She admitted that she had made some mistakes and that "technically they were right in the reasons they gave for not admitting me. But then they kept my scholarship money! Even though I wasn't allowed in!"

That made her furious. It was her second letdown by a Christian institution, and the second involving money that should have come to her. She felt cheated and betrayed. "So at that point I chucked it all. I just dropped out. I quit going to church, reading my Bible, praying, everything. I'd had it with anything called 'Christian.' And I stayed away for months and years until finally I came back out of sheer need."

Having been on both sides of the table in terms of ministry-related institutions, I could well imagine that there were reasonable explanations as to why Meghan had not received what she thought was her due. On the other hand, I was struck by the apparent loneliness of her situation. She was dealing with two well-established Christian organizations, probably neither of which was out to take advantage of her. Still, she had no one to look out for her interests. She was negotiating on her own, and she was unfamiliar with the system.

And there *is* a system in the Christian world—a power structure, a funding stream, a way decisions are made, a leadership hierarchy, a slate of institutions, and a set of assumptions about why people come into the system and how they will act inside it. Much of this is informal and most of it is unacknowledged. But the system is there.

I grew up in the system, so I know something of how it works. But a person like Meghan comes to it blind. In youthful naïveté she accepts what she is told at face value. Not that anyone is lying to her, necessarily; but no one is looking out for her interests, either. I doubt that most of us who have been in the faith and its institutions for years and years appreciate how intimidating all of it looks to newcomers.

Most of the time the system probably works adequately. But when it doesn't, there can be casualties, as almost happened with

Meghan. In her case, as in others, her confidence in the faith itself was shaken because at that stage in her development the gospel and the institutions promoting the gospel were virtually indistinguishable. Problems with the messenger invariably call into question the reliability of the message.

ROGER

Roger was a philosophy student at a nearby community college. I could tell right away that I was dealing with someone who had a quick mind and an aggressive approach to intellectual and theological issues. For that reason, I almost groaned when he told me about the highly authoritarian church he had been attending.

Yet it was not an intellectual crisis that finally sent Roger stomping out of that church, at least not directly. Rather, he recounted a long, tortuous account of deceptions, ethical compromises, gossip, political games, and cult-like tendencies among the leadership. I was hesitant to take everything he said at face value. Yet if even half of it were true, then he had left a church that was more committed to the control of its people than to their spiritual maturity.

For example, he described shaming tactics, such as leaders belittling members in front of the group or ridiculing their position in the community. He told of a series of conflicts that he had had with one of the pastors. As a result, the pastor had contacted Roger's employer, who happened to be a member of the church, and spoke about Roger in a way that caused doubt about him as a person—justifying the call using Scripture, of course. Roger believed that ultimately that call led to the termination of his employment.

Some of the conflicts were over doctrine. Roger frequently challenged the church's teachers, citing biblical texts and theological principles that seemed to contradict their teaching. Their ultimate retort, he said, was a frequently used line, "Other churches teach their interpretations, but we just teach the Bible." A more personal rebuke was "You have a divisive spirit."

Perhaps the final straw for Roger was when he learned that church leaders were planning a money-making scheme with a particular ministry organization. Previously, the church had taught strongly against that group. But now that there was potential for financial benefit, the teaching had suddenly changed.

One would like to think that this church was an uncommon chancre on an otherwise unblemished complexion of the body of Christ. And perhaps it was. Yet it only takes a handful of authoritarian churches like this one to convince unbelievers—as well as some believers—that Christianity is all about control and manipulation rather than freedom and eternal life.

Of course, one would also like to think that people would see right through groups that operate like this one. The tragedy is, many don't.

SCOOT

The fellow who introduced himself to me as "Scoot" was so warm and winsome that I felt as though a long-lost friend had suddenly re-entered my life. His infectious smile and gentle demeanor suggested that perhaps he worked with children. And sure enough, he told me that his church had recruited him to play the guitar and lead songs with a group of preschoolers. The position was a perfect match. The children enjoyed him, and he enjoyed them.

But he noticed one boy in particular who seemed to be having trouble conforming to the program and controlling his behavior. One Sunday the little fellow was causing such a disruption that Scoot suddenly raised up his guitar as if to smash it over the boy's head. Terrified at this sudden reaction by an adult, the boy stopped dead in his tracks, at which point Scoot broke into a big smile and laughed. He told the boy to sit down, which he did, and the class resumed.

At the end of the hour, the boy came up to Scoot and began strumming at his guitar while Scoot encouraged him to start practicing some self-control when he returned the next week. They parted on what Scoot felt were friendly terms.

Later in the week, however, Scoot was called to a meeting with one of the pastors and an elder, where he was told that he could not play guitar anymore in the Sunday school program. When he asked why, he was told that someone had complained about the incident. Scoot felt that the pastor had not checked the facts, so he challenged the decision and asked for a reconsideration.

At that point the elder blurted out, "Are you questioning a pastor's authority?" Scoot could see that it was pointless to argue, so he left.

On the next Sunday, he approached the woman in charge of the children's program and described what had happened. "Oh, that's ridiculous," she said. "I was right there and saw what happened. Let me go talk to them and explain it."

The next week he ran into her again. "I was wrong," she said, to his complete shock, "you *did* mistreat that child!" Then she added, "I think it would be best if you didn't play your guitar anymore around the children."

"It was obvious that someone had gotten to her," Scoot said, shaking his head. "I went and asked some more questions of the pastors, but I got nowhere. Obviously I disagreed with their position, and I told them so. Finally they told me, 'Look, you don't belong here anymore.' So that's when I left."

Once again, I was hearing only one side of a story. But it sounded mostly like a case of misunderstanding. What intrigued me was that Scoot approached me, a complete stranger, to tell me this story in connection with why he had left a church. It reminded me of the research of Dr. John Savage of L.E.A.D. Consultants. He found that most "dropouts" occur as a result of some crisis incident in the experience of a church member—a relationship that suddenly ends, a conflict that goes unresolved, or, as in Scoot's case, a conflict that is resolved in what seems like an unfair way.

Dr. Savage found that once a person decides to leave a church, there is a six- to eight-week window of time during which he waits for someone from the church to contact him. He wants someone to listen, and he also wants to know whether he is even missed. If no one contacts him within that period, he moves on.[7]

Perhaps Scoot approached me to get the impartial hearing he had apparently never received from anyone in his former church. I was not in a position to assess blame, as I didn't have all the facts. But I wondered how different the outcome might have been, both for him and the church, if someone outside the immediate situation had been asked to intervene and at least allow this gentle brother to tell his side of the story.

PHILIP

It was late in the evening when Philip sat down to tell me about his mother-in-law, Jane. "She had breast cancer," he explained. "She was going to this church that believed real heavily in faith healing. It was not a church that I agreed with, but I thought, if that's what she wants to do, then fine by me.

"Anyway, her doctor told her that she had breast cancer and needed an operation to have it removed. But she told her church about it, and they said, 'No, no, God is going to heal you.'

"So they sent this couple over to her house, what they called a 'prophet' and a 'prophetess.' They came to her house to pray over her. I was there, my father-in-law was there.

"These people start praying and all, and all of a sudden this guy, this 'prophet,' starts having what he said was a 'vision,' and he says, 'I see God! I see God coming down . . . and removing . . . yes! removing Jane's tattered breastplate of righteousness! He's removing that tattered breastplate of righteousness and replacing it . . . He's replacing it! . . . with a *new* breastplate of righteousness!'

"Then he starts laughing hysterically, and I thought maybe he was playing a joke or flipping out or something. But instead he says, 'Wait! Wait! God is giving her husband a new name. A new name! His new name is . . . Blazer Man!'"

By now *I* was laughing, convinced that Philip was the one playing a joke. But he was shaking his head, smiling to be sure, but with a look of real pain in his eyes.

"Man, I was so embarrassed," he said. "I mean, here's her husband, and he's like not knowing what to do or say, and my mother-in-law's writhing on the floor. It was just a mess.

"She ended up having to have that operation anyway," Philip continued, shaking his head in disgust. "But you know what's sad? All the way to the end she was blaming herself. She kept saying, 'I just don't have a strong enough faith. I just don't have enough faith.'"

I agreed with Philip. It was a sad tale. There was nothing in the incident that would encourage someone outside the faith to want in, and there was much to encourage someone inside the faith to want out.

NOTES

1. As quoted by George Barna, *The Invisible Generation: Baby Busters* (Glendale, Calif.: Barna Research Group, 1992), 167.

2. Eileen M. Crimmins, Richard A. Easterlin, and Yasuhiko Saito, "What Young Adults Want," *American Demographics* (July 1991): 26.

3. See Daniel Cattau, "'Baby busters' seek religious truth, author says," *Dallas Morning News* (December 21, 1992): 25A.

   See also William Strauss and Neil Howe, *Generations: The History of America's Future, 1584 to 2069* (New York: William Morrow and Company, 1991). Strauss and Howe posit a theory of generations that could prove remarkably useful to pastors and other church leaders. They point out that eighteen generations have lived on

American soil since the 1620s. Each one has lasted approximately twenty to twenty-five birth years.

The researchers claim that generations come in very predictable cycles of four distinct "generational personalities" or styles: *Idealists* (e.g., the Puritans, the Transcendentalists, the Baby Boomers); *Reactives* (e.g., the Gilded generation of Ulysses S. Grant, the Baby Busters); a *Civic Generation* (e.g., Thomas Jefferson's Republicans, the children of the Baby Boomers?); *Adaptives* (e.g., Woodrow Wilson's Progressives, the parents of the Baby Boomers).

These four repeat in exactly the same order, decade after decade, century after century. Therefore, the key to understanding the next generation—always a concern to pastors and others who want to make their programs appealing to up-and-comers—is to see where it fits in the cycle and therefore what its characteristics are almost certain to be.

4. Cattau, 25A.

5. This was the only occasion on which I gathered interview material in a "public" setting. All of the other stories in this book came from conversations that were set up and conducted on a private basis, usually through a third party.

6. Cattau, 25A.

7. For more on Dr. Savage's research, see p. 24.

11

John

*There is a moment between intending to pray
and actually praying that is as dark and silent as
any moment in our lives. It is the split second between
thinking about prayer and really praying. For some
of us, this split second may last for decades.*

Emilie Griffin[1]

D rugstore magnate Jack Eckerd once told me the story of what he calls his "spiritual awakening." "So many people think that all Christians are those who have hit bottom," he explained, "who've gotten on the bottom with drugs, alcohol, bankruptcy, or whatever; or who've had a terrible tragedy in their lives, like losing a son or wife under bad circumstances. They think that's where Christians come from—people who are in desperation and turn to God.

"I can almost see God saying, 'I want some guys and gals out there for just the opposite—who've got everything going for them all their lives, but still, they finally realize that without Me, they don't have anything. They aren't happy.'"

That was Mr. Eckerd's situation. "Here I was, extremely wealthy. I had seven children and fourteen grandchildren who were all doing relatively well, especially compared to some of the sad stories I hear from some of my friends, or read about in the newspapers—just terrible tragedies! I had a very supportive family, and good health all my life. So what more could anyone ask for? But I wasn't happy. I had a dry, empty feeling. I found out finally what it was that I was lacking."

What Mr. Eckerd told me was lacking was a relationship with his Maker. Despite incredible success, he felt dead inside. He was far from despair, but he knew he needed something. That something turned out to be spiritual life. Like the rich, young ruler who encountered Jesus,[2] he was the man who had everything—everything but a Savior. "I'm very happy that God picked me to be one of those examples," he said with a smile.[3]

I was reminded of Mr. Eckerd's story after talking with John. John had a similar experience in that even though he met with substantial success, he still found himself dissatisfied. The irony is that John's success was not in business but the ministry, and his struggle with emptiness came not before he met Christ but after.

For the sake of privacy, I will not disclose the specifics of John's accomplishments, but they were impressive; some would say spectacular. In fact, one could easily generate a list of hundreds, perhaps even thousands, of men and women today who date the turning point of their spiritual lives to their involvement with John and the ministries he created.

The remarkable thing is that John decided to study for the ministry *even before his own conversion.* "I felt that at college in 1958, '59, there was a lot of emptiness and aimlessness on campus. I felt that there was someplace—in the church—an answer to the basic questions. But I didn't really know what it was. So I decided as a freshman to go into the ministry. But I was not yet really a genuine Christian.

"I had grown up in the church—a conservative, [doctrinally] orthodox church. But there was no real life there. I mean, the doctrine was correct, but the life was lacking. The church preached the resurrection of Jesus from the dead, the virgin birth, the substitutionary atonement, and so on, but the implications were never spelled out— that if Jesus rose from the dead, He's alive today, and you can have a relationship with Him."

It was not until John's sophomore year in college that friends invited him to a weekend conference associated with a burgeoning renewal movement of that era. The speaker, a young Presbyterian minister, spelled out the relational side of the gospel, of knowing God in a personal way. The message immediately hit home for John, and he accepted it.

Nurtured by that parachurch organization, he entered what he calls the first stage in his spiritual journey, "the excitement, the first-love stage. I went to a lot of conferences. There was a genuineness, a reality—and no legalism. People were excited about the Lord. It was very spontaneous—small groups, a sharing emphasis, a lot of life and people just spontaneously getting together and sharing and praying. So those first three years were fairly exciting. As I say, that was the first-love stage.

"The second stage ran roughly from 1963 to 1977, and that was the 'be the good Christian, the good evangelical' stage. It meant going to seminary and getting a theological education. The emphasis there was on Greek, Hebrew, exegesis, theology. That was interesting and was a time for me to think through my theology—what did I believe, etc. But it was also a time of 'this is what good Christians do, and this is what good Christians don't do.'"

After graduating, John finally launched with high hopes into the ministry. It was hardly an auspicious beginning. "My first position was as an assistant in a basically dead, liberal church. They had never had an evangelical on staff before, so they thought they would try something new. I lasted eight months, and if I hadn't resigned I would have been fired. The senior pastor had been there eighteen years, and he was one who believed in the fatherhood of God and the brotherhood of man, and that was about it."

Fortunately, a pastor with far more conservative beliefs picked John up and recruited him onto the staff of his church. "My confidence after that first eight months was shattered. So I was really needing a confidence-building experience, and that was what that opportunity turned out to be."

It was a providential job of salvage, because John's next assignment turned out to be an unusually fruitful ministry in a very influential church. In fact, by any measure of success—attendance, giving, evangelistic outreach, missionary activity, quality of leadership, reputation, rate of growth—John's ministry was a supernova of spiritual light and life that in many ways fulfilled his dream of addressing life's basic questions and affecting countless people with the reality of Christ. Indeed, ripples from that work can still be felt throughout the world today, twenty years later.

But it was not to last. Even as he presided over a multi-staff ministry achieving spectacular results, "I began getting restless. I was thinking that I had probably gone about as far as I could in that situation. And also I wanted to do something a bit more creative. I think my creativity began to diminish in the latter part of that time."

So he began to examine his options. One day, while having lunch with a colleague, he says, "I was bemoaning the condition of churches and so on. Finally at one point in the conversation the man said, 'Well, why don't you go start a new one?' That struck me. So instead of going back to the church, I drove to the beach. Looking out over the ocean, a full-blown vision for a new church emerged—where it should be, what it should look like, and so on."

Several months later, the new church was planted. Once again John was focused and full of energy. "The experience was exciting," he recalled. "I mean, it was starting from scratch with a nontraditional approach. We wanted to be a different kind of church in the affluent suburbs. That's the type of person we wanted to attract and appeal to in a nontraditional way."

The strategy succeeded right from the start. "We quickly began to gather some strength. Some adults started coming. The first two to three years were kind of a heady experience. I was preaching and teaching, counseling, working with vision, boards, committees. I was doing all the things that I loved to do, that I felt I was created to do. I had a wonderful group to work with. I mean, we were young, we were flexible, we were creative. It was by no means an ideal situation, but it was about as good as you could look at—to be able to do what you love to do and have a wonderful group of people."

I was familiar with the environment John was describing. Having grown up in a seminary professor's family and having been around ministers and ministries all my life, I've known quite a few "entrepreneurs" in churches and parachurch organizations. Like newborn babies, start-ups are always exciting and convey a sense of progress, vitality, and expectation, especially when they succeed. They have an Early Church feel in that everything is happening for the first time and the experience is firsthand.

But I also had a hunch about where John's story was going to go next. For just as Scripture raises our expectations with the book of Acts, it also adjusts them with the book of Ecclesiastes. Granted there are varying points of view on how we are to understand that dark portion of the Old Testament. But it's hard to get around the book's sober opening: "All is vanity."[4]

The word "vanity" is *hebel,* which means fleeting, vaporous, futile, enigmatic, or profitless. That pretty well describes life in a fallen world. Life is not absurd or meaningless; but it does have a certain fleeting quality like smoke that quickly vanishes away. For a while our achievements seem impressive and our progress seems assured. But somehow those moments of brilliance never last. Nor do they ever satisfy—not in any ultimate, fundamental sense—even though we crave that they (or something) should. This is as true for believers as for unbelievers. Believers in Christ, however, have the advantage of a sure hope that will outlast this present world.[5]

I call this quality of *hebel* the Ecclesiastes Factor. I had an inkling that John had tasted of it. He confirmed my suspicion by describing a third stage in his spiritual life—disillusionment. "Here I was, doing all the things that I loved to do. I had a wonderful group of people. But very gradually I discovered that on the inside I was empty. I was active, I was busy, I was committed. But inside there was an ultimate kind of loneliness. There was a longing, an ache, an emptiness that began to surface that I had never experienced before and had no capacity to understand."

Life in a fallen world. Sometimes it means inexplicable emptiness in the face of senseless, horrible tragedy. Here it meant inexplicable emptiness in the face of galloping success—success in ministry, no less, "the Lord's work," as many regard it. The man had been faithful, obedient, dedicated. He was following what he perceived to be God's will. He was not involved in presumptuous, ongoing sin. Indeed, it was evident that the hand of God was on his work. Why, then, did he feel so empty?

He also wondered whether anyone else felt the same way, especially others in ministry. He felt sure that many of his colleagues did. But he was deeply disturbed by what he and his fellow pastors did with those feelings. "I saw a lot of hypocrisy, shallowness, game-playing, clichés. I would go to pastors' meetings where thirty or forty pastors would gather for fellowship. What did we talk about? All the 'wonderful things' God was doing in our lives and ministries," he said with biting sarcasm.

"Well, I knew better. Here were some guys that were on the verge of leaving their churches, some that were on the verge of getting kicked out, some that were on the verge of leaving the ministry, family trouble. But what did we talk about? All the 'wonderful things' God was doing in our lives. There was very little honesty."

There was also little substance. "I would go to seminars and workshops every six months, you know, whenever a new 'pony show' came through. 'This is going to be the secret to your Christian life.' I would see the same people with their notebooks and their tape recorders sitting there soaking it up. Then they would go back and 'inflict' it on their churches. Six months later, they'd have to go get something else and inflict that. Finally I said Enough! I am not going to pastors' meetings anymore. I am not going to seminars and workshops. I haven't applied 90 percent of what I know anyway, so why should I just get more information?"

The assessment sounded brutal, almost unfair. But I had to keep in mind that this was a minister talking, not an outsider. Moreover, it was hardly the first time I'd heard a pastor talk about unreality among the clergy.

But what about John's immediate circle of acquaintances? Could he not find a handful of soulmates who might understand his situation or at least support him in the midst of it? As a matter of fact, there was such a group. "There were six of us who would meet one day a month just to pray for and support each other, and we did that for ten years."

Ten years struck me as a long time. "Yeah, it was, but in retrospect I think it didn't go as deep as it should have—I mean, for being together for nine or ten years. We talked a lot about ministry and prayed for one another. It was a support group. It was where you could come and sort of unburden, talk, pray, and share. It was about as good as you could find, I guess, at that period.

"And yet, as I began to share with the group the disillusionment and the emptiness that was setting in in my life, I don't think they really understood what was going on in me—and certainly *I* didn't."

So, despite a burgeoning church, John felt the bottom falling out of his life spiritually. He felt himself drowning in emptiness and loneliness. He began grasping for something to hold onto. "I tried everything I knew to deal with it. You know, I had learned in the Christian life that you have your ups and downs. The down times, you ride them out, or you learn some of the tricks of the trade: if you're feeling depressed, despondent, pray more, read the Bible more, spend more time with Christians, get a change of pace, take a vacation, get away, go the beach, go to a ball game, do something totally different. I knew all those things, and those things had worked for the first seventeen years of my Christian life and the first ten years of my ministry. Now they weren't working. This emptiness was just going on and on and getting worse."

Meanwhile, the relentless nature of success afforded him little opportunity to catch his breath. In fact, it almost seemed to mock him. "I had to continue preaching, teaching, leading a church. So on the one hand I was performing. On the other hand, I was dying inside."

Where did he think the root of the problem lay? Was he starting to question the faith? Was *he* the problem? Or did he just not know? "I don't think I was sure. My tendency was to think that somehow I was the problem and that if I did the right things, I could get out of it." In other words, if he just had more faith, more honesty, more commitment, more whatever . . .

"And that was basically the history of the first seventeen to eighteen years of my Christian life—that kind of teaching: 'If you just do the right kinds of things, God is committed to doing this, therefore you will get out of this. So hang in there. Pray enough. Do enough. Confess enough.'" He paused and then said with great care, emphasizing every word: "Every single thing that I knew, had been told, had been taught to do—I tried and it didn't work!"

It was a sobering statement. I could only imagine the number of sermons, seminars, books, and Bible studies that he must have been exposed to over the years. He was hardly untaught. On the contrary, he had sat under some of the most renowned and effective Bible teachers of this century. Moreover, he had himself taught on the Christian life, to the benefit of many. Yet here he was, "dying inside."

He was, in fact, entering what he described as the fourth stage of his journey, a state of paralysis. "It just came to the point where something had to give. There was nothing happening on the inside, and how long could I keep performing on the outside?"

One of his mentors, a seasoned veteran of the faith, offered a grim analysis. "I see people go through three stages, particularly in ministry," the man told him. "Number one is tired. Number two is numb. Number three is burnout. You're at numb, heading for burnout." John asked him what he should do. "You've got to get out! Take a year off if you can, six months absolutely basic."

The most John could manage was ten weeks. The break gave him some temporary relief and little else. "But at least after about six weeks I began to feel like a human being again. I went back after the ten weeks and nothing had really changed."

It was a mystery. "Nobody really understood. And I didn't. I was very much alone. It was a very perplexing time. 'Lord, what is happening? What is going on?'"

It would be Christmas of 1980 before John started to get answers to his questions. A couple in his church gave him a book entitled *Turning: Reflections on the Experience of Conversion,* written by Emilie Griffin, an advertising executive in New York. Her husband, William, was the C. S. Lewis editor at Macmillan. *Turning* traced the different stages of conversion that many people go through on the road to faith.

It told the stories of C. S. Lewis, Dorothy Day, Thomas Merton, Bede Griffiths, and Avery Dulles, as well as Emilie Griffin's. These very intelligent, educated people went through years of struggle before finally choosing to believe in Christ.

As John read the book, he found that his own experience of conversion was quite different. "The Presbyterian minister at that weekend conference had said, 'Jesus is alive, and you can know Him,' and I said, 'Hurrah!'" Nevertheless, John identified strongly with the fourth chapter in Griffin's book, "Struggle," in which she described "the crisis of conversion: the most difficult time of all . . . both a struggle against belief and a struggle against the self . . . accompanied with a sense of uneasiness, of being cut loose from one's familiar emotional moorings, not knowing when, if ever, one will touch land again."[6]

"I saw that for me, the struggle was not before conversion, but after," John explained. The same could be said for many a believer, I thought. "There was one chapter where she was describing the experience of C. S. Lewis. Lewis thought that Christianity was for little old ladies and children. Then some of his best friends started becoming believers, and he knew they were not intellectual midgets. So it forced him to reevaluate Christianity, and he came to the very unsettling conclusion that it was probably true. And if that were the case, the only thing he could do with integrity was become a Christian. So as he describes it in *Surprised by Joy,* 'I was dragged, kicking and screaming into the Kingdom of God, the most reluctant convert in all of England.'[7]

"As Emilie Griffin was describing that, she was talking about God's pursuing love, how God pursues us far more than we pursue God. And at that point, I saw very vividly: I had been a Christian for twenty years, and for twenty years God had been pursuing me—and I didn't realize it!"

Then John described the turning point, the actual moment of insight that finally broke the spiritual stagnation that gripped him. "There was a picture—I hesitate to call it a vision—a picture that flashed in my mind. I saw myself walking down a street. It turned out to be a dead-end street. What do you do when you get to the end of a dead-end street? Turn around and walk back down. Another street—a cul-de-sac. Another street—a cul-de-sac. One dead-end street after another.

"I kept walking down all these dead-end streets. Then I saw myself walking down a large city street, like in New York, and there were skyscrapers on one side, skyscrapers on the other side, and all of a sudden, skyscrapers in front. So I was walled in on three sides by buildings. The only thing I could do was turn around and walk back down the street. Only this time, as I turned to walk back down the street, I was confronted with a large, imposing figure—and it was the person of Jesus.

"I looked at Him, and He looked at me, and I saw in Him a love and a compassion that I had never seen before. And this is what he said: 'Have you had enough? Have you had enough of the dead-end streets? Don't you understand? *I'm* what you're looking for!'

"And at that point, I had to make a decision—whether I would walk around Him and go on my way down the street, or whether I would stop. I decided to stop.

"Now, at that point, I sensed that something was happening. I didn't know what, but I sensed that Jesus was doing something in my life. What were all the dead-end streets? They were all the different approaches to the Christian life that I had tried for the better part of twenty years. When I became a Christian, the emphasis was on lay witness, talk-it-over groups, sharing. At my college, with one of the parachurch groups, the emphasis was on Bible study, missions, prayer, and doctrine. At seminary, it was get your theological house in order, learn to think properly. Then there was the discipling ministry approach.

"There was nothing wrong with any of these approaches. The problem was, I would jump onto an approach, milk it for all it was worth, and then it would come up short, and I would find something else a couple of years later. Then something else. Then something else. So for the better part of my Christian life, I was moving from bandwagon to bandwagon, from approach to approach. And finally what happened was that God in His mercy swept them all aside and none of them made any sense any more."

A "severe mercy"? "Exactly! Exactly! I could try any approach I wanted, but they didn't cut it anymore. They were all gone, and that left me with one thing, and that was Christ Himself. Everything was stripped away down to that basic reality."

The idea of God stripping things away was a theme I heard often in my interviews. Why would God do such a thing? My brother, Bob, reminded me of the truth of Hebrews 11, that "without faith it is impossible to please Him."[8] We often go to great lengths to insulate ourselves from God. We create elaborate safety nets to keep from having to rely on Him, even as we say we want to trust Him and please Him. Thus God is in the position of having to kick out the props from under His children until we have nowhere else to turn but Him. After all, *He* is what we are ultimately seeking. "He is a rewarder of those who seek *Him*,"[9] or, as John understood Him to say, 'Don't you understand? *I'm* what you're looking for!'"

John felt a glimmer of hope in what he was discovering, but he still was not clear what it all meant. Nevertheless, he tried explaining it to others. "They were excited on the one hand and apprehensive on the other, like 'What's going on with this guy?'"

He remained in a rather perplexed stage for a month or two. Then one day he was browsing through the stacks of a bookstore. "All of a sudden, almost literally, a book jumped off the shelf at me. It was Henri Nouwen's *The Way of the Heart*. I had never read anything by Nouwen, but I knew he was a really well-known author. So I pulled the book, and it was subtitled *Desert Spirituality and Contemporary Ministry*, and I said, 'Oh, give me a break!' The cover had a picture of blue sky and pink rocks.

"So I was about ready to stick it back into the bookcase, when something said, 'Take that book.' It was almost like a voice: 'Take that book.' So I opened it up to skim through, and it was talking about driven, compulsive people in ministry who are performing on the outside and empty on the inside. He was describing me right down the line! So something said, 'Buy the book.'

"I bought it, went home, and read it. Basically that book was God's word to me at that point. It was describing me, diagnosing the problem, telling me who I was and what needed to happen in my life—that there was no simple formula, that I needed to learn how to wait on Jesus through solitude, silence, and prayer.

"Now I had been a Christian for twenty years at that point, but in all honesty I had never concentrated on this whole matter of waiting on the Lord, being quiet in the presence of God. Quiet time was another performance, another activity to add to an already too-busy schedule. It was another way of earning points with God. So as I read the book, I thought, 'Whoa! I need to make some major changes here.' So I started setting aside two- and three-hour blocks of time in prayer—not to keep prayer notebooks and agonize in intercessory prayer, but to get before God and be quiet, to be open and see what happens."

It was an impressive accomplishment. Many people talk about the need for more prayer. But how many actually pray?

Yet prayer can be a dangerous thing, as John found out. "As I began to wait upon God and listen, God began to speak. Problem: I didn't like what I was hearing! Because this is what I began to hear: 'I want you to leave the church, leave the ministry, and spend a year alone with Me.' I said, 'That's crazy! Ridiculous!' But it kept coming back, week after week. 'Leave the church, leave the ministry, spend a year alone with Me.'

"I began the arguing stage. 'Leave the church? How would they get along without me? I'm the founding pastor!' 'Spend a year alone? I have a hard time spending an *hour* alone with the Lord, never mind a year!' 'Leave a good-paying job? What if after a year I can't get re-hired?' 'What will the Christian community think of this?' That one really scared me. I imagined people asking, 'Well, John, what are you up to?' and I'd have to say, 'I'm going to go spend a year with Jesus.' 'You are, huh?' I knew people wouldn't understand this, that they would think I had flipped out. And you know, some people did."

For months he argued against what he was hearing, like Moses arguing with God at the burning bush.[10] "Finally, I came to the point where I was so miserable that simply to relieve the misery, I had to do it. I just couldn't go on. So I resigned, preached my last sermon, loaded my car as best I could with as much as I could, and went to spend a year alone with the Lord."

However, this was anything but a vacation. He was, in fact, reluctant to spend the year by himself. But to ensure that he would make a good use of the time, he determined to have as little to do with people as possible. "That was a period of almost absolute, quiet solitude," he told me. "That year, I did a lot of walking the beach, an enormous amount of time praying, reflecting, some journaling, reading. I found myself sort of going through a process of withdrawal. I had to get rid of all the baggage that I'd accumulated for twenty years. For twenty years, well-meaning Christians had pumped me full of all kinds of stuff about what the Christian life was all about. I found that I had to discard about eighty percent of it. 'Lord, let's push the clear button. It's you, it's me; let's start all over again and build from scratch.' And that's exactly what happened."

I wondered whether starting from scratch meant abandoning the fundamental beliefs of the Christian faith. "No, my theology stayed pretty much the same. Some of the emphases that came out of my theology shifted, but basically the belief system stayed the same. But my whole view of the Christian life shifted about a hundred and eighty degrees. In the context of Luke 10, away from the Martha syndrome to the Mary syndrome.[11] Away from the busyness and the performance and the activity and the identity in *doing* to learning what it is to sit at the feet of Jesus, to 'choose the better part,' to find my identity in Him and then let the doing flow out of the *being* and out of the sitting. I had never seen that before.

"A lot of the reading was in the Catholic contemplatives—Thomas Merton, Saint John of the Cross; some old Quaker stuff such as Thomas Kelley, and the writings of A. W. Tozer. In all my years in the Christian life, I had never been exposed to the contemplative current. I didn't know it existed. So this was like discovering gold from a new mine.

"My whole view of ministry and the Christian life shifted dramatically. I didn't know if I was crazy or not, but at least in terms of reading and then beginning to talk with people, I found that other people were discovering similar things."

If I was anticipating some climactic ending to John's year of solitude—for example, a dramatic encounter with God, or a profound new insight, or a wisdom-filled manuscript, or a call to great sacrifice or service—I was in for a disappointment. Quite matter-of-factly, John said that he returned to the pastorate. It was as if one day he was walking the beach in solitude with God, and the next he was back in a church. Nor was it a church that I would have expected. John himself described it as "one of the busiest places in the Christian world," which I knew to be an understatement. Moreover, its "corporate culture" seemed to be a far cry from the experience of the desert Fathers.

"That was rather ironic," John admitted, "but, in a sense, it was God's doing, because I had to go back to work. I had to start earning a living. I had eaten up all my savings taking a year off."

But there was another reason for taking the position. "I knew that I wouldn't be there long-term. But it gave me the opportunity to test in the laboratory whether what I had been discovering about the nature of the Christian life and Christian ministry could stand the test of a highly pressured, structured situation. I sensed that in the future my ministry was going to be broader, to clergy and laypeople across the country, and I knew that it would be very easy for people to say, 'That kind of lifestyle is all well and good for you because you can spend half your time in contemplation. I can't take a year off.' So this was an opportunity to test what I had discovered. The bottom line was, it worked."

As in his two previous positions, John watched his ministry flourish, both in numbers and impact on people. But this time, "I was able to maintain my sanity."

Then in the mid-80s, he sensed that God was calling him to an at-large ministry emphasizing intimacy with the Lord and making one's relationship with Christ the priority in one's life. And that has been his work for the last eight years.

"Every place that I have gone, virtually without exception, I find the same thing: active, busy, committed Christians who love the Lord and love each other, who are up to their necks in Christian activity. Elders, deacons, pastors, assistant pastors, youth directors, choir members, Sunday school teachers—you name it—people who are up to their necks in activity saying, 'What I am experiencing is not enough. There's got to be more to the Christian life. This is not meeting my deepest needs, and I don't know where to turn, and I don't know what to do.'"

I had no doubt that he was telling the truth. But it was not a truth to make one comfortable—to think that vast numbers of churches would be producing people who are not alive to their spirituality nor intimate with their Savior. It tends to raise the question, *What's the point?*

John did not pretend to have all the answers. But he did have some answers. He told me that he finds two currents running through his life and ministry now. One is intimacy with Christ. "Intimacy with Christ is the priority from which everything flows. I've been astonished by what I've seen in Scripture about relationship to Christ. The simple concept of *knowing* Christ. Or *knowledge* of God, which biblically is not primarily intellectual knowledge; knowledge in a biblical sense is experience, relationship."

The second current has been grace. "If somebody were to come up to me today and say, 'OK, John, you've been a Christian now thirty-three years. What is the single most important truth that you've discovered about the Christian life?' my answer would be: as a Christian, not only am I saved by grace, but I live, serve, minister, and lead by grace."

John described a study he did on the word "grace." "There are over one hundred and twenty references to grace in the New Testament. That's a lot! Grace is one of the major currents. It's not mentioned at all in the synoptics.[12] But beginning in John 1 and all the epistles, one hundred and twenty-plus times. I discovered an amazing thing. The overwhelming majority of times when the New Testament speaks about grace, it has nothing to do with [conversion] salvation. Now there are bedrock grace passages—Ephesians 2:8–9, for instance.

No question about that. But most of the grace passages refer to different aspects of Christian living." John mentioned a large number of examples.[13]

Then he made this powerful statement: "Almost any evangelical church worth anything will teach that salvation is by grace. You won't be around an evangelical church very long without hearing that you can't save yourself, that salvation is not by works—you can't perform, you can't merit it, you can't earn it. But after somebody accepts grace—faith in the grace of Christ—then grace is virtually forgotten, and the Christian life becomes some combination of faith and works. My conviction is that *most churches preach grace and live works.*"

I could almost hear the blows of Martin Luther's hammer as he nailed his ninety-five theses to the door of the chapel at Wittenberg. I could also hear the strident objections that he—and John—must have faced in advocating "grace alone."

"The church, by and large, I think, is frightened of grace," John said. "A lot of pastors and laypeople will say, 'This grace stuff is nice, but if there's too much emphasis on it, people will end up getting away with murder.'" (By coincidence, three other people within as many days told me exactly the same thing.)

"We wonder why there is such a poor performance level in the church, and why people's lives are falling apart. It's not because we're preaching too much grace that people think they can get away with murder or adultery or whatever. It's that the grace hasn't gone deep enough. When the grace goes deep enough, it touches the deep rootedness of desire that causes me to *want* to please God. In 1 Corinthians 15, Paul says, 'His grace to me was not without effect.' It was the grace that produced the statement 'I worked harder than all of them.'"[14]

I thought about John in relation to the church. For a year he had pulled away from the church to spend time alone with God. Then he had returned to minister in a church and now was traveling widely, speaking in churches about the spiritual life. But I wondered whether he was part of a local body of believers. Did he maintain a membership in a local congregation?

He answered with great hesitation, choosing his words carefully. "I have a very difficult time there," he said. "I have, you know, good friends . . . well, certainly, part of what I have is a small board of directors for my ministry. You know, to become legal and tax exempt, we incorporated and all that. There are about six of us altogether. And then, a fellowship team that does a seminary course. So I have good support people.

"But it's so difficult, Bill, because, for example, I go to a seminar in a certain part of the country a couple of times every year. We do a Friday night and all-day Saturday seminar. And we'll get thirty, forty, fifty people that come to these things and we share and they get all excited. Then they go back to their local church. It's just squeezed out of them. So the problem is that there are so very few grace-filled environments, that when people begin to catch it, there's not a place that they can go and relate to. And, you know, I search in vain throughout my area to find those kinds of churches. They're very few and far between."

John seemed resigned—and perhaps better suited than most—to a tenuous connection with the local church. He is networked with people with whom he has close bonds. And he thrives on the encounters he has with groups of believers in his travels. "I see myself as a facilitator," he explained. "The best I can hope to do is challenge people to get into the presence of the Lord and let Him be their Teacher."

Does he see himself making any difference? "Yeah, I find myself alternately encouraged and discouraged. I'm encouraged by the hunger of people, the longing for something more, something deeper. I see people hungering, questing, searching, and finding answers, oftentimes in alternative places—offbeat ministries, recovery groups, that type of thing."

John's own ministry might be considered "offbeat" to many, especially with its emphasis away from programs and toward individual, personal intimacy with God. I admired the results that his work seems to be having on a handful of people around the country. But I wondered how his call to solitude, silence, and prayer could find widespread acceptance in a culture—and often a church—devoted to very different values.

But then, God is a pursuing God. John had described the process by which God had stripped away all the layers until John was left with nothing but Christ alone. If God could do that for an individual, might He not also do it for a group of His children, even an entire congregation of believers, perhaps even for a body as large as a denomination—or the church in North America?

It's an intriguing thought. But should it ever happen, the outcome will depend to a large extent on how one answers the large, imposing Figure that blocks one's path: "Have you had enough of the dead-end streets? Don't you understand? *I'm* what you're looking for!"

NOTES

1. *Clinging: The Experience of Prayer* (San Francisco: Harper & Row, 1984), 1.

2. Luke 18:18–30.

3. Interview with Jack Eckerd, February 3, 1988, Washington, D.C., for Career Impact Ministries newsletter, "Christianity at Work."

4. Ecclesiastes 1:1, NASB.

5. This is the message of 1 Peter 1:3–5. The fact that Christians are not immune from the Ecclesiastes Factor is demonstrated by Romans 8:18–25.

6. Emilie Griffin, *Turning: Reflections on the Experience of Conversion* (New York: Doubleday, 1980), 91–92.

7. This is John's paraphrase of Lewis. The exact quote given by Griffin is: "In the Trinity term of 1929 I gave in, and admitted that God was God, and knelt and prayed; perhaps, that night, the most dejected and reluctant convert in all of England. . . . The Prodigal Son at least walked home on his own feet. But who can duly adore that Love which will open the high gates to a prodigal who is brought in kicking, struggling, resentful, and darting his eyes in every direction for a chance of escape?" (Griffin, 137–38).

8. Hebrews 11:6, NASB.

9. Ibid. (italics added).

10. Exodus 3:13–4:17.

11. Luke 10:38–42.

12. The synoptic gospels are the first three books in the New Testament—Matthew, Mark, and Luke.

13. Such as John 1:14–17; many passages in Romans; 1 Corinthians 3:10 and its preceding context; 1 Corinthians 15:9–10; 2 Corinthians 12:7–10; 2 Timothy 2:1; 2 Peter 3:18; and Revelation 22:21.

14. 1 Corinthians 15:10.

12

Anthony

*No church can create enough meaningful jobs for
all of its members to do something in church.
In fact, only one-third of the membership of a
local church can be given a job doing church work.
So if you think that serving the Lord means doing
some work in the church, then two-thirds of you
are doomed to frustration and disappointment.*
Clayton Bell[1]

During the 1980s, doctors across the United States began seeing patients who complained of a strange, flu-like illness. At first, they treated the malady as just that—an unusually tough strain of influenza. Symptoms included a low-grade fever, mild headaches, pains in the joints, a loss of energy, and other indications of a pesky virus. As one might expect, they prescribed little more than aspirin and bed rest.

Yet after months and even years, patients' symptoms failed to go away. They didn't get worse; but they didn't get better, either. What was going on? Researchers began a frantic program of investigation, trying to isolate a cause for this odd malady. But nothing turned up.

Nothing definitive, that is. There was no end of speculation. Some suggested that a new influenza virus had entered the country, one that had "learned" how to outsmart the normal human immune system. Others posited that perhaps a nonlethal strain of virus similar to HIV had emerged.

Other theories noted the fact that many of those with symptoms were young professionals. Soon the condition was dubbed "Yuppie flu."

This invited a psychological interpretation: the problem was a form of burnout, an occupational hazard of ambitious, Type-A overachievers. Yet some dismissed the whole "epidemic" entirely. If there was a disease, they said, it existed only in the heads of doctors, not their patients.

In the end, however, there were too many cases of genuine suffering to dismiss the phenomenon as a false alarm. No one knew exactly what they were up against. But the medical community began to accept the diagnosis of "chronic fatigue syndrome." There is still debate over the exact nature and cause of the illness, but researchers have isolated the Eppstein-Barre virus as a likely pathogen.

After hearing Anthony's history of involvement in the church, I began to wonder if some Christians are not afflicted with a spiritual version of chronic fatigue syndrome. Like Anthony, they have not left the faith; they may not even have left the church. But somehow they have little energy for involvement in a congregation—though they did in the past—and they seem to suffer from a low-grade virus of discontent.

"I don't know what's happening to me," Anthony told me, almost as if I were a doctor taking his patient history. "We're at a church now, but I don't know what's going to happen. Somehow we're not jumping in with both feet. It bothers me in some ways. I'm not looking for the perfect church. But I'd like to have something that clicks, and this doesn't seem to be really clicking."

How would you have diagnosed this man's condition? Perhaps the same way that physicians diagnosed early cases of chronic fatigue syndrome. Just another touch of the flu. Just another case of boredom with a church. Nothing serious, nothing fatal, nothing unusual—indeed, almost to be expected.

But if you hear that hacking cough of joylessness enough times from enough people, you have to start wondering what's going on. Why is it that so many people don't really *like* their churches—yet don't dislike them enough to leave, either? At least, not until something happens to trigger an exit, such as a conflict or an alternative that looks better?

I'm no epidemiologist on the ills of the church, but my guess is that perhaps a majority of Protestants feel toward their churches somewhat the way Anthony feels toward his. There's no easy way to prove that, of course. But it is significant that at least *half* of those who claim to attend church attend once a month or less[2]—not exactly a fervent loyalty to the program.

Perhaps, then, because he seemed so representative of so many people, I listened carefully to Anthony's story. He was no newcomer to the faith or the local church. In fact, this middle-aged executive had participated in numerous congregations during the course of his life— beginning with what he called "a very heavy Italian traditional" Roman Catholic background.

"I knew that God existed. I believed in God. But I didn't know anything about Him, certainly none of the personalized aspects. It was more superstition than anything. I had no concept of God on a personal level. I knew He existed, but that was as far as I could go. I just didn't know much else."

One thing he did "know," however: God was someone to be *feared.* "The priests made me fearful of God in an unhealthy way. For instance, suppose you went up to the tabernacle.[3] It was all gold and was probably worth ten million dollars or something. I remember a priest telling us in catechism class that if you ever opened that door, God would shoot out a beam of light and rip your eyes out! Burn your eyes out! Because God is holy, and you can't go in there. Only the priest can open it up and take out the challis.

"So that was pretty heavy hocus-pocus for a kid. I had some real unhealthy fear of God. Not reverential fear, but unhealthy fear, that if I did something wrong, God might zap me."[4]

Yet ironically, God did just the opposite at a critical moment in Anthony's childhood. "When I was seven I almost died. I had a kidney problem. I found out years later that my mother had sent all this money to an orphanage in Italy where they would pray for people. You'd send a check and a name and they would pray for you for days on end. I was healed. It was a miracle. I lost a kidney, but I survived.

"My mother always attributed it to prayer—to Saint Anthony, specifically. That was our family's patron saint, so to speak. We talked about that experience all the time. It was the idea that God gave Saint Anthony the assignment because he was special and not like us. That's why he was a saint. Who knows? Maybe He did. I'll take it either way!"

Some might be bothered by the theology involved, but Anthony's recovery had a hand in bringing him to a personal encounter with God years later. His mother was stricken with a life-threatening illness, and her doctors held out little hope. So Anthony, recalling his childhood experience, determined to send money to the Italian orphanage to buy prayers for his mother. But when he was unable to locate the facility quickly, he reluctantly agreed to have a risky operation performed on her.

As he was leaving the hospital after scheduling the surgery, he encountered a priest who urged him to "have faith." Willing to do so, but puzzled about how, he began praying in his car on the way home, using renditions of prayers that he had memorized as a child.

"I really gave it the best effort I could," he told me, "and I prayed all night. I got home and I prayed until I went to sleep. Then I prayed the next day. The same prayers, over and over. I must have said a million of them. Finally I said, 'Look, that's all I can do. I'm prayed out. I don't know what else I'm supposed to do.'"

Miraculously, his mother recovered. Even the surgeon admitted that he had no medical explanation for the favorable outcome. "Soon, my mother came home. And then it started to set on my mind that something really significant had happened to me and to my family. It dawned on me that I had had an encounter with God. I wasn't quite sure. I didn't see Him anywhere. But I was sure of the results. I was *sure!*"

His curiosity piqued, Anthony began to take a strong interest in spiritual things. He began reading the Bible and discussing it with a coworker. He talked about the faith with a Catholic cleric. Then, through some friends in business, he began going to a nearby church.

"God gave two gifts in a row!" Anthony recalled with a surge of joy. "Not only my mother's experience, but then He put me in a church that had this pastor who was a wonderful man of God. The first night I met him, I invited him to my house. I said, 'Look, I want to talk to you. I've had this encounter with God.'

So the pastor came over and began answering Anthony's numerous questions about the Bible and the faith. He was able to explain the gospel in a way that Anthony could understand and accept.

"Now I'm not one of these people who can say to you [that my conversion] was on December third at eight o'clock on such and such a street. I don't remember that at all. It was a process for me.[5] I wasn't ready to jump in until I knew more. Was this the real thing? Because what was really paramount to me was that I'd had an encounter with God—the most powerful force I had ever seen! This Guy was big! He was able to do stuff that no one could explain.

"So I had a new power base I was after. It was no longer money, money, money. It was this Person who had brushed against my life. I had to make sure it was the right place, because I didn't want to end up with some weakling or some impostor. I wanted the right one. I wanted the real thing.

"It took a process of probably a few weeks before it was in me. And I said, 'Man, this is the real thing!' I had met Him. Now I knew who He was. I knew where He was. I could indeed have a relationship with God. So God did a double miracle."

It was a remarkable story of conversion. In fact, it was the way conversions are "supposed" to work: Something causes an unbeliever to pay attention to his spiritual condition. He starts investigating. He hears the gospel. He responds in faith. And then, as a new believer in Christ, he is "folded" into a supportive church. Don't most conversions happen that way? Perhaps—except that new converts don't always find an acceptable church home. That's why Anthony called his experience a "miracle."

"God sent me to a church that was . . . well, no one is perfect, but they were pretty close to being accurate in all areas. They weren't overzealous, they weren't underzealous. They were in the middle of the road and they were biblically based and they had good, sound doctrine. They let people be who they were. They didn't try to make you this model Christian where you had to look a certain way.

"I remember one day I said to the pastor, 'I'm sorry I didn't see you in church Sunday. I was just tired and we all wanted to stay home and watch a game together as a family.' He said, 'That's so spiritual.' I mean, I'd never heard a pastor say such things! He wasn't afraid, you know? He was one of the few pastors I've ever met that wasn't afraid. If everybody wanted to leave, they could leave. 'It's not my church, it's Christ's church.' So I was very fortunate to have found him."

One of the few pastors who was "not afraid." What a fascinating comment! I had never really thought of pastors as fearful. Not all are, certainly. But it took me back to a conversation I had had years earlier with a friend who makes a study of pastors and churches. He was coming through Dallas, so I met him for breakfast at a coffee shop in the atrium of the Loews Anatole Hotel.

During our conversation, I asked him about the potential for enlisting churches to use some small group curriculum for business and professional people. The idea was that churches could distribute the material to laypeople for use in small group discussions that would meet in the workplace. "It'll never happen," he answered matter-of-factly. "You'll never get them to buy it."

Surprised, I asked, "Why not? Are you telling me that churches wouldn't be interested in a program to help their people be more effective on the job?"

"That's not the issue," he replied. Then he looked up at the spacious atrium that ascended above us for maybe a dozen stories or more. There must have been hundreds of rooms fronting on the expanse, and hundreds more in the other wings of the hotel. "The church is basically like this hotel," he said, "and the pastor is like the manager. The manager of this hotel has one job to do—fill up all these rooms with people. And once he gets them filled, his job is to keep them filled for as long as he can.

"It's the same thing with most churches. The pastor's job is to fill up the church. And once he's got people in there, he wants to keep them there as long as possible. The last thing he wants to do is have them go outside the church for a program like the one you've described."

It was a cynical point of view, for sure. But I had to concede that there was merit in what he was saying. One has only to look at the real estate that many churches occupy to appreciate what some pastors face. All too often pastors have the job of not only getting people to come but then motivating them to help pay for the infrastructure before they leave—all the while, tending to their spiritual needs as well. No wonder Anthony had met few pastors who weren't afraid.

In any case, Anthony's new church had no problem either attracting people or helping them grow spiritually. "It was wonderful. We did a Bible study program. We were supporting missionaries. People had prayer ministries where they would pray for the sick and they would get healed. We had home churches going, cell groups. The church started to grow. I mean, it was so refreshing!"

Apparently the leadership also did an excellent job of using church members as volunteers in ministries and opportunities, based on their gifts. Anthony was recruited to teach—but in an unusual way.

"I got the pastor and said, 'One of my coworkers came to Christ today. It was awesome! But we've got nowhere to send him. We don't have any classes here for beginners that explain the basics.'

"I'm going on, all excited, and he says. 'Well, Anthony, we do have a class for beginners.' I said, 'We do? Who does it?' And he said, 'You do.' I said, 'Me! I can't teach God's Word!' He said, 'Suppose you were in front of a boardroom full of executives, making a presentation.' I said, 'Yeah, but that's business stuff. I could talk in front of a whole stadium and it wouldn't bother me. But I'm not going to teach this [Bible] stuff.'

"He said, 'Can you tell someone why you love Christ and what happened to you?' I said, 'Yeah.' He said, 'Can you talk about the book of John a little bit, now that you've studied it?' I said, 'Yeah.' He said, 'Well, then, you have a class.'

"And that's the way he was. He didn't make me go through five years of study. 'Just tell them how you love Christ. This person's a beginner. He doesn't want to talk about eschatology or hermeneutics. He wants to know, why does Christ love you? What did He do for you?' I said, 'I can do that.' So that's where I started. I had been a Christian maybe five or six months and I was a Bible teacher!"

An effective one, too. Anthony had a lot of ability as a communicator, to which he added knowledge as he studied to prepare and experience as he conducted classes. "We had wonderful classes," he recalled fondly.

So after hearing him describe with great enthusiasm his warm memories of this dynamic church, I could only ask, What happened? Why didn't he stay there permanently?

"Somewhere along the way we got into this friction where some people in the church said, 'We're tired of all this teaching of the Bible on Sunday mornings. We've got Bible classes all over the place. Can't we have just some good preaching?' See, the pastor was not a preacher, he was a teacher. He would preach a message that was a teaching message. But a lot of the people wanted to feel motivated. They wanted to feel inspired. You know, they wanted the warm fuzzies."

It was obvious where Anthony's sympathies lay. But it was also instructive. Churches tend to develop their programs and style of ministry according to the unique pattern of gifts and motivated abilities[6] that the founding pastor or senior pastor happens to have. In this case, the pastor had the motivational style of a teacher, so not surprisingly the church perhaps felt more like a school than a church.

There's nothing wrong with a congregation's building on its pastor's strengths. Indeed, it is advantageous to do so—and virtually unavoidable. Yet in the process, there is a strong tendency to impose the pastor's unique style on the spirituality of others—the way they interact with God and accomplish His work.

For example, if the pastor grasps information by organizing it into systems and categories, he will tend to preach and teach that way, and is always in danger of running out of patience with people in the church who grasp information differently. Likewise, a pastor motivated to persuade people may emphasize evangelism or spiritual commitment and dismiss others who are not inclined that way as cowardly or uncommitted.

The point is that the pastor needs to be who God made him to be and allow each individual in the congregation to be the person God made him or her to be. Wherever the people's needs go beyond the pastor's gifts, someone else will have to be found with the gifts to satisfy those needs. After all, isn't that why Christ "gave gifts to men"?[7] A congregation has many needs that a pastor cannot meet, but other individuals can.

In Anthony's church, apparently some of the people not only wanted but *needed* the "warm fuzzies." They weren't getting them from the pulpit, as they expected. And for whatever reason, the church was unable to provide them through some other means. "So it kind of fell apart," Anthony explained. "It was sick. Eventually, God saved that church and it came back fine. But by that time, we had moved and decided that maybe we should look for another church."

Anthony ended up at a Pentecostal church that his wife had frequented. "It was very lively, which was fine. I didn't have any problem with the liveliness or the clapping or anything else. I was seeing all the conflict and tension at my old church and I thought maybe this was an alternative. It was obvious that my wife was getting something from this new group.

"So I gave it a chance. They made me a teacher right away because they knew I had been one at my other church. But we had constant conflict because I wouldn't teach their ten tenets. I didn't believe two of them, so I would only teach eight.

"The elders would call me in on that, and I'd have a theological debate with the pastor—which was easy because he didn't know that much about the Bible. I'm not saying that I was smarter than him. It's just that I had had [a virtual] college education in the Bible with [the people at my previous church]. He was a lightweight in the Scripture."

What "broke the camel's back," as Anthony put it, was a growing legalism in the church, especially over attendance. "I finally stopped going again, and finally the church went out of business. The pastor's wife left him because he was such a legalist. I'm not saying she was all in the right or anything. I'm just saying that's what happened. So here the church falls apart again, and I'm saying, 'I'm not doing this anymore.'"

I could understand why. More than anything else, Anthony craved authenticity in his faith, a sense that he was dealing with "the real thing," as he put it. This situation lacked that kind of reality. "I think what was happening to me was what happens to a lot of people of my age group and who are in the business world. You're out in the business world and you're seeing how the world runs, and you come to the church and they want to make everything like this hunky-dory fairyland that doesn't exist. You can't relate to it. There's no relevance there."

I had heard that complaint from countless others who feel frustrated trying to live in two worlds—the "real" world of work, family, community, and so forth, and the "spiritual" world of religion and the church. Some people may be able to straddle that dichotomy; Anthony could not—or would not.[8]

"So that church ended," he continued, "and that's when we decided to try a large church. Now this was a big church, a big-time facility. Beautiful place. First class.

"Unfortunately—and this is [something that I realized later]—a church can only be that big if it's program-driven.[9] And if it's program-driven, you've got a pastor on the top who is not so much into people, he's into programs. And he does good at it. I mean, this guy put a wonderful church together. I don't slight him at all. He did a wonderful job. Strong administrator. It was a corporate layout. And it worked fine for them. That was his style.

"But don't expect this guy to call you for lunch. Don't expect him to have a lot of chummy talks with you. It's not going to happen. But for me, I like to operate with the decision-maker."

That was a valuable piece of knowledge. Anthony had learned something important about himself and how he relates to a church. He had told me earlier that in his business most of his clients were medium or small firms. He had targeted those kinds of businesses because he needed access to the decision-maker. So why should things be any different at church? His bent was to relate directly to the senior pastor. But as he was discovering, opportunities for that were more likely to occur in a medium or small congregation than in a large one.

As a result, "We started going to a different church. The pastor there was a gifted teacher, gifted by God to really have a wonderful understanding of the Scriptures. Never went to a theological seminary. He worked under the auspices of another church with a pastor that trained him.

"So, we were going there and . . ."

Anthony had been talking for some time by now, telling me about each successive congregation. Suddenly he paused. Perhaps the thought had crossed his mind "Bill must be thinking that I sure change churches a lot!" For he threw in a disclaimer before going on. "I can't blame the church now anymore. I'm just saying that somehow we were not fitting in."

Then he continued, "I loved to go there and listen to this guy. He would get into some real heavy stuff and I'd say, 'Oh, this is exciting!' I'd get the Bible and look things up. It was very rich like that.

"But the church itself was hard for us. We didn't feel . . . I don't know what to say. We just didn't feel a comfort zone about it, with the people. It was a regional church; they had people who traveled an hour and a half to get to this church. They were from all over the lot. I can't . . . I wish I could give you a reason as to why we're not continuing there, because I really enjoyed the teachings very, very much. I wish I could put my finger on it. Something was missing there, and I don't know what it is."

Then, as if finding—and needing to find—a legitimate "excuse" for leaving that church, he latched onto a reason that made a lot of sense, given his makeup. "The problem, I think, was that this guy had so much on his plate. He was so much in demand. He would speak at other churches. So it was hard to get something going with him. I mean, if you wanted to have lunch with him, you're talking thirty or forty days away. He was booked every day with somebody for something. So it just didn't work."

By now there was a note of frustration in Anthony's tone. As he went on to tell me about his current church, the one where he was not "jumping in with both feet," I could see why he might be feeling a bit desperate. If one counted the Catholic church of his youth, Anthony had been involved in at least six churches in his life. Yet none of them had quite "worked" for him; none of them had really "clicked."

But somehow there seemed to be an underlying assumption that at least some of them should have. As a result there seemed to be an unspoken question Anthony asked himself: "What is your problem? Why can't you settle down in a church?"

There was a time when I might have asked the same thing. Over the years, I've observed quite a few "church-hoppers," people who seem to skip from church to church the way children play musical chairs. One week they suddenly show up in a congregation, all smiles and enthusiasm. Just as suddenly they practically flee in the night, like a band of spiritual Gypsies. "What is their problem?" I wondered. "Why can't they just stay put?"

Eventually I came to see that some people have a real struggle committing themselves to a body of believers. Wounds from the past make it difficult and sometimes almost impossible to sink down roots. In addition, factors such as a highly mobile, transient populace or changes in pastors or programs help to explain a relatively high turnover rate among many churches today.

But I also came to see something else. As a long-time churchgoer, I was evaluating church attendance on the basis of a subtle but extremely powerful expectation: that one should center one's spiritual life and growth around a local body of believers. This follows from a less subtle but equally powerful belief: that the local church has been ordained by God as the primary means of helping people grow spiritually. Therefore, it follows that if one is not committed to a local church, one cannot really grow spiritually. Not much, anyway. And if there's no commitment to a local fellowship, is there a genuine commitment to Christ?

I think Anthony was developing some skepticism about these principles. Not that he rejected them outright. Nor was he ready to give up on the church. But his understanding of "church" was changing. "I may be getting to the point in my life where I'm thinking that the church is not what I'd been taught it is," he said.

For instance? "Well, the church really isn't in the building. It's nice to go there corporately and worship God. There's nothing wrong with that. But I don't think that's what Scripture means when it says, 'Forsake not the assembling together of yourselves,'[10] which is used to get people to come to church. I don't think it means that at all."

I asked Anthony where he had come by his understanding of what a church is all about. Primarily from two sources, he explained. Most of it probably had come from his Roman Catholic upbringing. But a second source was other believers who, as he pointed out, pass along a great many stereotypes or archetypes "that you just catch. Nobody tells them to you; you just catch them."

One of the most powerful is the idea that "you meet God in a church building, that all the people assemble before Him like the people in the Bible did in the Temple. I mean, you physically had to meet God in the Temple. You couldn't meet Him somewhere else. And that mindset is still in the church—that we need to come to this place to meet God, because it's 'God's house.'

"Because you hear this over and over, you get this idea that you *must* go to church. And sometimes you go to church even though you don't want to or don't feel like it. You don't feel reverential, you don't feel like worshiping, you don't feel like singing. You're angry. You've had a bad day. Whatever it is. But you go robotically. It's an insult to God in my opinion. So now I'm getting to where I would rather get God mad because I *didn't* go than to go and pretend I wanted to go.

"Even Christians who have been taught well, who understand theology, who have been thoughtful of the idea that Christ set them free— they still have in the back of their minds that if they don't go to church at least sometime, something is wrong. I may be wrong, but I believe that's true for most people. And they don't know why! They don't know why this feeling is in there, but it's there. It's something that says, 'You need to go to this *place.*'"

Having rejected the idea of the church being defined by a building or place, Anthony had adopted a more dynamic view of what constituted "the church." It had a lot to do with Christians working together on projects and tasks. "I think every time I go to [my work with a local Christian youth ministry], I'm 'assembling together.' I think every time that I collaborate with other believers on a project to help other people, we're doing that. That's what church is to me. That's *part* of church.

"See, that's where Christ is working. I mean, if I did my job the best I could today, then I honored God. I did something that God would be pleased with. But it wasn't anywhere near a church. I'm not excluding church, but I don't think it has to be the traditional idea of church. And that's where I am right now, because I feel more productive doing things here in my office and in the youth ministry and in other areas where I volunteer work of some kind, or when I teach. I mean, I've seen people's lives changed, and that turns me on so much! It's hard to go back to something less."

There was a fire in Anthony's eyes now, a passion. I'd seen it earlier when he was describing the first church he'd attended after his conversion, especially in talking about his first experiences in teaching. Somehow teaching *mattered* to him in a profound way, a way that made so many other parts of church feel like "something less."

"One of the greatest things that's ever happened to me," he went on enthusiastically, "that God gave—this has been a wonderful gift—is that in most of the classes I've done, either Bible studies or seminars, people have come up afterwards, and you could see in their faces— some of them would even be crying—that they had seen how important this thing was [whatever I had been speaking on]. And I felt so good that I had had a part in that! Not that I did it, but I had a part in it. I was able to deliver something to make a difference, so that they would do something.

"You know, I've had a lot of people change . . . one woman who is now in a different business. She changed her life! I mean, it's like every time I drive to her store, I say, 'Wow, man! I had a part in that!' And that's fantastic! To me, that's where God is—in my gift. So I know that when I had a part in that, God was pleased. I mean, it was His gift in the first place. How can He *not* be pleased? He's got to feel good that I didn't neglect it, that I did something with it rather than, you know, hiding it under a bushel."

The change in Anthony's affect was stunning. Suddenly, I was face-to-face with an extraordinarily passionate individual. He was beside himself with excitement. Every part of him seemed engaged and motivated. I had no doubt that I'd reached the heart of what spirituality was all about for this man: "I've seen people's lives changed, and that turns me on so much!"

Could it be that I had stumbled onto a sure-cure for the spiritual form of "chronic fatigue syndrome" that had been afflicting this man's soul—a shot of teaching responsibility? He didn't seem to have any trouble jumping (or even leaping) into that with both feet. It obviously "clicked" for him. "God is in my gift," he'd asserted. It was a profound insight—probably the key to his walk with God.

Could it also be the key for countless other bored believers? Could the prescription for spiritual lethargy be the discovery and exercise of one's spiritual gifts? Imagine an entire congregation of people who felt as passionately about their God-given abilities as Anthony felt about his!

Yet the fact is, very few believers have as clear an understanding of what their giftedness—their passion—is as Anthony does: He *knows* that God has designed him to make an impact on somebody's life. But most Christians haven't the faintest idea what God has designed them to do. Nor have their churches helped them discover what their God-given design and giftedness is, or how to employ those gifts in *meaningful* assignments—"meaningful" as the person with the gift defines it, not as the church defines it. [11]

"This is what's turning off a lot Christians, and their churches may not realize it," Anthony explained. "It's this idea that no matter what need or challenge arises in the church, any Christian in the church should be willing, ready, and able to meet the challenge. That turns a lot of people off, because if they can't use their gifts, they feel guilty."

He began imitating a typical call for volunteers. "'No one has still raised their hand for watching the nursery next Sunday. Well, now, we're just going to have wait a few more minutes until the Holy Spirit speaks to someone.' What an insulting thing to say! I've heard stuff like that. Or they'll do it other ways. But the guilt is right out there. It comes like a wave. You can feel it.

"And someone gets so pressured because there's total silence that they finally say, 'I'll do it.' So what happens? The next Sunday the nursery is the loudest you've ever heard it. And that person hates every minute. Can't stand the kids. Doesn't want to be there. It's a tragedy! Why don't we start telling the truth and facing the facts? Until we have someone gifted in a particular ministry, we don't have one.

"I once asked a pastor this question," Anthony continued. I could tell by now that he loved to teach. "Suppose you paid fifty-eight bucks of your own money for a ticket to see the Chicago Bulls. And all the guys you went there to see were not there, but the guys from the Cubs baseball team decided to come in their place and put trunks on. They play the game and they get destroyed. They don't make one basket—a total bunch of buffoons! Would you think they were worth fifty-eight bucks? Of course not!

"The reason for that is because they were never asked by God to be basketball players. God gave them gifts and talents to be baseball players. But they decided they were going to play basketball. And it cost you money to watch them do something they couldn't do, and you did not enjoy any of it. You were insulted, as a matter of fact.

"The pastor said, 'That's right.' I said, 'Why are we doing that in church?'"

It seemed like a fair question. It also seemed like a question that contained a significant answer for why at least some people—people like Anthony—are leaving churches today: most of their God-given passion is neither acknowledged nor utilized.

"This is the way I'm looking at things right now," Anthony concluded. "Again, I'm not saying that there is something wrong with going to church. I'm not against it. I still go to church. I don't go as faithfully as I used to, every single Sunday. But I've gotten to a point now where that doesn't make me feel guilty. If I start doing that, I'm endangering my freedom in Christ, so I can't let that happen to me.[12] At the same time, I want to be useful. There may be a context in that building where I can be useful. But I haven't found that just now."

NOTES

1. From a sermon preached September 22, 1985, entitled "What's a Layman to Do?" at the Highland Park Presbyterian Church in Dallas, Texas, where Dr. Bell is the senior pastor.

2. George Barna, *The Frog in the Kettle* (Ventura, Calif.: Regal Books, 1990), 132.
   Other data show that North Americans maintain a remarkably consistent and fairly conservative set of beliefs—for example, they hold to the existence of God, the divinity of Christ, the integrity and authority of the Bible—yet have less desire than ever to join or participate in a church on a regular basis. In other words, "believing has become divorced from belonging. According to his own scale, [George] Gallup rates the [religious] commitment of only about one in ten Americans as high, four in ten as moderate, and five in ten as low" (Reginald W. Bibby, *Fragmented Gods: The Poverty and Potential of Religion in Canada* [Toronto: Irwin Publishing, 1987], 217, citing George Gallup, Jr., *Religion in America, 50 Years: 1935–1985* [Princeton, N.J.: The Gallup Report, no. 236, May 1985]).

3. The tabernacle, or *ambry* as some traditions call it, is a box or recess in a wall that holds the elements for the Mass.

4. Note that this is Anthony's recollection of his Catholic upbringing. Obviously, not all Roman Catholics have had the same experience. Nor does the form of Catholicism to which Anthony was exposed necessarily represent official Catholic teaching or the teaching of all Catholic priests.

5. As it is for most people. Nevertheless, the strong tendency among many who have a passion for evangelism is to treat conversion as an event rather than a long-term process. It is both. To be sure, there's great value in a person's knowing exactly when he or she "crossed the line" of faith in Christ. For example, it can prevent subsequent doubts about whether one is truly saved. On the other hand, it can create real pressure to "make a decision" based less on a willful, informed choice or commitment than on a hurried prayer prayed in ignorance. Obviously, God works in all kinds of ways. But people who take pains to investigate and think through this most important of decisions often make some of the strongest believers. Anthony is a case in point.

6. The term "motivated abilities" was coined by Art Miller of People Management, Inc., whose thinking informs this paragraph. Art's thesis is that every human being has been individually designed by God with a unique pattern of skills and abilities, as well as the motivation to use those abilities to seek a desired outcome. This "motivated abilities pattern" is more than just a list of a person's activity preferences or even a measure of one's "potential." It is a picture of how God has designed an individual—a design as distinctive as a fingerprint or a coil of DNA. See Art Miller and Ralph Mattson, *Finding a Job You Can Love* (Nashville, Tenn.: Nelson, 1982), and *The Truth About You* (Berkeley, Calif.: Ten Speed Press, 1989).

7. Ephesians 4:7; see also 1 Corinthians 12:7. However, there is a legitimate question whether most churches are set up to take advantage of the enormous human resources at their disposal.

8. Doug Sherman and I have addressed this problem of two worlds in *Your Work Matters to God* (Colorado Springs: NavPress, 1987). We point out that "most professionals, and especially most men, hold a mild skepticism toward the faith. They feel that it can't stand the rigors of the street. They attend church on Sunday, and so forth. But religion is a sort of weekend hobby, like golf or fishing. Come Monday, it's time to put away those toys and get back to the 'real world'" (19–20).

9. By "that big," Anthony meant more than 1,000 in attendance. His assessment that such a church can be that big only if it is program-driven was his opinion.

10. Paraphrase of Hebrews 10:25. Anthony was clear that he did not see this passage as talking primarily about church attendance. However, he did not say exactly what he did understand it to mean. It may be that a majority of Bible readers would agree with him that the writer had a much larger view of the church in mind than meeting together in a building. At the same time, he is correct that some Christians use this passage to enforce compulsory church attendance.

11. Again, Art Miller's thinking has had a large hand in shaping my perspective at this point. What I particularly appreciate is that not only has Art developed a "theology of persons" that makes sense, he's also developed a proven technology (the System for Identifying Motivated Abilities™) with which to find out how God has designed each person.

12. The issue of freedom in Christ is large and complex, and Anthony only alluded to it without explaining his understanding of it. I understood him to imply that his standing before God is based solely on the merits of Christ and on *nothing* that he either does or does not do. Thus prayer, Bible reading, church attendance, and other spiritual disciplines and habits may affect his relationship with God, but not his standing before God. Therefore, he refused to allow himself to feel guilty about not attending church. As he explained, it was not that he was against church attendance. But he refused to let that be a litmus test for his spirituality.

13

Daniel

Blest be the tie that binds
Our hearts in Christian love!
The fellowship of kindred minds
Is like to that above.
John Fawcett

A farmer went out to plant his crop. As he scattered his seed, some of it fell on the roadside, where it was quickly spotted by the crows, who ate it up. Some of the seed fell on shallow soil, where it soon sprouted. But lacking deep roots to find water, the plants withered in the scorching summer sun. Other seed fell among weeds, which slowly choked the life out of the tender shoots that otherwise would have made good plants.

However, much of the seed fell on rich soil and grew rapidly into strong, healthy stalks. As harvest approached, the farmer began to anticipate the yield. At the least, he estimated, his field would produce a third more seed than he had planted. Some sections might render twice that. And the best parts of the land might even double his investment.[1]

One morning, as the farmer walked his rows, enjoying the smell of loamy soil and the silky swish of stalks against his legs, he came upon a plant that looked pale and droopy. Stopping for a closer look, he saw that its leaves were rubbery and fevered, as if some microscopic scorpion were stinging their insides. Comparing the sickly shoot to the plant next to it, he found that it, too, looked limp and hot. He continued his gaze down the row. Plant after plant was bent over, like a line of retching soldiers.

The farmer stood up and looked across the field. Perhaps half an acre showed signs of this strange blight. Yet the rest of the crop seemed fine—at least for now.

The next day, the affected plants were dragging their leaves on the ground. By the third day their stalks had collapsed. By the fourth they were clearly gone. Their leaves, rather than drying and curling, began to rot, fouling the air in that part of the field with a putrid stench. Meanwhile, the rest of the crop continued to grow.

This man was a modern farmer, part-scientist, part-businessman. So he shoveled some of the decaying mounds into a box, along with samples of soil, and sent the package off to the agricultural extension service for testing. Two days later he received a call. Someone would be coming out that afternoon—along with a representative of the Environmental Protection Agency.

Before long the farmer's land was crawling with trucks and technicians. Samples were taken and field-tested. Test wells were drilled. Maps were drawn. Photographs were taken. Markers were pounded into the ground. And finally a large sign was posted: DANGER! TOXIC WASTE SITE.

As later research would reveal, the property had once been owned by a man who ran a factory nearby. Having no regard for the land, he allowed his men to bury several drums of hazardous waste in his fields. For years the vessels had held their noxious contents, unknown to anyone. But eventually, when moisture finally broke down their aging seals, the toxins leaked out, poisoning the farmer's plants and rendering that portion of the soil unusable for years to come.

Very few people come into the faith today without drums of toxins buried inside them. For most of us, things that happened prior to conversion—and for some, sadly, even after conversion—and our responses to those experiences have left latent but active wastes buried inside us. No one can say when or how those poisons will seep out. For some they never do. For others, decades may go by, and then suddenly, almost inexplicably, vibrant spiritual growth is knocked down by troubles that leach out of the past.[2]

For that reason, one cannot pay too much attention to the history of a person—especially when it contains experiences such as those that led Daniel to the faith.

"My father died when I was in high school," he began. "Died of cancer. You know, cigarettes, the whole thing. Fairly quickly. I remember we found out in May and he died by August. So it was all fairly

fast news and fast coming. And then, a couple of years later, my mother developed breast cancer. That metastasized later, while I was finish-
ing college, and she died."

The death left Daniel with one older brother, who happened to be
struggling in a troubled marriage. In fact, during their mother's extended illness, Daniel had been "pretty much in charge and the caretaker."

I could only imagine what life looked like to Daniel at that point.
The world must have seemed like a pretty wild and meaningless place.
"Yeah. I don't think I really took time to think about it. I mean, at that
point I just took on the responsibility that something was wrong, and I
was—in some denial sense—determined to make it all go away."

"Making it all go away" included an attempt to bargain with God.
"I remember during my father's death sort of doing the typical wheeling
and dealing with God. You know, if my father lives, I won't go away to
college and I'll live at home, or whatever."

The God with whom Daniel tried to strike a deal was a God he had
grown up with in his culturally Jewish but semisecular home. "I grew up
in a conservative temple, mostly religious on holidays. And I didn't have
a set of grandparents who were alive, like a lot of my friends' families,
where the grandparents may have kept kosher and you probably had to
be a little bit more religious. It was mostly for them, because they were
the ones it was important to.

"For us, that wasn't there. We didn't keep kosher. So, yeah, [reli-
gion] wasn't a strong thing. It was more identity, family."

Given his age after his mother's death, the loss he felt, and the
relative neutrality of his Jewish background, it was not surprising that
Daniel was open to the gospel. "After my mother died, I was pretty
confused. The summer before I went to grad school, I was approached
by one of these evangelical street people.[3] I used to ignore them and
really had no interest.

"But one day, for some reason, I got into a conversation with
some guy on 34th Street in Manhattan, and he invited me to some
conference out on Long Island. For some reason, I had a certain interest in going and went.

"It was a typical Christian conference, and at the end they asked
people to come up and say they accepted the faith, and I did that. I'm
not sure I knew exactly what I did, but I did that."

Hearing Daniel's retelling of his apparent conversion, I could already begin to see the potential for problems later on. The clue was his

admission that he hadn't been sure exactly what he was doing when he "accepted" the faith.

I've heard Christians who do lots of evangelism say that they try hard to get potential converts to make some kind of decision, whether or not the people understand everything that's going on. "After all, how can anyone appreciate all that's involved in their salvation?" they argue. "The main thing is to present them with the facts of the gospel, and then push for a declarative action of some sort—coming forward, praying, raising their hand, whatever. People can sort out later all the whys and wherefores of what they've done. What matters is not letting them get away without some decision for Christ."

I won't debate the merits of that approach here. But in Daniel's case, I'm certain that a lack of understanding at the time of his conversion contributed to a lack of understanding later in his Christian experience. It was not that he misunderstood why Christ died, but that he had not fully grasped why Christ needed to die *for him*.

I remember a pastor once telling me that when he talked to people who had come forward for an altar call, his initial question to them was, "Why have you come?" He explained that not only did that give him clues about the people, it gave the people clues about themselves—particularly their motives for coming forward.

Had someone asked Daniel that question, perhaps he would have discovered that the main attraction of the gospel to Daniel was its novelty. It was a message Daniel had never encountered before.

"I think I was looking for answers. I was looking for a sense of truth. I don't remember thinking of it as [an explanation for] 'this is why my parents died.' I mean, I'm not thinking that at all. It was more what had gone before somehow didn't really make sense. And all of a sudden, I was being presented with something very new to me. And that, I think, was a big part of the appeal: a whole new way of looking at life."

True Christianity certainly is a new way of looking at life. For that reason, it is not unlike marriage, which, as some wedding rites point out, ought not to be entered into "unadvisedly or lightly." Can one ever "rush into" the faith before he is ready? Is there ever a time to say to a person, "No, you can't become a Christian yet. You don't understand what you're doing. Let's wait a while until you do"? Perhaps Daniel's experience can shed some light on that question.

After he returned from the conference, he had a vague sense that whatever he had done or decided, he needed to act on it. But he wasn't sure how. "It seems somewhat interesting to me that there was never really any follow-through," he remarked. For example, "I never really connected myself with a church in New York."

Nevertheless, when he moved to a different city in the fall to enroll in a graduate program in education, "I went there thinking I had done this thing and that I needed to do something about it. It seems interesting to me that I didn't sort of let it go."

Again, he was in an ideal position to be recruited by religiously inclined people. "I was at school, and like so many universities do, this one had various groups on campus. I ended up running into a Christian group that had other Jews involved in it. I think that in particular helped, since that was my background. So I felt a little bit less isolated. I talked with some of those people and ended up going to their meetings and getting to know them better, and through them hooked up with a church.

"So I started to become involved in that and sort of entered the church, the whole world of church. Particularly at that point in my life, I found a real appeal in it. There was a real sense of community, a real sense of people who seemed to know each other and seemed to be talking about deeper things. It made sense and felt attractive to me. I had just moved to this new place and just lost family, so it felt very attractive. People seemed to have a heartfelt faith or something. They were basically involved in each others' lives."

In light of what he had told me about his conversion, I pressed Daniel on what he found so attractive about the church. "It was all new. It was all novel, engaging. I mean, here were all these people involved in each others' lives, and people were always inviting you places. And here I was in a new place. I was a grad student so I wasn't living on campus. But I was meeting people fairly quickly and felt fairly comfortable."

It sounded like an exciting church. Nevertheless, newness and excitement can have a downside, especially for a neophyte, as Daniel was. Not knowing exactly what to expect—since the situation is totally new—yet feeling intensity and excitement, one tends to form a perhaps overly optimistic impression. Since Daniel had never encountered a church before, he had no idea what he was looking at. He had no trouble seeing the positives; he also had no way of evaluating or anticipating problems.

"I don't remember feeling pressured to be at things," he told me, "but there was a certain sense of always being invited to things. I remember expectations starting fairly quickly—you know, that you should show up for things. And yet I think the attraction overcame any sense of pressure. It was sort of like, 'Why *wouldn't* you want to show up?'

"I don't remember stopping and thinking, 'Do I really want to go?' I didn't seem to feel like I'd question that. It seemed to be where I wanted to be. The church itself felt very attractive to me. I liked meeting the new people and it starting to feel more like home there.

"And when I started being invited over to where some of these people lived, I found that particularly appealing. Here was this lived-out community, people really trying to make community real. My own personal living situation wasn't that way, so I was very interested in hooking up that way.

"And I think, too, for me the church had a sort of attraction because it gave me a place to use certain strengths and talents or gifts or whatever in a meaningful way. In other places I didn't seem to be able to do that. In the church there seemed to be a place for me to get a sense of where some of my strengths and skills were. And I still look at that as a very positive thing. There were some things I got to do during my time at church that I enjoyed, and it was just very much me."

To me it sounded like an extremely positive introduction to the local church. There was good teaching, the members were working hard at building Christian community, and the congregation was making use of Daniel's gifts.

Not that things were perfect. "I was never all that comfortable with what I would refer to as 'spiritual talk.' You know, 'This thing happened and I prayed and I know this was meant to happen. I needed this job and I prayed and I got the job. I prayed and this person came along.' It didn't quite work that way for me. It didn't feel that clear to me.

"I think this goes on in the church: You do a lot of comparing of yourselves. You hear people talk about their relationship with God or what a relationship with God should be like. You find yourself questioning whether or not it's like that for you. And very often, it didn't feel that way, partially because of who I am and the way I approach things.

"But that whole sense of direct connections—'I prayed and this happened,' sort of feeling like special things are going on during quiet times and all that kind of thing—that was tough for me. It just didn't feel that black-and-white to me. I mean, despite what I was saying or feeling or teaching, to me even if it did happen, it was just very easy to feel like it could have happened anyway.

"I remember thinking, 'I don't know. I don't know if I'm getting those experiences or not.'"

I asked him whether he ever blamed himself for not experiencing what others apparently were. "Oh, sure," he affirmed, "I assumed that the problem was me, that I must not be spiritual, or I'm doing it wrong, or there's just something that I'm somehow not doing right or approaching right or believing right."

Then he added, "Perhaps I made up for that by being active. I mean, I think on some level I could feel more spiritual by doing a lot of things, like enough action would somehow create the right result. Often when I kept going back to the learning part of it, or preparing for teaching things, then I'd see myself get excited about stuff, or it having real meaning to me."

Some of those meaningful activities included leading a cell group for which Daniel put together a very successful retreat, tutoring kids in the inner city, teaching a singles Sunday school class, counseling, teaching, and leading small groups. In addition, after completing his graduate program, he became a schoolteacher.

And so Daniel continued in the faith for a number of years. He was a regular in the church, where he was admired as a stable, faithful, growing believer. "I'd say I was making progress," he reflected. "I felt like intellectually—and that's how I tend to approach things anyway—[Christianity] continued to make sense to me. I was learning things through the years that continued to come out the same. I was feeling fairly affirmed that this made sense."

To all outward appearances, then, Daniel was a picture of spiritual health—a man whom any pastor would have been overjoyed to have had in his congregation. Then one day, unexpectedly, Daniel's spiritual vitality withered as he hit what he called a "personal crisis."

He didn't go into great detail about what happened, and I didn't pry. But he did tell me that "I finished a fairly full church year and a fairly full teaching year. I was dealing with a lot of feelings about my parents. And it's like everything sort of stopped. I think it was a mix of burnout and being tired but, ultimately, I think it was just grief. All that activity ended and I was in a relationship that ended. There were a fair number of endings that went on that summer; it was a summer of loss.

"And I think, basically, a lot of things caught up with me. I think what had happened to me before I even left New York caught up with me—about my family." In other words, feelings of grief that had percolated deep inside him for years finally boiled over. "Exactly. It came on pretty strong."

I asked him whether, in all those years since the death of his parents, anyone had ever helped him come to terms with that loss. Had anyone ever challenged him to stop and examine what meaning it might hold for him? Had anyone ever encouraged him to do his grieving?

"No," he replied. "I mean, I can't say it didn't come up. If I ever talked about where I'd come from, it did come up. I had moment conversations or individual conversations around it. But . . ." His voice trailed off.

It was hard to fault anyone for not paying attention to the pain Daniel carried all those years. Probably no one knew it existed. Yet I couldn't help but feel that someone *should have* probed. Someone *should have* asked questions. Where was Daniel's family? Where did he go on holidays? What happened when his parents died? How did that affect him? Why did he always seem so . . . alone?

Some people would insist that questions like these are none of the church's business. If Daniel didn't care to volunteer information, then pastors and others leaders were right to have left well enough alone. But that goes directly against the New Testament's teaching about community in the body of Christ.[4] It also conflicts with the purpose of the church: to develop people and bring them to maturity in Christ.[5] How can one attain spiritual maturity when toxins such as unresolved grief may be poisoning his system?

At any rate, regardless of whether Daniel's crisis could have been avoided, once it hit he turned to his church for support while he weathered the storm. But that proved to be an even greater crisis in his spiritual pilgrimage.

"It came to a point where I was having a real hard time. I mean, what ended up being hard was that I had friendships and relationships where I taught, and I had what I thought were my more important relationships, at church. So that's where I went. And I'm not going to say that there weren't individuals in church that stood by me, because there were. My friends stood by me.

"But I did not get the support that I needed during a time when I needed for people to reach out to me. I felt very much on my own. I ended up having to deal with it on my own. My love for the church and the community that I connected with—I didn't feel like that's where I got my support. And I found myself with a lot of anger and a lot of disappointment.

"The difficult thing for me was, time passed and it was like no one came looking for me. That was the thing that probably hurt the most. People knew I was in pain. I mean, that was sort of interesting. The church was the place where I *didn't* keep it a secret; at work was the place that I did, except for one or two people that I let know.

"But when I was kind of missing for a while, I ended up getting a gift from the teachers I worked with, who really weren't even supposed to know, and a note saying, 'We're thinking about you.' Again, there were friends from church who came to see me and were in touch with me. But there was no real follow-through from the church community."

There could be many reasons why Daniel's church pretty much overlooked him in his hour of need. I don't know all the facts. What matters is that he felt abandoned. However, some might argue that if Daniel needed help from the body, it was his responsibility to be more aggressive than he had been in seeking it out.

But is that fair? Consider the context that had helped to form Daniel's expectations at that point, the countless messages over the years, both explicit and implicit, to the effect that "We're the body of Christ. We care. We're here to help. We're going to weep with those who weep. We'll show the world what true community is all about."

Yet the most helpful support seemed to come not from Daniel's church but from his own community of friends, whether believers or not. As for the handful of friends from church who did reach out, he perceived them as acting more from humanitarian than spiritual impulses. In short, he came away from the experience feeling that simple human friendship had been far more responsive than Christian community.

"I think that was the thing that hurt. I guess I anticipated that the community that I had committed myself to and seemed to be giving a lot to would come through for me. But you know, what came out was, whether it was work or church or family, it was the people who were just friends because they were friends or for whatever reason—*they* came through. And the church and community and all that seems to go with that didn't know how to.

"Some of my closest friends are still people I knew at that church. A lot of them are disconnected church people as well. I came away with some very important and deep friendships from that time. But I'd say that I came away really kind of angry and hurt—by my expectations perhaps—of what I *thought* the church community was about."

I asked him where those expectations had originated. "Because of where I come from, I don't think I had any real expectations," he replied. "I think I became disappointed or disillusioned by what I started to become or I started to expect over time, because I don't think I came in with any expectations."

In other words, he felt that the program itself led him to expect that certain things would happen if a member found himself in trouble. Yet when he was the person foundering, Daniel didn't find his fellow parishioners responding as he had anticipated.

Looking back, did he feel that some of the people in his church community were guilty of "false advertising," that they promised him more from Christianity and Christians than either one delivered? He paused a long moment before answering. "I'd say that the Christianity that the church projects does. Yes. Yes, I think based on my experience and other people I've talked to, I'd say that happens."

It was a grave mistake, because Daniel's disappointment led to a massive shift in his perceptions about the faith, as well as the community of faith. "It seemed to cut off something in me," he explained, "what I described earlier as a real attraction and enjoyment of a place to express a special side of myself, to be involved, and to be involved in a community. I just had no desire to go back. I mean, I just found myself not wanting to be there.

"I'd say most of that was a certain feeling like I needed to take care of myself. I needed to stop thinking that the right family or the right community was going to do that for me. It was the work that *I* seemed to have done that got me out of [the crisis]. I hope and like to think that God was a part of that. But it certainly didn't seem to have much to do with the church."

And so Daniel stopped attending. He realized that his former church was the only congregation he had ever known; perhaps others were different. But he had no desire or energy to look for another body of believers. "I truly don't have the energy. And I think with being older, it doesn't have an appeal to me, because the idea of being part of a group where there's always a sense of 'You need to start being in agreement for the group to work'—you know, that somehow does not have the same appeal as it did before."

I asked him whether anyone from the church had contacted him to ask why he had dropped out. "No, nobody really did. And that hurt. I can't say I hurt anymore, but that hurt for quite awhile—I'd say for a good year.

"I kept thinking it was going to happen. And it didn't make sense to me that it didn't. I mean, I'd go over in my mind again all the stuff that I did, particularly that last year. It's like I needed to validate to myself this feeling I was having that I deserved [some sort of a visit]. Not in any big way, but I wasn't some guy sort of sitting in the pew. I had paid my dues. I'd been a faithful member. I'd been in leadership. I'd been involved in the programs and I deserved somebody to kind of hear my side of the situation.

"The reality is, you know, who's to say that if that call had occurred, what I would have done."[6]

It is indeed hard to say what might have happened. As it was, the church's silence only confirmed Daniel's conclusion that all the talk about Christian community had been just talk. It was bad enough to feel abandoned during his crisis. Now he felt ignored after leaving.

So I was not surprised to learn that his spiritual life has lain dormant ever since. "I'm not sure much has changed in the last few years," he said. "I can't say I've come to terms with myself spiritually. I don't think I've allowed myself to become real close to that. I don't know. I think about it sometimes, but not a lot."

I was curious whether he still believed in the basic truths of Christianity. "I guess I'm sort of in a fairly agnostic place all around. I feel like I had a very strong exposure to Christianity. I learned a lot. I haven't shut it off. I don't feel like it was a phase that I went through.

"I also don't feel angry anymore, and I don't feel negative about my time there. There are things there that perhaps I need to get back to and think about again. There were reasons that this had such a strong attraction for me. But I'd say that my focus the last few years has been on me, which I feel has been good no matter what terms I come to spiritually.

"I've reconnected with extended family, reconnected somewhat in terms of my roots. You know, I get myself to the Passover seders, probably just to connect with family and probably because I grew up with that and always liked it. And I go to temple on Yom Kippur. That is the one day I often do think about my years at church, because from the Jewish perspective, that's a fairly significant day spiritually. It always reminds me that I have yet to work that part of it out."

I pointed out that some readers would question whether his conversion had been genuine in the first place. If not, they might argue, that would explain why Daniel had "fallen away" when faced with a crisis. Sure, he may have been involved in a church; but was he ever a *"true* believer"?

"I ask that question myself," he admitted. "I ask that question, too, though I think if I heard someone say that to me, I'd probably argue with them. Because despite where I am now, I feel like I knew myself well enough to say there was something real going on there for me. I'm not comfortable giving things names so easily, and I think that's an outgrowth of leaving the church. There, everything was given labels. But the whole world of black and white does not work for me anymore or even make sense for me anymore.

"But I can't say that there was not something there. It was always important for me to have friends outside the church, and I had relationships going on other places—you know, through my work. And that part of my life was important to me because it kept me in touch. The reality was, I was talking with them about my faith."

Another indication that Daniel's conversion was genuine was that despite the hurt and disappointment he felt and his lack of enthusiasm to rejoin a fellowship, he missed the opportunity to exercise his gifts among other believers.

"There are certain things that go along with communities that I do miss—some of the things I talked about earlier, such as counseling. Because the church attracts such a varied group of people, it's a place where I had the ability to make a difference. Or I *felt* like I was making a difference. I miss that."

So where does he see his spiritual life going in the future? "You got me," he replied in a flat tone. "I'd say I really don't know." Does he think about it much? "I don't. I can't say I think about it a lot. Knowing myself the way I do, I think I could see myself getting back to it when I have a sense of where my life is going. Right now, everything else feels so much bigger. [Spirituality] doesn't feel 'handleable.'"

To me it seemed that Daniel was back where he had started: on his own, lots of questions, few answers. I had to wonder what good his exposure to Christianity (and to Christians) had done him. If any part of him needed salvation—and all of him did—it was the deep reservoir of loss buried in his soul. Yet as far as I could tell, nothing (and no one) in his Christian experience had quite touched that grief. As a result, what chance of long-term survival did the seedlings of his faith really have?

But Daniel felt more optimistic. "Too much has been learned and too much has taken place," he told me. "So I see my faith more as dormant than as lacking survival. If my faith is genuine, I'm still a 'believer.' Perhaps it's just my faith in the church—particularly the evangelical church—that hasn't survived."

After talking with him, I realized that a moment of crisis not only tests a person, it also tests the church. It tests it against its own ideals of love and community. Yet it does not test it in an ideal world but with real people in a painfully real world.

The church can expect to face more and more such tests every day, especially as Baby Boomers return in large numbers. Some leaders hail the Boomers' renewed interest in religion as a hopeful sign for the future, pointing to the enormous resources that they bring with them.

Yet in reentering the church, the Baby Boom generation is not exactly the great army of God coming to conquer the world's ills. By contrast, many are limping in with arms and legs blown off, spiritually speaking. They are recovering from broken relationships and addictions of every kind.

Nor are these wounds always visible on the surface. As in Daniel's case, many a Boomer suffers from "internal bleeding." No one knows there's a problem—least of all the hemorrhaging person—until something ruptures. Then comes the test of the person—and of the church, which claims that Christ is the Lord of history. If so, then we must accept that on any given day He may call us—not just individually, but corporately—to resolve ancient conflicts and reclaim lost ground polluted by the past.

NOTES

1. So far, this follows the parable of the sower, Matthew 13:3–9, 18–23.

2. Some readers may wonder: doesn't salvation in Christ wash away the sins of the past and make us new people? The answer is, of course it does. 2 Corinthians 5:17, for example, says, "If anyone is in Christ, he is a new creation; the old has gone, the new has come!"

   However, there is nothing in this verse (or any other) that obligates God to instantaneously remove emotional pain from our past or even to remove the fruit of our past sins. We are "new people" in Christ but not "other (or different) people." We can think of Jesus after His resurrection by way of analogy. He was "new"—for example, He had a new body; but He was still Jesus, not someone else. In a similar way, in Christ we are "new"—for example, we have a new capacity to relate to God, a new destiny, a new source of power and life; but we are still the persons that God originally designed and purposed: same abilities, same background, same DNA.

   Second Corinthians 5:17 is a difficult verse to translate, even more difficult to interpret. I hardly intend to suggest a summary statement of spiritual transformation or sanctification here. But I'm aware that verses like this one are often cited as evidence that Christ changes "everything," if one will but turn to Him. Although I don't disagree with that principle in spirit, I think it borders on false advertising to state it that way. Things are not quite that simple, as so many people have found—including the person in this chapter.

3. That is, Christians approaching people on the street with a gospel message.

4. For example, Philippians 2:1–4; 1 Thessalonians 5:11; Hebrews 12:12–13; James 5:13–16.

5. Ephesians 4:11–16.

6. Daniel's experience here confirms the extensive research on church "dropouts" that Dr. John Savage has conducted. See p. 24 (chapter 1, footnote 10). .

14

Peter and Sheila

*An artist is virtually never able to succeed alone.
He needs a community to back him up: if he fails it
may be his fellow-Christians who are at fault, failing
to give him the positive response he needs. But without
this creativity we shall not be able to show the real
validity of an art and life based on Christ our Lord.*
H. R. Rookmaaker[1]

Martin Luther's advice to Christians was never to become a priest, a prostitute, or a banker. Were he alive today, he might well add artist to the list. Not because art is intrinsically shameful or sinful—it is neither; but for the same reason that Paul advocated celibacy: "those who marry will face many troubles in this life, and I want to spare you this."[2]

Artists face countless trials and tribulations. But Christians who are artists—that is, artists who happen to be Christians—are called to a special burden. To them is set the lifelong task of solving two difficult problems: what it means to be a Christian and how to survive as an artist.

How convenient it would be if answering either question helped to answer the other. But that does not always happen. Quite often, advances in one's spiritual life pose a severe challenge to art and expression. Just as often, artistic achievements raise troubling issues in one's spiritual pilgrimage. I do not pretend to fully understand why this should be the case; I just know many artists for whom it is.

The situation is made worse by the fact that art today has become highly politicized. So much so that the serious Christian-artist[3] stands with a foot in two worlds—the world of art and the world of the church. Neither seems to understand very much about the other. And what little is understood is hardly respected. Indeed, holding "two different conceptions of the sacred," each side "profanes what the other holds most sublime."[4]

So I wasn't surprised—though I was saddened—when Sheila, an opera singer with a background in theater, stated emphatically, "I get more understanding from my non-Christian friends [in the theater] than from Christians!" It was a painful statement that revealed many things. For one, it suggested that Sheila finds herself somewhat alone when it comes to talking about connections between her faith and her work. It also suggested that most of the Christians Sheila knows apparently are not patrons of the theater.

Yet that has hardly stopped some of them from challenging Sheila's spirituality. "While I was discovering a vocation in the arts," she recalled, "people in the place where I was living were *praying* for me because I was involved in the theater! That was 'evil'—intrinsically evil. They were so involved in the cultural separation of the church from society that happened around the turn of the century—'You don't get involved in culture because that's not who we are as Christians'—that they *feared* who I was. They suspected who I was."

Fear and suspicion. Could there be a worse introduction to Christians and the church for a budding young artist? Yet apparently that was the climate Sheila faced when she entered the drama program as a freshman in a Christian college. It was her first major exposure to the institutions and culture of evangelical Christianity.

Ironically, she enrolled in the school she did because she was looking for a church. "I'd heard about this Christian college. I had not found a church, and I expected I'd find the right church, which is why I went there.

"I'd read in the Scripture that the body of Christ didn't mean *a* church, but I was sure that I was going to be able to find *one* of the churches in that area where there would be nourishing growth. My dad was all concerned when he heard I was going off to this place. He opposed it! But I was just dead set that that's what I was going to do. I thought at this school I would live among Christians and finally get into the 'Promised Land' of the faith."

Naive and idealistic? Perhaps. But then, every bid for freedom contains an element of wishful thinking. And that's one thing college represented for Sheila—a chance at freedom. Her dream was to escape the nightmare of her background and to embrace something she saw as positive and effectual—a community of Christians. "I came from a very troubled family background, with a lot of alcohol. There was *always* alcohol. I remember when my mother would taper off her drinking, my dad would drink more, and vice versa. So I was used to a lot of screaming and yelling, and it was a real troubled family. A lot of garbage.

"I found Christ right in the middle of that sort of almost unbearable pitch. I was twelve and my cousin had become a Christian. It was funny. She was the original horrible child—horrible, awful, awful child! And my aunt was so used to her being that way that when she became a Christian and changed totally, it freaked my aunt out! She said she was going to go find out what had happened to her little girl!

"My aunt went to set her straight and heard the gospel and became a Christian. So one day I was sitting in the backseat of their car and heard them talking, and I just came to the place where I said, 'What are you talking about?' And they got out [a tract that explained the gospel].

"I had been part of a denominational church—dropped off, picked up, didn't know what in the world was going on—and my whole response when I heard this was, 'Why didn't anyone ever tell me this?' I said, 'Yeah! This is great!' It was the total 'yes' of a child; it was just, 'Yes!' I was sort of crying for it because of my background."

So Sheila's relationship with Christ was born. She had almost no resources to guide her as a new believer. Nonetheless, she nurtured her new faith as well as she could on her own. "I had no church. My mother asked me what I wanted for Christmas, and I said I wanted a *Living Bible*. I had seen them at K-Mart and I wanted one. I've still got that Bible from that time. I mean, the New Testament is just shredded! It was amazing.

"So my initial encounter with Christ was really *an encounter with Christ*. I was just a child with [little more than] that *Living Bible*, and I would read the gospels and read the gospels and read the gospels. And I would pray all the time. It was a real sweet time. I felt like I had somebody I could talk to that I'd never had. So I prayed a lot."

One of her most common prayers was that God would rescue her from the pain in her home. Eventually He did, through the college she attended. But while she was still in high school, her aunt took her to a seminar where she was urged to submit to the authority of her parents, and especially her father. In her case, that advice proved simplistic. Yet having had no other substantial Bible teaching with which to compare it, she innocently accepted it at face value.

"OK, so you're in a desperate situation," she remembered thinking. "You're looking for *anything* that calms this unbearable storm. Submit to the authority of your father because all men are in authority over women? Fine! Fine!" Then, as an aside, she added, "This is a big part of my problem with the church now—that it basically does not respect women."[5]

Then she continued, "I must say that God was *really* gracious to me through all of that. I could see Him protecting me from some of the worst emotional shocks. You know, once I put myself under the authority of my father, he abused me. I mean, what do you do with that? I don't know. At sixteen . . . For some reason, I had a barometer in me [that helped me discern what was truly of God and what wasn't]. I know [what is true]. I *know!* And I think that's grace."

It was remarkable grace that she survived childhood at all, either emotionally or spiritually. The teaching she received, while no doubt well-intentioned, seemed completely insensitive to the reality of her situation. It put her in a bind between living "holy and wholly," as psychologist Donald Sloat has so aptly described it.[6] It was the kind of no-win situation that many Christians face today as they struggle to apply the ideals of Scripture—such as healthy respect for parental authority—in a fallen, dysfunctional world.

"I was looking for a fix, a quick-fix to life," Sheila explained. "The church does offer a quick fix to life. If you do A, B, and C, you'll get X, Y, and Z. It's a quick fix.[7] And being naive and young, I wanted it. I wanted somebody or something to get me out of there. I'd do *anything* I could to escape. I'd just do *anything* for God to take away the pain."

Which helps to explain her choice of a college. Her letter of acceptance seemed like a ticket to freedom. However, not surprisingly, her experience at school did not quite live up to her expectations, many of which, she admits, were not only too high but just plain wrong.

"You know, I was still looking for someone to fix [the world] for me," she recalled. "I had bought into that seminar: if I just had the right person to be in authority over me—a pastor, a husband, a deacon—I thought that would fix it. You know, let's get the right man or get in line with the right program and then . . .

"Hey, as a woman, you're not even *expected* to take care of yourself! In fact, many consider it 'godly' *not* to be responsible! 'Responsible for your own spiritual life in front of God? No, no, no, no, no! Put yourself in the proper authority relationship and *he* will take care of it.' I laugh at that now, but it's been a painful thing."

Excruciatingly painful, I was to learn. The concepts that Sheila had so readily adopted from the seminar were not unlike the advice followed by many Jews in Nazi Germany: Obey the authorities. Do whatever they say. Don't resist. But such prescriptions turned out to be poison. "It is poison, and I think poisonous systems like that are created by frightened people," she said.

"It's not that I was told that God wouldn't be there in my pain, but that I should *forget* my pain and it would all go away, as long as I did this and this and this and this. It was very much interested that I had 'the mind of Christ.'[8] It was very interested in my mind, but not at all in my feelings."

The approach to Christian living that she was describing is based on a view of humans that exalts reason but disparages emotion. A popular expression of that point of view can be found in the formula: FACT-FAITH-FEELING. The argument goes that Christianity (the truth) is based on facts; one must place one's faith in the facts; then feelings will eventually follow along.

It is truly amazing—and tragic—that such a simplistic conception of people and the gospel would find such widespread acceptance among Christians today. Perhaps its popularity lies in the fact that it contains a core of truth: Christianity as a religion does rest on a bedrock of propositional, historical truth. It is not derived from mysticism. That means that we can *base* our faith not on subjective experience but on objective realities—"facts," if you will.

But does that render subjective experience (such as feelings) meaningless or without value? By no means. Emotional reactions are just as real, just as valid, as any "fact." More important, they are human in a way that no historical "fact" can ever be. Therefore, we ignore them, slight them, or abuse them to our peril.

Yet as Sheila discovered, some Christians talk about conversion and the Christian life in a way that can be very damaging to people's emotional health. For example, 2 Corinthians 5:17 is often cited: "If any man be in Christ, he is a new creature: old things are passed away; behold, all things are become new" (KJV). Either explicitly or implicitly, this verse and others like it are often used to encourage new believers to just forget about their pasts, essentially to bury negative memories, to avoid whatever pain and problems may have preceded conversion.

As a burgeoning mental health industry (both "Christian" and "non-Christian") and its patients can attest, that is not good therapy. Neither is it good theology.

Yet that was the foundation on which Sheila was trying to reconstruct her life—with little success. Fortunately, she had a handful of friends who kept her from becoming totally despondent. "I was going from one caring Christian to the next in sort of a chain of grace," she remembered. "They were really holding me together. God did a *huge* work of grace in providing individuals. It was like an underground railroad."

In the end, however, she needed professional help as she began drowning in pain from her past. She began to have uncontrollable fits of crying. Then, in a moment of misguided magnanimity, she decided to pay a visit to her father and seek "reconciliation" in the relationship. The outcome was not what she had planned. "My dad started screaming at me, and it just fell apart."

Back on campus a few days later, "I was walking to class and I sort of veered off the sidewalk and sat down. I just sat there and said, 'What is it? What's going on?' Finally she showed up at the dean's office, where all she could manage to blurt out was, "I'm crying! I'm crying!" The school took her to get help at a nearby clinic.

That proved to be a turning point. Upon her return to campus, she threw herself into theater with a renewed passion. It was a path that led her in some interesting directions. First, it helped her begin to accept herself as an artist—which is to say, as someone with a different outlook on life. The drama department was one of the counter-cultures of the school.

"My college was a very 'jockish' sort of place. There was no problem with Christian athletes, no problem with physical education and that kind of thing. That was OK. But the drama department was kind of suspect because the stuff of production was mostly secular stuff. How many times are you going to do *Godspell?* How many times are you going to do *A Man for All Seasons?*"

She continued reading and studying the great playwrights of English literature. In the process, she started to rethink her understanding of "truth."

"I prayed a long time ago, 'I want to know what the truth is,'" she told me. "Finding the truth has been the story of my life. When I was in college, I was doing a Bible study, I was going to chapel, I was involved in a parachurch group, I went to this church and that church. I went through so many different cultural manifestations of the church, thinking that the truth was there.

"Then one day I realized: These people are worshiping the Bible! These people are worshiping their system of belief! I am involved in learning how to worship a *culture*—a tiny system which spells out in a very careful, idiosyncratic, cultural way, what a real believer is—and not being challenged to seek a living God. Otherwise you end up being a good girl with your head covered who doesn't say anything in church. You don't drink, dance, or smoke—and you don't go out with boys who do!"

These last words were delivered with heavy sarcasm. But her point was clear: she was learning the difference between "the faith that was once for all entrusted to the saints"[9] and the various cultural manifestations of that faith throughout history and around the world today. Most of those at her school practiced a form of Christianity that placed a high value (she would say too high a value) on the Bible. She was in no way opposed to the Bible, but she felt that their overemphasis on Scripture led to a cerebral faith, a faith concerned mainly with right and wrong, truth and error. To her it seemed like a faith devoid of passion or personal encounter with God or other people—the very things for which she longed.

In other words, she was creating options for herself. She was discovering that there were more possibilities for how to live as a Christian than the handful of models to which she had been exposed.

It was in this context that "I finally decided to quit keeping the pledge," the school's list of rules by which students were expected to abide. "I went out and bought a large bottle of rum and invited a friend over, and we got completely drunk. I don't know how I stayed at the school after that! I mean, it was a stupid thing to do, given my background. We got completely smashed! But it was a political statement.

"The funny thing is, I had to be up at six o'clock the next morning to visit a highly liturgical church as part of a class I was taking in theology of worship. It was the kind of church where there were no pews, so I had to stand, and I was so hung over! I mean, I smelled that incense and it was awful. I nearly fell over. But the professor waited for me. He was looking at me like he knew what was going on."

Actually, the professor seemed to know a great deal that was going on in the lives of many of his students. "In a class on Christian culture, he was the first one who ever explained to me what happened to the evangelical church around the turn of the century with the whole [modernist-fundamentalist split], and the turning away from the culture, [10] and I thought, 'Oh! I get it!'"

It was at that point that she joined a more liturgical church "because I wanted a creedal church, a church that was centered around creeds, that no matter who we were as people and how we lived out our spirituality, we got together once a week and said what we believed. We *said* that we believe in Jesus, we believe in the Holy Spirit, we believe in God the Father, we believe in these things, we believe in salvation, we believe in the church—these are things we believe in. We can stand together before God and say these are the things we believe in, these things are central. This is the bottom line—very important."

In choosing to affiliate with a high church tradition, Sheila was following in the footsteps of many artists. Of course, there is no way to know for sure how many other Christian-artists end up in liturgical churches. But often that spiritual "climate" and approach to worship seem to appeal to believers who work in the arts.

They certainly fit with Sheila's understanding of art and worship. "I have strong feelings about what theater is culturally," she explained. "I think its roots are in worship. Worship is a theatrical experience in a way. We act out what we believe, and we do so because we are incarnating beings. Liturgical churches don't see matter as bad or nonspiritual. It's the stuff that Jesus chose to inhabit.

"So we need an incarnational approach to worship. We not only need to *say* it to remind ourselves who we are, we need to *do* it—to hear the Word and then do the Word in the Eucharist. So I'm into a liturgical worship, where you have the liturgy of the Word and the liturgy of the Eucharist. You *hear* it; you *do* it.

"And I go to the theater because there I see people act out situations that become universal, and I need to know that. I need to learn. I need to see it. It feeds me. There's much spiritual truth in all the arts. Truth can be found in the strangest of places: on a New York City stage, in a painting, even by a well in Samaria chatting with an adulteress. [11]

"I remember seeing *Medea* in New York City and realizing I had seen something very true about mothers and children and the relationships between women and men which really affected my life."

Thus, in many ways the theater became as vital to Sheila's spiritual life as attending church. After graduating, she migrated to New York to pursue theater professionally. Her career blossomed. But her search for a church proved less fruitful: "When I left college, I went to New

York not expecting to find a church, and I really never did. I mean, I told God, 'I don't know if I can hang onto You, so You'd better hang onto me.'"

She described feeling "alien" whenever she entered most of the churches she visited. "It was hard to go into a church where we all face front, we all hear the sermon, we all do this, that, and the other, and everyone leaves or talks to their friends. It's hard to really get in touch with spiritual life."

During a trip, she ran into a friend who listened to her talk about her life in Manhattan. Sensing that Sheila was languishing emotionally and spiritually, the person encouraged her to move elsewhere. "Sheila, you don't *have* to go back there," she told her. "You don't *have* to stay in New York City."

"I thought, 'She's right! I *don't* have to stay here. I can choose something else.'" That led to a relocation to another part of the country. Soon she began attending a church, and it was there that she met Peter.

Sheila's husband, Peter, was not a professional artist. It was not that he lacked talent; actually he was quite accomplished as an actor and musician, and he often directed dramatic performances at the church. But Peter's upbringing in an upper-middle-class family that attended a conservative denominational church seemed to preclude a career in the arts.

"I became a Christian when I was seven," Peter told me, "and at eighteen a reawakening and the really personal part of my sojourn began as a Christian for whom God was real. I was involved in a lot of evangelistic crusades and teaching. At college I participated in Christian student groups, and when I left college I went on staff with a student ministry.

"I expected my faith to make me successful. I thought it would just overcome my faults in a somewhat automatic sense. In fact, there's a very standard evangelical path toward overcoming faults: you fellowship, pray, study the Bible, and witness. Those are the four bedrocks. Do those things and you will grow.

"So I was always disappointed when I had trouble being a good student and the non-Christians were great students. I wouldn't get around to it. I wouldn't plan right. I was always late. I'd always be catching up. Yet somehow I thought my faith was supposed to make all that go away by the pursuit of God. Live heavenly minded and it will conquer the earth, as it were."

Peter realized that a lot of the motivation behind this thinking "was not coming from Christian theology; a lot of it was right out of my own personality and history. It also was strongly influenced by my family. But I do think the Christian theology made it worse at times. I had the idea that I would be successful somehow, that the work of God in me would help me to be someone significant and someone great in the world, and meaningful."

In essence, Peter had adopted a "sanitized" version of prosperity theology. Prosperity theology is the idea that if a believer does what God wants, God will bless him with success—especially financial gain or restored health (thus the teaching is also known as a "health-and-wealth gospel"). The corollary, often implied, is that if one is not successful, there must be something wrong in one's relationship with God. Sin or a lack of faith must be blocking the person from receiving God's blessing.

Most conservative evangelical groups, such as those with which Peter was associated, rightly reject the crass materialism implicit in this heresy. It's a doctrine that puts greedy humans in the driver's seat and turns God into a celestial Santa Claus obligated to reward good behavior.

Yet many who denounce the health-and-wealth gospel of slick TV preachers nevertheless promote their own "sanitized" version of the same flawed thinking. Peter mentioned a "standard evangelical path toward overcoming faults: fellowship, prayer, Bible study, and evangelism." Few would teach that these four disciplines lead to an increased bank account. Yet many suggest that they inevitably lead to spiritual riches and a better standing with God. It's as if God *owes* something to the person who honors these habits—namely, semitangible fruits such as joy, peace, a sense of direction, a sense of significance, and success in the spiritual realm. Underneath it all is often a subtle attempt to earn God's pleasure and favor.

"I did recognize just a teeny bit of responsibility on my part to learn to work," Peter admitted. "In fact, I wanted to work, and do things well, and be disciplined, and get things done, and all that. I wanted to be effective." In other words, he wanted to be a great student, mostly because he thought he *ought* to be a great student. Never mind that God might have made him to learn in other ways than are commonly offered in an academic environment. Yet, like many believers, he expected his faith to change who God had made him to be.

"Absolutely! And boy, I had Bible verses right on it, you know. 'It's in my weakness that I rejoice; and His strength is perfected in me.'[12] I kept looking for that to happen! And it didn't happen for me. It did some. There were some changes, but . . .

"I left college, and I always assumed I would be some kind of a full-time Christian person because I wanted to do something significant, and because that was the 'real' person. The 'real' person was a full-time minister. Deep down I knew that was wrong thinking, but deep down I was also desperate to be significant, and that was the only acceptable way of being significant."

I smiled as Peter talked about this "wrong thinking," because I have written on it in some detail.[13] Countless people have assumed that the most "significant" careers are those in vocational Christian work. They thought that by becoming a minister or missionary they were joining God's "first team." In Peter's case, the choice proved perilous.

"Not surprisingly, I crashed and burned in a *big* way. I went off with this group and was out to change the world. I wanted to change the world for Jesus. I thought that I *would* change the world. But I had a lot of growing up to do back then. And it wasn't just spiritual growth.

"So I was left very shaken with my horrendous faults, and ultimately, sins, and just feeling like 'I have no idea how to be a Christian.' I really crashed and burned by the time I left that ministry. My question was: 'What's different about me? What makes the Christian different from the non-Christian? We're supposed to be so different; *I'm* not different! I don't *feel* different. I can't do anything. What's different?' And on and on: 'Well, if God is, how does He make a difference?' And it's still a difficult question for me.

"Maybe that gets at the real challenge of my faith. The church doesn't help me answer that question very well. Some people in the church do." But not all. He pointed out that many congregations major on minor concerns. "In my church growing up, the length of hair was the issue. That was a spiritual issue! So churches are not [always] helpful with these questions."

Fortunately, Peter was able to "limp into" a church where he found safe harbor while he patched up his tattered soul. "At that church I did ministry for a while—music—and that actually formed a bright spot for me. There were a lot of good things about that church. One thing was that the pastor and others accepted people who really were quite faulty, but still worthy.

"But over time I got more and more away from church involvement. I went through about a year and a half of counseling, which helped pull some things together for me. And then I started reevaluating, 'Well, what am I going to do?' What I really gave up at that time was art—theater. Even though I had always [expected] to do ministry, part of that, I thought, would be to do 'great theater.' I thought somehow that would just happen. But eventually I came to see that that would take an awful lot of work. And I got to a point of recognizing, in spite of a church drama troupe I'd started . . . I said, 'I just don't have the drive. I just don't have what it would take to keep at it.'"

It was a fork in the road that confronts many young artists. The myth is that creative people should just follow their dreams and sooner or later everything will work out. The reality is that many a talented person has had to divert his artistic élan into an avocation or else shelve it altogether while he earns his living in another way. (This is one reason why congregations do well to provide opportunities for creative expression. The church is sitting on massive untapped reserves of artistic talent.)

"You don't just matriculate into it and start off the bat," Peter explained. "So I dropped it. I finally got to a point of saying, 'You're not going to do that, so what are you going to do?' Through the counselor and a woman I was dating and primarily through a book called *What Color Is Your Parachute?*,[14] I did some reevaluating of my past, wherein I saw some bright spots regarding one-to-one work with people. And that's what led me toward the idea of counseling and some sort of social work."

Today Peter works in the mental health field. "It was a good answer and I enjoy it very much." But he added, "That [career decision] was the first time I wasn't taking the next step with the idea that 'God would lead me into it,' as opposed to making the best choice based on the information I had. It felt like going against the faith, to take control of my life and say, 'I've got to make a decision.' I felt like for me to have to make a decision was being not submitted, and I had to come to see that as untrue."

This was a monumental development in Peter's spiritual pilgrimage. It involved far more than a new way of thinking about God's will; it posed a challenge for his *feelings* about God, as well. "Ideas about my relationship with my father, and my relationship with my heavenly Father, and what direction by God *is,* and what my purpose in the world is, were just little shifts that happened in my therapy.

"I remember one day I was riding my bike, and instead of the idea that 'I have to *know* what God's will is; I have to find that next step, or else I'm in sin'—which is the feeling I had—I had the notion of, 'There's a world out here, and God is saying, "What I want you to do is learn how to be wise. So take a step, and if you fall, you fall."' I can remember gliding along, feeling this freedom and thinking, 'Whoa! So the real path is not to find the next step and make sure I don't make a mistake. I need to make choices, to work this thing out.' And it felt very good."

Peter recalled another incident that showed just how much his thinking was changing. He went on a retreat with some men from a church he was attending. During a prayer service, one of the leaders began praying over Peter. "Part of his prayer for me was that the Holy Spirit would 'come and take control of my heart.' And I stood there and said to myself, 'No, God! I don't like this language! I'm going to be submitted to You, God, but 'take control of my heart' is that robotic language that I left behind. I want to *choose* You. I want to *give* my heart. I'm open to You. I love You. But I don't want You to take *control* of my heart. I want to give my heart.'

"The ironic thing is that he prayed over me twice. The first time, nothing happened. The second time, he started saying, 'Praise Jesus! Hallelujah!' Later he told me that he saw the signs of the Spirit at work. I stood there and thought, 'If you only knew what I was thinking!'"

Eventually Peter began attending the church where he met Sheila. He was well on his way toward pursuing a career in the mental health field. He was also making tremendous strides spiritually. Still, to the extent that he had said "no" to the stage, he felt a certain regret, a loss that he still carries with him.

"I still yearn to do something significant," he told me, "and in fact, more and more I have kind of a sense of, 'What am I doing here? With my life? What is significant about that?'"

He went on to say that a series of recent events has convinced him that he is likely to find his greatest sense of significance through artistic pursuits. One of the most important was an artist's workshop, where he concluded, "I *am* an artist; this is true of me. And in some of those experiences when these certain things have happened, I've just felt a life and a flowing that I don't usually feel. And that has been as spiritual as seeing God on a mountaintop or something."

As a result, he plans to do more acting as opportunities permit, in order to express his creative side. Nevertheless, he remains a bit puzzled as to how to fully satisfy that impulse. And because it is so tied up with who he is and how he relates to God, he remains to a large extent a person who is starving spiritually.

The same is true for his wife. "I've gotten to where my toleration is low," Sheila said, commenting on what she sees as a lack of artistic sensibility in most churches. She told me about an incident in the church where she and Peter met and were attending for a while.

"They were doing this series about the arts and Christianity, and there was this Christian artist there with his paintings. I saw his work, and he was actually an illustrator—more of a Norman Rockwell type. His work was in acrylics; to me acrylics is plastic and the medium is plastic. You don't do realistic work with acrylics. An artist sort of observes that.

"Anyway, this man was painting in acrylics, and he was painting Christian art in sort of biblical themes. He obviously had brilliant talent as an illustrator. He had painted the earth from the perspective of beyond the moon. But he had needed to make it 'Christian,' I suppose, and he'd put a little bit of red where the Red Sea was, and you could see a cross, and I thought . . .

"That would have been fine, except that I was discussing this with a man in the church. I was saying how unfortunate I thought it is that the church really embraces photo-realism as a sort of 'Christianization'—as the only way Christians express themselves in art. And the rector heard that. He had no background in art, but his response was, 'Well, I've never seen any Christian art that wasn't realistic.' I mean, you know, it was kind of a put-down, like, 'What are you quibbling about?' Whereas I'm starving for [some artistic integrity]. It may be a small point to some, but I finally just had to say, 'Yeah, it may be minutia or something, but I'm starving!'"

I've seen sidewalk sales of art promoted by a group calling itself Starving Artists. Sheila and Peter were two artists "starving" artistically in the church. We talked about why that might be. Why is it that so many churches—which once were a fountainhead of the arts and culture—now seem to many artists like cultural wastelands?

"Part of it is just the cultural differences," Peter explained. "I've met people for whom, as far as I can discern, God is in their lives, and I'm really glad for that. But the way they express it in language, and just kind of who they are because of what their subculture is . . . I just don't like them. You know, I just can't relate well to them. Their sensibilities are so different from my sensibilities. So it's hard to worship well [together] on those bases. And they wouldn't want to do that. Or, if we worshiped the way I would or talked about things as I would, they would look at me with either, 'What in the world is that guy talking about?' or, 'Is he really a Christian?' You know, 'This is strange stuff!'

"And I don't blame them. A lot of people just can't hear what I'm saying. It just sounds too frightening to them. But where I start to blame is when the whole church gets institutionally that way. Then I feel like, 'Someone should know better here! Someone should be able to realize and accommodate out to the other direction—not everyone accommodating to the culture of the church.'"

He went on to tell me about a book he had recently read that analyzed people in relation to communities. The author, a psychiatrist, made the argument that two basic needs people have are conformity and individuality. Peter pointed out that the church is supposed to be a community, so it ought to be a place that satisfies both. The church certainly helps people conform to a common belief system and, to some extent, a common set of behaviors, he said.

"But I haven't seen the church as a whole be aware of the need for individuality or individuation. They don't see that as their mission. And it should be their mission."

He illustrated his point by referring to the novel *My Name is Asher Lev,* by the Jewish writer Chaim Potok. "One of the things that struck me was that the rebbe [rabbi] was able to see that 'there's just something unique about this individual, and we need to accommodate to that individual.' So he sent him to a tutor. He actually condoned, if not approved, that he would have to draw nudes and things like that. He kind of said, 'There's something different.' It's not a happy ending, but at least there was a place to send him.

"So that was a great example to me of a very clear culture and a very clear doctrine, but also of someone with the wisdom to know that individuation was necessary and important, in addition to the conformity. Now that was a unique, very special situation, and you rarely see people like that at all, especially in the church."

The word "especially" was painful to hear. Again, why should that be? Why is it that the church so often seems impotent at producing people of craft? Walt Whitman said that to have great poets, we must have great audiences. In that light: What kind of audiences do today's churches make? When congregations show up on Sunday mornings, are they yawning from having stayed up late to attend the theater, the symphony, the opera, or the ballet? And is their haste to exit the sanctuary at twelve o'clock sharp due to irresistible impulses to be present when the doors open at the local art gallery?

It has been said that in ancient Greece, art killed religion; later in Christian Europe, religion killed art. That alone is worth some reflection. But we can add that in modern America, entertainment is killing both art and religion—a situation that leaves very little space for the Christian-artist.

Sheila, Peter, and people like them crave space. If they cannot find it in the church, they can be counted on to find it elsewhere. They are like the stage-players who roamed England in Shakespeare's day, "glorious vagabonds" in search of a patron and, failing that, anyone who will but attend their art.

NOTES

1. *Modern Art and the Death of a Culture* (Leicester, England: Inter-Varsity Press, 1970), 245.

2. 1 Corinthians 7:28.

3. For the purposes of this chapter, I wish to hyphenate the term "Christian-artist" to draw attention to the difference between the person who is doing "Christian art" and the artist who happens to be a Christian. "Christian art" has come to mean artistic work that in some way identifies and distinguishes itself as "Christian." (It may or may not be good art.) Those who do such art often style themselves as "Christian artists."

   By contrast, what I prefer to call the "Christian-artist" is a person who happens to be a Christian working with art *of whatever kind,* whether "Christian" or "non-Christian." (Again, it may or may not be good art, though in my experience, true Christian-artists make a conscious effort to concern themselves with the best art they can.) This distinction may seem insignificant to some readers; it is of first importance to many others. (I will not get into a discussion here about what constitutes "good art.")

4. James Davison Hunter, *Culture Wars: The Struggle to Define America* (New York: Basic Books, 1991), 249. Hunter's entire chapter 9, "Media and the Arts," explains a great deal of the tension between the two worlds in which the Christian-artist is trying to live.

5. I don't know for sure, but my perception is that Sheila was criticizing Christians who do not respect women rather than making a sweeping judgment about Christianity's view of women. See chapter 19 for more on the issue of women and the church.

6. See *Growing Up Holy and Wholly: Understanding and Hope for Adult Children of Evangelicals* (Brentwood, Tenn.: Wolgemuth & Hyatt, 1990). Dr. Sloat finds some chilling parallels between the families of alcoholics and the families of dysfunctional Christians.

7. Again, while I cannot say for sure, Sheila seemed to be challenging the notion that some in the church (such as the creators of the seminar) imply that life's problems can be solved through easy answers, through a spiritual "formula" or "quick fix"; but she was not saying that she now regards true Christianity itself is a "quick fix."

8. 1 Corinthians 2:16.

9. Jude 3.

10. See p. 207 for more on the Modernist—Fundamentalist split (chapter 15, endnote no. 2).

11. John 4:1–42.

12. A rough paraphrase of 2 Corinthians 12:9.

13. See Doug Sherman and William Hendricks, *Your Work Matters to God* (Colorado Springs: NavPress, 1987). Peter had heard of the book, and after the interview I sent him and Sheila a copy.

14. By Richard Nelson Bolles, published in annual updates by Ten Speed Press.

15

A Letter from Mark

I was a-trembling, because I'd got to decide, forever,
betwixt two things, and I knowed it. I studied a minute,
sort of holding my breath, and then says to myself:
"All right, then, I'll go to hell."

Mark Twain[1]

March 9, 1993

Bill, Hello!

I was glad to meet you and have this chance to tell my story. It's a hopeful sign to me that someone would have interest in doing this project.

It's hard to know how to tell my story on paper. I've often felt that the telling would be too personal or biographical, straying away as I have from direct contact with the church. I've deliberately scaled back the more personal details, not because I'm unwilling to talk about them, but they may not be as pertinent to the topic. Anyway, I hope this contribution has some value to your book.

I grew up in a conservative religious home. My parents were founding members of _____ Church, where I have my first memories of church at age 3. I cannot remember a time when I did not believe in God. The church was very fundamental,[2] and they described their belief in the fundamentals with all the fervor that fundamentalists are always accused of. A portion of that, I think, is great. But I'm not convinced they knew a great deal about what it was they were so vehemently defending. At any rate, I certainly couldn't tell you anything about most of the systematic categories of doctrine from having been there.

In first grade, I was bussed an hour's drive to a private Christian school. They had a variety of teachers, some former missionaries. We learned the Old Testament Bible stories (in King James) along with the Three R's. Since most of my friends were connected with the school, I knew few of the kids in my neighborhood.

At church, I was awarded my first Bible for Scripture memory. I was also thrown out of Sunday school classes for the usual offenses, was baptized, learned to wear polyester, and became acclimated to the social life of the church. The drive there Sunday mornings often seemed to be the time and place for domestic disputes between my parents.

We went through a succession of church buildings, pastors, and Sunday school teachers. Through them all, I was instructed in my duties towards spiritual growth and all the items that people who were "serious" with God were supposed to do for Him. I went through periodic "rededications" and a seminar on conflict between parents and teenagers (a hot topic for me).

Through the later parts of high school, I was at odds with my parents so much that even the suggestion that I might grow my hair longer when I went away at college led to pushing and shoving; the refrigerator was relocated a few inches. Eventually, riding a motorcycle with a learner's permit, I sampled other congregations. But I wound up at the church my parents selected because the Sunday school teacher was talking about relations with parents.

In our church, the college-bound *always* attended one particular conservative Christian school, and then ideally went on to a particular seminary. For me, though, as college approached, the thought of not being able to attend movies, play cards, dance, etc. seemed too much to bear, especially after I visited a different Christian school that had a beautiful campus. I gladly signed up to go there [because of its more tolerant atmosphere]. Don't misunderstand, I had no intention of avoiding Christian responsibility. My efforts at self-discipline towards spiritual growth were completely sincere and ongoing.

My church's approach to spirituality was a serious issue. The forms were diverse—things like Scripture reading and memory, prayer, tithing. Witnessing was a big one. While today I have no problem with any of these works, the method of enlisting help and promoting these acts bore no small resemblance to mercenary coercion. The adults were harassed to make financial contributions, to serve on committees, etc.

One of the lower points was when the pastor chewed out the congregation because no one had come forward at the end of the sermon.

That's my childhood church in retrospect, from the eyes of a child. [The presumption was that] only "moral midgets" would disagree with the "spiritual" task of the day. And while it would not often be said directly, the message was clear: without these works, you were at best a second-class Christian, or at worst had a faith that was seriously in doubt. The "victorious life" was assumed to be the pursuit of every sincere believer. So one could not go long at church without hearing about someone's spiritual "success."

College was intense. Academic probation, a failed romance, and a coworker contemplating suicide were more than my trust-and-obey training[3] had prepared me for. I had grown up reading the Bible, attending Sunday school, and doing all the extracurricular things that were attached to the church. But now I felt very foolish and very lost.

I did not have a good orientation towards what it was that I believed. The only thing I had knowledge about was eschatology.[4] When it came down to doctrines where there were many different positions, I had never heard of any others [besides the one my church taught]. Why it was that the group I worshiped with believed the way they did, evaluating the pros and cons of its position—that type of thinking wasn't really encouraged. It seemed that the focus wasn't what you believed, it was how you behaved. Again, I have no problem with wanting good behavior. But in my case, driving towards it made me behave much, much worse.

It was about that time that the thought of rejecting the faith first presented itself. However, I felt I had too much experience of God's effect on my life to completely deny Him, even though at that time I felt like I had been either abandoned or targeted for seemingly arbitrary punishment.

Within the culture of my college, there was no mention of spiritual failure. There was certainly no place to talk about pain, failure, or frustration. The "proper" topic was victory—how some righteous act had led to blessing or insight. The focus was on the Christian's righteousness, not on the redemption of the miserable sinner. I was now pretty miserable.

Finally I gave up. I decided to stop trying to please God, keep His commandments, or be in any way apologetic to Him for my behavior. Up until then, God had seemed like an arbitrary Judge and Punisher. I would no longer grovel under that tyranny. I started avoiding church.

However, I continued to pray, though sparsely. A small dose of hedonism prevailed, which by today's standard would probably be considered very mild. I also developed some relationships, some of which helped my pursuit of pleasure, but some which also built my self-esteem and confidence.

In retrospect, I now value this time as my real conversion experience—not the defiance of God, but knowing I had no righteousness to offer Him.

Meanwhile, concerned friends asked how I was doing with God, where I was in my "Christian walk," and what I was doing with my spiritual life. My closest friend (and hero) from high school came to visit and had the same questions. Having lived for about a year with my new "game plan," I explained to him where I was at. "I've given up trying to keep the Law.[5] I cannot do it. I absolutely cannot do it. I refuse to beat myself up. It was making me very depressed, to the point of instability. I cannot keep doing that. I'll wind up killing myself trying."

I had, however, noticed two phenomena in my spiritual life. First, after I stopped trying to keep the Law, I felt that my prayers gained a dimension of sincerity that I had not previously known. For years I had watched how the church's [over]emphasis on spiritual growth bred congregations of Pharisees. Now my abandonment of piety had me speaking with God as a lost sinner. There was no attempt to speak to Him with the pretense of my efforts at righteousness.

The other thing that happened, strange as it might seem, is that I felt that I was actually sinning less. Skeptics might say that I just had a seared conscience, so that I wasn't even aware of sinning anymore. But if I were them, I wouldn't want to have to defend that. If my conscience were really seared, I would have felt free to tell God about how righteous a person I was and how successful I was spiritually, and how He ought to be so pleased with me. But all I had to bring to God was a very broken person, and one who was very angry. I was angry because I couldn't even imagine how my circumstances might possibly "work together for good."[6]

You see, if God's job description was to be a Caretaker, then I thought He stunk. I sure was not well cared for. Honestly, that's exactly how I was taught to think about God: as a Caretaker. Somehow He was responsible for whatever condition I was in, not me. There's a whole bunch of confusion and misinformation spread that way. It's the idea that if you obey God, He will bless you. I obeyed, and I got punished. People may have said that my reward wasn't in this world, but I thought, "Well, that's good, because I may not be in this world for long, at this rate!"

I remember thinking, "Do I feel like God does not exist, and I've been fooling myself?" For whatever reason, guilt or conditioning or whatever, I could not deny that I believed God existed. I'm sure that skeptics could have fun with that, with whether my upbringing even allowed me to genuinely doubt His existence. It was not a very logical thing to me. But for whatever reason, I could not deny His existence. Yet I had serious doubts about His character.

Still, for all the emotional brutality that I feel came my way through the church or in the name of God, I'm grateful that [the church] was also the place where the most healing came from. I had a doctrine professor who became and still is a very close friend. His name was Thomas and he was a Lutheran.[7] All I knew about Lutherans was what I had picked up from my parents. Lutherans supposedly believed some crazy things about baptism and the Lord's Supper. They were sort of Protestant Catholics and, from my parents' point of view, closet Nazis.

My parents' only experience with the Lutheran church was in the early forties, before the end of World War II. The Lutherans in their area all attended a congregation that was heavily populated by Germans, and so it was perceived as if they were at some kind of a meeting of the Third Reich on U.S. soil. The sentiment was very strong that way, and that was not a popular thing.

At any rate, I was ignorant about Lutheran theology. But in Thomas's doctrine class, he would categorize all the various systematic topics of theology and what the different traditions believed—Roman, Calvinist, Lutheran, Wesleyan, and so on. After that class, I had to admit that there was no portion of my motives that was not tainted by pride or greed. My best efforts in the pursuit of righteousness were still stained.

Of course, my upbringing would have had me ignore or rationalize that fact by "declaring victory" and moving on to the next spiritual conquest. I suppose most of the people in my childhood church felt like they were experiencing victory, but in my gut I thought they were doing a really bad job of self-evaluation. You either got to be a Pharisee, or you got suicidal. Either way, something was just not working.

For years I enjoyed the friendship of Thomas, reveling in the colorful language of Luther and avoiding contact with church, where the Law was used like a club to bludgeon children into fear and trembling. It was kind of amazing. For all the violence that had come through the church, I found it amazing that I could have a relationship that could be so powerful with somebody who loved theology. "Theology" was a good term to him rather than being what it was in my youth—something almost antispiritual.

Looking back, I wouldn't describe my relationship with Thomas as primarily academic or instructional, I would describe it mostly as being very personal and tremendously healing. After a while, I came to agree with him that both truth and health (especially mental health) could coexist in the theology of the Reformation and Luther, where Law was not rationalized and grace was not just for conversion.

As soon as I found work that provided the necessary health insurance coverage, I sought help from psychotherapy. I was fortunate to have been introduced to a therapist who had a tremendous grip on family relationships. As Fritz Pearls says, "Therapy is only as high as the therapist." I was fortunate to have found a very high one. In therapy, my many conflicts could be addressed directly. The issues were depression, guilt, and low [self-]esteem, among others. Today these demons don't seem to have the same power they enjoyed in my teens and early twenties. But I do find it necessary to continually remember the reality of having had such a hard time.

Some issues have been more challenging than others. Still, even though the process of change has been ridiculously slow, my images of God and the church have undergone changes of their own. I came to see that my image of God as an arbitrary Judge and Punisher was as warped as my guilt and low [self-]esteem. I had actually learned to read the Scriptures to the virtual exclusion of passages that pronounce grace to the believer, not just to the unsaved. For example, I had ignored the import of Paul's failures in "this wretched body of death," and his response of "thanks be to God!"[8]

Actually, I remember coming across those kinds of verses in high school, and I even read some books that talked a lot about grace. But when I went to my pastor and asked him why he wasn't preaching grace in all its entirety, the way the Bible presented it, he told me, "Yes, I know the Bible says that. But we can't teach grace that way, or else people might start taking advantage of it." Even now, my parents tell me they don't understand when I speak of needing to hear the gospel [the "good news" of grace] every Sunday. To them, the gospel is for conversion. For spiritual growth, a book like James will do.

I also came to see that the Law was every bit as bad as I had been told. Actually, it was a great deal worse. The Law was even harder to keep than I had been taught, and I had even less ability to keep it than I had been taught. That made the cross so much more required, substantial, and dramatically needed. For the longest time, I had been real happy to avoid the abuses of piety by avoiding the church. But eventually, I came to see that that was only good at avoiding the negative; it gave no positive input.

So I asked Thomas where I might find a church that believed and preached grace. The reply was sad and frustrating. [He said that many] modern Lutheran congregations had departed from the Reformation, confusing Law and gospel, or else easing the Law at the expense of the truth—a rationalization of another sort.

One weekend, while driving with Thomas, I told him that while I was glad and somewhat proud to have abandoned the perverted sense of spirituality that I'd had, I now realized that it had been a long time since I enjoyed hearing the truth about God from a pulpit or learned more about what I now believed. It had been a long time since I had heard the gospel, and I was sad about that. I also felt sad that it was not available at every church. Most of all, I told him, I felt far from the faith.

I'll never forget his response. It was so terribly gracious. He said, "The church is very far from the faith, and it doesn't surprise me that you can't be part of it." I felt like someone had just pronounced absolution! Suddenly there was no more defiance towards God. I even got to where I didn't care who the people were in church, I just cared about what was being said from the pulpit. I wanted it to be the truth. It needed to be the gospel. I've gotten to where I actually look forward to hearing the Law as well as the gospel. But if I hear the Law without the gospel, I'm just livid.

The times I did attend church were whenever Thomas held services in a congregation as an interim pastor. Having heard him in the classroom, the thought of hearing his theology borne out in the pulpit was almost too good to be true. However, most of the churches were not local, so attending regularly was not easy to do, and sampling the other local parishes was more than I could do for a long time. Usually I'd hear either the Law preached again or some empty fairytale.

Later, I did start attending a local church where Thomas was called as an interim. It really was good to hear his preaching, not for its finesse and delivery per se, but because I felt I was hearing the truth of the gospel, and it was wrenchingly emotional to me. My attendance became more regular. However, with the call of a full-time pastor, I often wait for the monthly Sunday that Thomas preaches.

My current outlook on the church is still very guarded, even pessimistic. But there are pockets of hope on the horizon. The pessimism is partially due to my disgust for bureaucracies, and the church is inevitably a bureaucracy. I expect the violence historically done in God's name to continue. I still see churches and believers holding agendas equal to or higher than the gospel. I expect piety to continue the lead in this area, to the minimizing or exclusion of the gospel.

It also appears that in a desperate attempt to be "relevant," many churches are futilely trying to reach people via their other life needs, such as pop psychology, health-and-wealth, or whatever the society has explored and abandoned as a panacea. It seems to me that churches often lag behind the culture by five to ten years. With all these attempts at relevance, the gospel competes unsuccessfully with the other agendas.

But there are hopeful signs, too. There are some groups and some escapees from the [more Law-driven] backgrounds that have noticed those other agendas. I thank [one particular group with which I have been associated] for being a gadfly to the church. I've resented the anti-intellectualism of the churches like the one in which I grew up and welcome the challenge to know what I believe. If there had been no scholars and committed laity in ages gone by, we would have no Bibles in domestic languages and no ability to explore the Word or test the spirit of our church leaders, etc. Today, though, it's as if the Christian community has gone numb or brain-dead towards what it is they believe.

Bill, I find the topics you are addressing in your book to be very important ones. Why do believers leave the church? What will the shape of the church be in ten or twenty years? What would we want it to be? With people asking these kinds of questions, I'm encouraged about the future of the church. Yet sometimes I fear that future generations will look at the late twentieth century and wonder (in Thomas's words) if any intelligent thought occurred. The answer is, quite possibly not: we have been too busy introspecting.

I wish we had the scholarship of a Warfield, Chemnitz, Pieper, and the like with the communication skill of a C. S. Lewis. We do have some power hitters, but the culture of the contemporary church would appear to prefer Spirit-filled aerobics!

Anyway, I wish you the best in this and future projects. Thank you for the opportunity to tell my story. It has been an emotional journey, so I'm unable to tell it without some force or fury and some soap-boxing. But however it goes, I hope you have some fun working it all up!

Best to you and yours,
Mark

NOTES

1. *The Adventures of Huckleberry Finn*, chapter 31, "You Can't Pray a Lie."

2. Mark uses the term "fundamental" in its technical sense, meaning of or relating to "fundamentalist" doctrine. The term "fundamentalism" has taken on many new meanings and connotations during the twentieth century, mostly negative. But originally the term defined a movement of conservative Protestants who, in the early years of this century, set forth a handful of essential, interconnecting, "fundamental" beliefs: the verbal inspiration of the Bible (which led to a literal interpretation or *hermeneutic*); the virgin birth of Christ; the substitutionary atonement of Christ; the bodily resurrection of Christ; and the imminent and visible second coming of Christ.

   In 1910, a series of ten popular booklets summarizing these doctrines and their implications was published, entitled *The Fundamentals: A Testimony to the Truth*. Three million copies were distributed to pastors, seminarians, and other church leaders. The five "fundamentals" not only served as an outline for fundamentalist teaching, but became the touchstone for testing orthodoxy.

   Mark is saying that the church in which he was raised followed in the fundamentalist stream of doctrine and culture.

3. An allusion to the hymn "Trust and Obey."

4. The doctrine of "last things" and the end times.

5. Mark uses the term "Law" in the same sense that the New Testament uses it to describe any moral expectation that people must fulfill to meet God's holy standard.

6. Romans 8:28.

7. Thomas was not the professor's real name.

   I have made an exception here by letting stand the reference to Thomas as a Lutheran. My policy elsewhere in the book has been for the most part to delete denominational names and labels. Here, however, Thomas's theology had a direct impact on Mark's thinking and to leave it unidentified would have been both cumbersome and unfair. However, I do not mean to imply that all Lutherans hold to the things that Thomas was teaching, or even that Thomas was necessarily representative of teachers in the Lutheran traditions.

8. Romans 7:24–25.

16

Norman and Judy

It is not a question of giving up sin,
but of giving up my right to myself,
my natural independence and self-assertiveness,
and this is where the battle has to be fought.
It is the things that are right and noble and good
from the natural standpoint that keep us back
from God's best. . . . Beware of refusing to go
to the funeral of your own independence.
Oswald Chambers[1]

On July 20, 1969, astronaut Neil Armstrong took his famous "one small step for a man, one giant leap for mankind"—a leap that was as much psychological as it was technological. After Apollo 11, was anything impossible for human engineering?

But about the same time as Apollo and Soyuz pioneers were opening up the frontiers of outer space, mission leaders around the world were opening up the frontiers of missionary strategy. In fact, during the decade that began in 1970, the entire missionary enterprise seemed to take a gigantic leap of its own into the modern era. New terms and novel methods replaced old assumptions and time-worn traditions. Carefully researched goals were set and progress began to be measured systematically and objectively.

As a result, the nature of missions seemed to change overnight. The new-era missionary was far less likely to be sent to a remote, steamy jungle than to the "asphalt jungles" of the world's great cities. Nor was the worker as likely to be culturally insensitive or ignorant. Indeed, mission leaders were already paying close attention to "cross-cultural communication" twenty years ago—long before today's trendy preoccupation with "multi-culturalism."

One result of this new-style approach was that old stereotypes were laid to rest. It was no longer appropriate to think of the missionary as a fair-skinned, silver-haired colonialist dressed in khaki shorts and a pith helmet, accompanied by his homely wife. No, the missionary *team* was far more likely to be an energetic young couple right off Main Street, U.S.A.—a couple such as Norman and Judy, for example.

"I was an English lit major," said Judy.

"And I was a history and Bible major," Norman added. "I wanted to eventually teach history."

"We both wanted to get into teaching," Judy explained, "so we moved to an area that had a really great teachers' university. We'd never been real materialistic or ambitious as far as making a lot of money. We just wanted to help people. So we went to this school, and we got good jobs for students to have. Then, just about that time, we heard about New Horizons Missions,[2] and the whole story of Norm and Judy as missionaries started to unfold."

Norman recalled the process that started them thinking. "We read somewhere that there was this incredibly large number of Christian young people going to secular colleges just to go and be regular Americans, and we were two of those. And I think that kind of got under Judy's skin, because she always felt like she was destined for involvement somehow in God's plan. I never had those feelings, but I also didn't have any objections to doing it."

It was an interesting case of timing. Because it was the late-seventies, Judy and Norman were moving directly against the flow of the culture and especially their peers, the Baby Boomers. Societal trends were heading toward the so-called excesses of the eighties as many young adults were scrambling madly to establish careers and to start making good money. So for this couple even to be thinking about missions was very countercultural.

Yet a number of factors contributed to their increasing interest in missionary work. They took a course that introduced them to the status of Christianity around the world. They made a number of friends who were likewise eager to "finish the Great Commission."[3] And most important, they were actively recruited by a leader from a mission agency. Still, they did not make a quick, impulsive decision to go overseas. Instead, they gradually immersed themselves in what might be called the "missions subculture."

"The whole thing was to reach the unreached and the 'hidden' peoples,"[4] Judy said. "So among our friends it was kind of a hobby to look into different hidden-people groups and find the ones who were the least reached. We found what we thought would be the least reached people, [this particular] group. So we started getting ready to go and plant a church among them. We started a Bible study in our home—a prayer group, actually—and we started researching the people. We'd go to the library, and we each had to bring a different piece of information each week."

From the data they gathered and by consulting mission experts, they began to formulate a strategy. The group they wanted to reach was located in a part of the world that was politically and religiously closed to the gospel. So if their efforts were to have any hope of succeeding, Norman and Judy would need to plan carefully and move cautiously. Even then there was a high potential for failure, as missionaries to that area were routinely arrested and deported.

But the couple seemed energized rather than daunted by the challenge. "We fell crazy, head over heels in love with these people!" Judy exclaimed.

"Yeah, we were really in deep," her husband agreed. "In fact, the third week into this prayer group that we started, we happened to see on public television an hour-long program on this group, the ones we were really interested in. Here we were watching a video of them! That was really exciting."

"We were genuinely very intrigued and felt that affinity," Judy continued. "I would call it sort of a honeymoon—we had been courting this idea of missions and we were totally excited. It was the ultimate thing. It felt like being on the crest of the wave.

"We had met some resistance from both of our home churches as far as going to work with [that group of people]. Some people were afraid and didn't think we knew what we were doing and all that. Also, we were going to go with New Horizons Missions. It was relatively new and wasn't a name they'd heard of. And at that time there weren't a lot of mission boards doing work [in that part of the world]. But when we finally got our churches to where they understood what we were doing, they were totally excited.

"In fact, when we started raising support, we were given a phone number of a missions pastor at a huge church. So we called him up, and he totally freaked out that he was meeting real, live missionaries who were going to this particular people."

"New Horizons Missions was one of his favorite organizations," Norman pointed out.

"So he kind of connected with us and said, 'Hey, we're going to be one of your sending churches.' Of course, then our excitement built even more, and we definitely felt like, 'We are doing the *ultimate* thing of Christians!'" Judy paused for an instant before adding reflectively, "It was really like being set up. It felt great at the time, but as I look back on that, I'm not sure how healthy that was."

Suddenly a cloud seemed to have dimmed her bright enthusiasm. I made a mental note to revisit that last statement later. But first I wanted to ask them whether they felt as though they had ever received a "call" to become missionaries. This seemed important for several reasons. First, a sense of calling to the ministry has traditionally been a virtual requirement of many mission boards, churches, seminaries, and other institutions involved in training, ordaining, or sending vocational Christian workers.

In addition, I knew that some readers of their story would see it as important. A call to mission work would be God's imprimatur on the couple. Without it, they could not expect to receive His full blessing; indeed, their efforts would more than likely fail. With a call, however, they would be able to face almost any obstacle or hardship, confident that they were fulfilling God's will.

Norman answered, "I'm not sure there is such a thing as a call. In fact, I don't think there is."

I replied that it must have been very difficult to raise support if they were unable to describe a call to missions.

"Yeah," he agreed.

Judy joined in. "We did have a few people ask us if we felt like we were called, and we probably answered something like, 'We've really felt the Lord's leading, and one thing has led to another, and God has made things fit into place.' You know, you use all those phrases. It can sound OK, like, 'That sort of sounds like a call.'"

"Especially in certain churches," Norman added. "If you just say, 'The Lord is leading us,' who can argue with you?"

There was no intent to mislead. Judy and Norman definitely believed that God wanted them on the mission field. But they would not have been able to pinpoint a "call" to that work, certainly not in the sense that many have described it—for example, as an inner voice commanding them to go to a particular people or part of the world, or as a series of incidents too amazing to be coincidental. Readers will no doubt interpret the events that follow according to the importance they place on the need for a specific call. But to Norman and Judy, it wasn't an issue.

Eventually, they finished raising their support and finally left the United States. At last they were on their way, embarking on a strategy to plant a church among a group of people who had never heard the gospel. For the first few years in the country, their main goals were to master the language and culture of the people and to gain their trust. By accomplishing these objectives, the new missionaries would be "preparing the soil" so that eventually they could present the gospel message.

Things went pretty much according to plan. However, while the plan was actually quite well conceived in regards to the people to be reached, it was rather ill conceived in terms of the people sent to do the reaching—Norman and Judy.

"When we went over there we felt like this was the *only* thing to do, and you couldn't have stopped us," Judy explained. "But the reason it was like a set-up is that we weren't prepared for the alternative: What if it didn't work? I think we just assumed that this was going to work and we were going to be there the rest of our lives. We didn't really face what would happen if we *didn't* stay doing this forever and ever. And I think especially for me, that would have been a really good, key thing to talk about."

In fact, exploring the question, *What if this doesn't work out?* might have prevented a great deal of pain later. Yet that is one question people starting new ministries seldom, if ever, ask. Indeed, there is almost a taboo against asking it. After all, if one is convinced that "God is in this," then how could there be any prospect for failure?

Furthermore, the psychology of ministry start-ups tends to be such that there can be no alternative but to move forward. After all, didn't Jesus say, "No one who puts his hand to the plow and looks back is fit for service in the kingdom of God"?[5] The message would seem to be that one's only option is total, all-out commitment. There can be no turning back.

Add to this thinking a hefty dose of entrepreneurial enthusiasm and the practical need to instill confidence in potential supporters, and one can quickly create extraordinarily high expectations. In Norman and Judy's case, it was a perfect recipe for disaster.

Judy continued, "One of the things we didn't do before we went to the field—because our mission was new and they hadn't gotten into it too deeply yet—they didn't do any psychological [testing or preparation], which seems like a real good idea before people get out there.

"See, what happens is, you go out on the crest of the wave. You get to the field where the rubber meets the road, and it's really tough going because every day you are struggling to survive—mentally, physically, and spiritually. And any garbage you've got under the surface, under the skin, is going to surface. All the sudden, you don't have all this protective coating like you do in the States where you don't have to face those issues. You can just overlook them.

"So when I got over there and the honeymoon was over and I was facing the daily grind, all my stress came down and I said, 'OK, why am I really here?' And inside I was saying, 'I don't like this at all!'"

That question of why Judy was on the mission field would prove to open the door to countless unexplored issues in her inner, spiritual life—"garbage" rising to the surface, as she put it. For a while she stuffed it back down, perhaps hoping it would all go away. But then she and Norman returned to the States for their first furlough. While home, she met with a psychologist New Horizons had recently brought on board.

"To make a long story short, I really struggled with going back. I still felt like I should. But for the first time in my life I was saying to myself, 'I don't want to go back, and I don't want to do it for anybody else. And since I don't want to, I'm not going to, and I don't have to.'"

It's important to appreciate what a profound moment this was for Judy. To many readers, the idea of paying attention to one's likes and dislikes may seem so normal as to be unremarkable. But not in Judy's world. A common attitude toward ministries and missions, then and still today, is: It doesn't matter what you "like" or what you "want"; it only matters what God wants, and if He wants you on the mission field, then that's where you'd better be! Sure, you're going to have days where you want to throw in the towel. But if you're doing God's will, and trusting Him, and persevering in the task, then He'll give you the strength to surmount those trials. If you can't trust Him for that, are you really fit for Christian service?

"I took those feelings with me to my session with the psychologist," Judy recalled, "and he dealt me a lot of . . . mercy. He helped me see that maybe I needed to look at my feelings as friends, and we got into some wonderful stuff. I really felt freed after that session.

"For example, he brought up Jesus, how in the garden of Gethsemane, you know, why was He sweating drops of blood? Why was He up all night? [Because] He had to have been struggling with His feelings, too.[6] Feelings are OK and you can let them out.

"For the first time in my life I was getting in touch with my feelings. I don't think I was yet at the point where I could act on them, but I was getting there."

In the end, the couple did go back. "The first few years had been basically language learning. So when we got back from furlough, the understanding was that we would start getting into evangelism." Yet that wreaked even greater havoc on Judy's emotional life.

"My main problem was that we were there as missionaries. We had to be undercover. And I couldn't stand it. I'm a very open person. I couldn't stand my friends [among the people] not knowing what I was really doing."

She explained that, in that culture, the women did most of their work in the morning and then got together at midday for tea, knitting, and gossip. "I remember being at one tea in particular. There were probably thirty women in this living room. Of course, they all wanted to know about this American woman. They couldn't imagine why any of us would want to go over there. They all wanted to come here. They think it's heaven here, so why would we pick up and go over there? And we couldn't tell them why.

"At that point, Norm didn't have a job. We were both learning the language. I mean, in a normal situation, foreigners would come over there with an oil company or something. So I could kind of hear these women whispering, 'What do they really do for bread? How come they don't have to work? How can they just learn the language?' That gnawed at me, and I wasn't good at covering up."

It didn't help that the newspapers frequently carried stories about missionaries being found out and deported. In fact, one day a major article appeared under the headline "We Are Invaded by the Missionary."

"It described us to a tee," Norman recalled with a chuckle. "It said that missionaries will be a couple in their late twenties or early thirties with a couple of kids, usually from America. They'll live in a nice apartment, and they'll leave the country every three months and go to [a nearby free country]. We were doing all of that!"

Judy had little concern about being exposed, however. In fact, if she could have had her way, she would have been a great deal more open. "I didn't care that much about getting kicked out. For me the issue was I didn't know how I would face my [local] friends if they looked at me and said, 'So *that's* why you're my friend!' I just wanted to be real and have the same kind of struggles they did.

"And I think, to tell you the truth, one of the things that factors in at this point is that I felt like I didn't really know what I had been saved *from*. It wasn't like I had this great testimony of how God had changed my life, because really, all I had memory of was trying to please people, and I had learned the whole thing under that kind of umbrella."

Anyone who has ever tried to convince someone else to accept the gospel knows how important her own story of faith can be. Yet Judy seemed to disparage hers as somewhat insignificant. I asked her to take me back to the first steps in that journey, which had started decades before and thousands of miles away.

"My father was a minister," she began,[7] "and I was the youngest of eight kids. I remember at a very, very early age—I think I was about four—[to believe in Jesus] was a very natural thing for me because I was always hearing at church and at home that I needed Jesus as my Savior and Lord. Somehow, even at that young age, I was old enough to at least understand that I wanted to be with Jesus, and that I needed to ask Him into my heart. So I remember doing that at that young age, and then growing up in two or three different churches where my dad was the pastor.

"As I was growing up, I was basically the kind of person who wanted to please people. We were in a small town of a few thousand people, so I really spent my life trying to make my parents happy and protecting my father's reputation as a minister.

"In my high school years, there was a lot of guilt as far as if you weren't going to have a goal of being in full-time ministry, then somehow you were less than the best. It was very covert. It was never spoken, but it was there. For instance, one of my older sisters was a missionary, and hers was the only picture in my father's study, on his desk.

"I remember when missionaries would visit in the church, I would stand there at the end of the service and there would always be not only an altar call, but a missionary call.[8] So I'd stand there as an eight-year-old and tremble and pray, 'Lord, don't ever call me to do this, because I don't want to.' But there was always in my heart the feeling that I was going to have to do this someday in order to ease my conscience."

I doubt that many adults appreciate the far-reaching impression that rituals like a "missionary call" can have on a child—especially a child as eager to please as Judy was. A child can hardly process such an appeal rationally; she mostly responds emotionally. Faced with a passionate, persuasive, perhaps even archetypal figure in the pulpit whose voice cries out about the fate of the lost and the desperate need for workers, often to the moving strains of an organ—what other reaction can a sensitive child have but fear and an uncontrollable urge to do something?

In addition, "There were strong feelings, especially from my mother, that if it feels good, it's wrong. If you want to do it, if it makes you happy, then you better do just the opposite. In fact, I've heard it called 'masochistic Christianity,' where as long as there's this death-to-self at the forefront,[9] which is where my mother was at constantly, then you were OK. But if you really wanted to go to certain colleges and really wanted to go into a certain field, you had to really stop and pray about that for a long time. Make sure that was what God wanted."

In other words, a sense of one's self—personal choices, feelings, preferences—didn't matter. Self was the enemy; it was not to be trusted. It all sounded terribly unhealthy. Indeed, "masochistic Christianity" seemed like a good name for it.

Judy eventually left home for college, where she met Norman. He, too, had grown up in a large family that was strongly committed to a church. "Every time there was a meeting at church, we all had to be there. I grew up with a real strong knowledge of the Bible because that's all we did. I wasn't really rebellious about it, because I just thought that's the way life was."

However, Norman was a year in college before he "truly became a Christian," as he put it. "Before that, I knew all the right answers, but I don't think I ever really made a commitment. I don't think I ever really felt like I was in."

I asked him what caused him to consider the gospel on a more personal basis. "You know, it sounds really stupid, but it was Three Dog Night's last album.[10] They had become Christians. Their last album had all these songs on it talking about their journey and how they found the Lord and all this stuff, and I thought, 'I can relate to that.' I think that was a big part of it. That really sounds weird, doesn't it?

"Anyway, I started getting really involved in church on my own terms. I just started doing a lot of things, and it wasn't my parents making me do it, *I* wanted to do it." For example, he taught a Sunday school class for youth, started a college group, and worked at a Bible camp. "Then my best friend started getting letters from a girl in college. He said, 'Do you want to go there?' So I said, 'Sure, I'll go there,' and we went to the college because Judy was there."

Before long, Norman and Judy married and then transferred to the teachers' university, where they ultimately decided to go into missions.

"After we were married for a year and a half or so, I was overwhelmed with feelings of guilt," Judy explained. It was easy to see why. "I felt guilty that I'd never gone to the mission field. We ended up having a big long talk—"

"Actually, we had this big argument," Norman corrected, "mostly based on Judy's built-up guilt feelings of 'We aren't doing squat with our lives!'"

Whatever the case, "We basically said, 'Lord, put us in the world where You most want us,'" Judy continued, "and the very next day we went to visit my parents and my mother showed me all this information about New Horizons Missions, and it started at that point."

It was a scenario I had heard many times before, and I could almost predict how it would come out. There was certainly nothing wrong with the couple's prayer to be placed wherever God wanted them. But the underlying guilt that Judy had picked up from her past rendered the prayer almost meaningless. It was not unlike a death row inmate praying, "Lord, I'll go wherever you want me to go." Fine prayer, but realistically there can be only one place for him to "go"— through the door to the death chamber.

Furthermore, having prayed that prayer of submission, Judy and Norman were highly vulnerable to using circumstance as a way of determining God's will. Again, there was nothing wrong with New Horizons Missions. But their enthusiastic leap at it as the first opportunity to come along reminded me of countless others who have managed to discern divine messages in coincidental events, or "fleeces."[11]

I once met a man who admitted to having proposed marriage to his girlfriend on nothing more certain than the change of a stoplight: "I said, 'Lord, if you want me to marry Becky, let that light turn red.' The light turned red. So I gulped, stopped the car, and asked her to marry me."

In a similar way, I've heard of people buying houses, giving away money, changing careers, taking jobs, quitting jobs, going into the ministry, witnessing, even filing for divorce based on some coincidence that happened soon after a prayer was prayed.

Far be it from me to disparage anyone's walk with God. No doubt God can and does sometimes arrange matters in a way that leads us into His will. But does that exempt us from responsibility as humans to make wise choices based on sound information?

Judy concluded, "The point is that the guilt I carried around with me finally kind of exploded, and it wasn't until years later that I realized that was probably the main motive of why I went into missions at all."

I wondered how many others have ended up in missions and other ministries out of similar feelings of guilt. It's as if they had no choice. The only way to ultimately please God is through "full-time" Christian service. And of course, for many, the ultimate service is foreign missions.

"That's the key word—*ultimate*," Judy agreed. "Because of the kind of person I am and was, it was within me to make other people happy. And the ultimate way to make God happy was [missions], because I perceived Him through what my parents projected."

Norman pointed out that even in deciding where they would work, they tackled one of the hardest mission fields possible. "Yeah," Judy agreed, "we went to [this particularly tough part of the] world. It was like, you know, the crest of a wave. That was where we wanted to be. It was like, 'Let's do the most *important* thing.' Of course, you can imagine the ramifications of that when you turn around and decide to come home."

Judy recounted what happened. "After we'd been back on the field for about five months, things really came to a head. I just got to the point where it was difficult for me to even make it through a day without struggling over [being there]. Then one day Norm sat me down and said, 'What if we pursue leaving?' I looked at him dumbfounded! I actually went in and put on a tape of the 'Hallelujah Chorus'!

"I think that was such a key moment for me—not just in my mission experience, but in my whole life. Nobody had ever said to me, 'It's OK for you to do what you want to do.' I felt like a butterfly who had just popped out of a cocoon, and I said, 'I'm free!' It didn't even matter at that moment if we were really leaving or not. It mattered that it was OK if we decided to go.

"So the following week we prayed and read Scripture and really sought out the Lord and our own feelings about everything, to see if this was the way to go."

During that week, a small but significant incident took place. As Judy remembered it, "One of the devotional books that I grew up reading—basically because my mom did—was Oswald Chambers's *My Utmost for His Highest*. And if you read it with the perspective that I had, it can be damaging. During the week of our decision, a passage that we used was John 7:38: 'He that believeth on Me, as the Scripture hath said, out of his heart shall flow rivers of living water.'

"And Oswald Chambers's interpretation of that is that the point isn't for you to be fed, the point is for people to be fed through you. And by the time I got to the bottom of his thoughts on this given day, I felt so awful about myself because I felt like God was saying to me, through this man's interpretation, 'You shouldn't be worrying about how you feel about being [here]. You're here for other people. So you should stay for their sake.'

"In other words, my feelings don't matter. I need to be a broken vessel for these other people who are going to go to hell if I don't tell them about God. And so I felt so defeated. I felt like everything that had been freed within me was all of a sudden a closed fist again."

I checked the indicated selection in *My Utmost*. For September 2, Chambers writes: "Our Lord's teaching is always *anti*-self-realization. His purpose is not the development of a man; His purpose is to make a man exactly like Himself, and the characteristic of the Son of God is self-expenditure. If we believe in Jesus, it is not what we gain, but what He pours through us that counts. It is not that God makes us beautifully rounded grapes, but that He squeezes the sweetness out of us. Spiritually, we cannot measure our life by success, but only by what God pours through us, and we cannot measure that at all. . . .

"It is time now to break the life, to cease craving for satisfaction, and to spill the thing out. Our Lord is asking who of us will do it for Him?"[12]

Judy was right. Given her background and emotional condition—chronic guilt, a habit of ignoring her own feelings, an unhealthy need to make others happy, a belief that missions was the ultimate way to please God—Chambers's message could be damaging. In her case, it was almost devastating.

"But then," she continued, "I don't know where it came from—I think it was from the Lord—but out of the blue was this thought that, 'This is this *man's* interpretation of a verse. Let me go back and see what the actual Scripture says.' I looked up the verse, and found that Jesus was quoting from Isaiah. So I went back to the verse in Isaiah, and it was the verse about 'You will be a well-watered garden.'[13]

"That gave me a whole different feeling. It wasn't the idea of a broken cistern with water pouring through it. It was a picture of, 'Hey, I'm well watered, and people are going to come to me to partake of something that God is giving to me.' It's not that He's giving it through me and ignoring me. He cares so much about me that I'm also going to be well fed. And that was a real breakthrough for me, I think. It was the beginning of me building my own faith. I had to believe it from within my own self."

It was a breakthrough, all right, and long overdue. At last Judy was growing up and coming to a sense of her own self. And by finally paying attention to her feelings, she ended up turning *toward* God, not looking for a way to be rid of Him.

Furthermore, while fans of Oswald Chambers (of whom there are millions) might not like it, one of the surest evidences that she was on the right path was her willingness to question the validity of this renowned man's interpretation. I admired her courage. She was right to go back to the the Scriptures and examine what *they* had to say rather than rely on someone else, no matter how celebrated, to do her thinking for her. At last she was taking responsibility for her own spirituality.

At the end of the week, "We went and talked to our team leader. It was such confirmation. He said, 'You know, this really feels right.' He didn't discourage us at all and our whole team accepted it. I was overwhelmed, because I had that other fear that I grew up with—that if I stopped doing this, I wouldn't be acceptable.

"That night we called the pastors of the churches that had given us their support. The first church was like, 'OK, you know, whatever you say.' The second church was a little bit more progressive and said, 'It's OK, you know, we're here for you.'

"Then at the third church, the large church, the missions pastor had been doing research and was on the cutting edge. In fact, he had just been at a seminar about missionaries coming home from the field for various reasons, and how they felt, and what kinds of things they were going to go through. I mean, it was incredible! He said, 'You're our heroes no matter if the church was planted or not. You did what you were supposed to do at the time.' That was really terrific.

"But then within the next few days, we had to call our parents."

Judy broke off, and tears came to her eyes. Clearly the calls home were the toughest to make. Norman took over the story and explained why. "It was because my dad was mad. He said things like, 'Oh, well, did Judy have a bad day, and you're coming home?' or, 'Did God change His mind?' I was like, 'Lay off it, man!' He really made me mad!"

"I think a lot of that was generational," Judy came back to say. "My parents didn't come off quite that bad, but I could tell they were disappointed. The feeling I got from Norm's dad was, 'I've been so proud to have kids on the mission field, and now I'm not going to have that anymore.' You know, I've heard doctors and lawyers talk about that—that if they stopped doing medicine or law, their parents would be disappointed in them. So it's not unique to missionaries.

"But that began—and this is really the key part of the story for me, and I'm not even able to talk about it—that experience with our parents began suspicion within my heart that the Christian church was not going to be behind us in [our decision to leave the mission field]."

But how could it be, really? The church is in the business of *sending* evangelists to the ends of the earth, so it can hardly be expected to celebrate when some of them come home, especially if they've left their task more or less unfinished. Yet Norman and Judy were not looking for a party. Indeed, they did not expect the church to support or even understand their decision. But they did hope that the body would stand behind them as people and trust their decision to return, just as it had trusted their decision to go.

"I think they just didn't know what to do with us," Norman said reflectively.

"Yeah, we were an anomaly," Judy agreed. "People didn't really know how to respond to us. I remember the first Sunday back at Norm's home church. Every other time we had visited there they had made a big deal about introducing us and stuff. And here we were back from the field, and they didn't even acknowledge that we were in the service! It was just a feeling that we were kind of an embarrassment. We were not very 'special' anymore, because we came back."

I asked them whether anyone at those churches had taken them aside privately and asked them the exact reason why they had returned from the field. "I don't think anyone ever did," Norman replied, and Judy agreed.

So apparently Judy and Norman were not the only ones to overlook the question, *What happens if things don't work out?* The churches that supported them had not considered the alternatives either. As a result, they greeted the returning missionaries with a climate of ambiguity instead of supportive concern and practical help.

Fortunately, New Horizons proved more astute at helping the couple through their reentry and eventual transition out of missions. As Judy recalled, "They were very understanding. Of all the mission agencies I've ever dealt with or seen, they were the most 'laid back,' in a good way. I mean, they were real organized and everything, and they were not into making anybody feel guilty. We really appreciated the grace that they dealt us.

"Still, I think, looking back, if we had somehow had a little bit of counseling from somebody who understood what we were going through, it would have been a good thing. But it's like we never really came to grips with what had happened to us. And so one thing led to another, and eventually we had to find a job, and then other pressures started happening."

"And if you've been a missionary for ten years, what do you do for a living?" Norman pointed out. Then he added, "Because of those painful experiences, at least for me, I started pulling away from church psychologically and saying, 'This is not a place that's going to meet my needs because I don't really fit in here anymore.' And I think that has been a gradual process ever since then—feeling less and less and less like I fit into any church that I can think of."

His wife had a similar reaction. "I have felt less and less like I belong," she told me, "and it seems easier not to invest in a church family and a church body because there really isn't anybody that I can relate to and who can relate to me."

I asked her to explain that. "It's just a real crisis of faith," she replied. "It all goes back to that moment when we called to say we were coming home. That's when I started getting suspicious of the church. That was the beginning of a departure from everything I had been raised to believe.

"I had trusted the church up until that moment. But then it stopped being there for me in some way, and I said, 'Hey, I'm not getting the support I need.' And that opened me up to say, "Maybe this whole thing is faulty! How do I know whether any of what I've believed is true? Maybe I've just been believing it for my parents or whatever.'

"So my mind started to question, what is the truth? If [the church] wasn't there for me, is any of this true? You know, you tend to see God through people and institutions and whatever.

"But I can't let it go altogether—which makes me think that it's more related to the church than it is to God, that there really is a core relationship, and that maybe I just need to come around full circle and rebuild."

Given these feelings, I asked them where they saw their spiritual lives headed. "Good question!" Norman responded. "We haven't gone to Sunday morning service in a while. I don't know, I guess my problem with church is not that I've lost my faith or feel like it's hopeless or that kind of thing. It's more that I'm bored with it. I go to church and I hear sermons and I think, 'I just don't want to hear this.' I don't know if that's because I'm dodging something. I really haven't sat down to figure out what it is."

"I feel like an outsider," Judy said, "and I realize for the first time what the rest of the world feels like, people who have been treated like outsiders. Nobody really knows I'm going through this, and I can't talk about this with very many people.

"It isn't that I have to have somebody convince me about the basic theology or something. It's my lack of the feeling that I used to have— and I don't mean to say that I depend on a feeling in this faith thing; there *is* a desire to know God and to know truth—but it's definitely a lack of desire to be involved with the churches I've known.

"I can't say I feel very guilty anymore. I think I'm kind of getting past the guilt stage. I feel like if God really loves me, and He's the kind of God I want to believe in, He's really hanging in there for me."

Then she returned to something she had said earlier. "You know, I was never saved out of anything. I was a four-year-old kid when I asked Jesus into my heart. It wasn't like my mom, who was saved out of this horrible pagan background. But now, it's like I'm being taken through that barren experience that a lot of people are saved out of. So, you know, maybe *this* is what I'm going to be saved out of. And maybe that's going be valuable to somebody someday who can relate to what I've been through."

I thought so. After all, consider John Mark. He made the "mistake" of returning home to Jerusalem instead of continuing with Paul and Barnabas on their missionary journey to Asia Minor. As a result, Paul marked him off as a failure. Having once "turned back" from the work, John Mark was thereafter viewed as unfit for service. (Apparently even the apostle Paul didn't know what to do with someone for whom a mission assignment didn't "work out.")

But the story did not end there, thanks to John Mark's cousin, Barnabas. Years later, John Mark probably traveled with Peter to Rome and, according to tradition, worked with Peter to write the gospel of Mark. And eventually even Paul changed his mind about his former associate. Toward the end of his life, he instructed Timothy to "pick up Mark and bring him with you, for he is useful to me for service."[14] Quite a change from Paul's initial assessment!

Early church tradition holds that John Mark went on to become the first missionary to Alexandria, Egypt, where he won many converts and became the first bishop of that city.

So I had good reason to believe that Judy and Norman's story would prove highly valuable. It seemed to be a timely tale for a church where there are far more John Marks than there are apostle Pauls.

NOTES

1. *My Utmost for His Highest* (New York: Dodd, Mead & Company, 1935), 344.

2. I have substituted this pseudonym for the actual agency that sponsored Norman and Judy as missionaries. To my knowledge there is no mission board or agency named New Horizons Missions, and any similarity between this name and any actual ministry or organization is purely coincidental.

3. The Great Commission is a general term used by many Christians for the church's mandate to take the gospel to the ends of the earth. Thus it has become a catchphrase for evangelism and missions. The term is also used in a narrower sense to indicate Jesus' final words to His disciples, a version of which can be found in each of the four Gospels and the book of Acts (Matthew 28:18–20; Mark 16:15–18; Luke 24:46–49; John 20:21–23; Acts 1:7–8).

4. "Unreached" and "hidden" peoples are semitechnical terms coined or at least popularized by missiologists Peter Wagner and Ed Dayton, and Ralph Winter respectively. "Both are speaking of very large numbers of homogeneous units—ethnically, geographically, culturally, and economically separate segments of mankind. Depending on how such segments are defined, there are thousands or tens of thousands of them.

    "The phrase, *hidden peoples,* is attractive. It calls attention to the huge neglected [from the standpoint of having had the gospel preached to them] majority of mankind"—Donald A. McGavran, *Understanding Church Growth* (Grand Rapids: Eerdmans, 1970), 73.

5. Luke 9:62.

6. Luke 22:39–46. However, notice also that in the Garden of Gethsemane, and later at Calvary, with the help of His Father, Jesus did what He didn't "feel like" doing.

    Likewise, Norman and Judy were not using their *feelings* to avoid their *responsibilities.* They were learning to understand that God does care about people's feelings; that He, in fact, works through and uses people's feelings, interests, and talents. They found that understanding freeing.

7. Judy was not the only "PK" (preacher's kid) I interviewed. However, in this book I have chosen not to highlight the impact of the ministry on her life or the lives of the others. That is a subject in which I have a personal interest, and I plan to deal with it in a later book.

8. A missionary call is similar to an altar call, except that instead of appealing to people to accept the gospel, the appeal is to commit oneself to a lifetime of service on the "mission field."

9. An allusion to Matthew 16:24–25.

10. Three Dog Night was a popular musical group of the late sixties.

11. See the story of Gideon, Judges 6:36–40. For a good discussion of "putting out a fleece" before the Lord, as well as the larger issue of determining God's will, see Garry Friesen, *Decision Making and the Will of God: A Biblical Alternative to the Traditional View* (Portland, Ore: Multnomah, 1980).

12. Chambers, ibid., 246.

13. Actually, no one knows exactly to which passage in the Old Testament Jesus was referring. There are several texts in Isaiah that seem to fit—for example, 44:3; 55:1; and 58:11, the one which Judy seemed to indicate. It reads: "The Lord will guide you always; he will satisfy your needs in a sun-scorched land and will strengthen your frame. You will be like a well-watered garden, like a spring whose waters never fail."

    There are also other texts that Jesus may have had in mind, including Psalm 78:15–16 and Zechariah 14:8.

14. On John Mark's initial return home, see Acts 13:13. On Paul's negative reaction and Barnabas's helpful intervention, see Acts 15:36–41. On Paul's instruction to Timothy, see 2 Timothy 4:11 (NASB quoted).

17

Tom

*Compared to the highest privilege of knowing Christ Jesus
as my Master, firsthand, everything I once thought I had
going for me is insignificant. . . . I gave up all that
inferior stuff so I could know Christ personally.*
Philippians 3:8, 10[1]

There is a splendid moment in Steven Spielberg's blockbuster movie *Jurassic Park*, when world-class paleontologist Allen Grant, who has devoted his life to the study of dinosaurs, suddenly comes face-to-face with real, live prehistoric creatures. He falls to the ground, dumbstruck. The reason is obvious. It is one thing to piece together an informed but nonetheless imperfect image of dinosaurs by picking through fossils and bones. But to encounter an *actual* dinosaur firsthand—well, there can be no comparison.

Later in the film, John Hammond, the wealthy impresario behind Jurassic Park, reflects on what motivated him to build his island menagerie: "I wanted to show people something that wasn't an illusion, something that was real, something they could see, and touch, and feel."

For many people, spirituality amounts to picking through the artifacts of faith that survive from long ago and far away. In that bygone era, humans saw God, heard His voice, and experienced His awesome, at times terrible, power. But that was then. Today, those kinds of gripping encounters with the living God are generally regarded as extinct. They might as well be placed in the same category as Jurassic Park: fun to imagine, but unlikely to happen. Of course, if one ever did come face-to-face with God—with a God who wasn't an illusion, but Someone who was real, Someone you could see, and touch, and feel—well, there could be no comparison.

And so people long for God. In fact, deep down they long for an *experience* of Him, no matter how passing, more than anything else in the world. That was certainly true of Tom, for whom three questions kept recurring: Does God exist? If so, what difference does He make? And what can I experience of Him?

"Basically, I found satisfactory answers to the first two," Tom told me, but the last one—it never happened. I never experienced Him."

Over time, that lack of firsthand experience led to a flood of doubts and ultimately the extinction of Tom's faith. I asked him to take me back through what happened.

"To go back to the beginning, I can remember my mother taking the kids to church when I was in kindergarten and first and second grade. She did it because she felt that was good for us. It wasn't something that was necessarily a personal faith of her own. She felt it was great for the kids."

As Tom described his mother's decision, I immediately thought of an interesting phenomenon taking place today. All across the country, millions of Baby Boomers are returning to churches they left in the sixties and seventies. The number one reason bringing them back is their children. Like Tom's mother, and perhaps like their own parents, many Boomers now want to expose their own kids to religion.

Understandably, church leaders are enthusiastically celebrating this development. But there's a dark side to it that I haven't heard mentioned. If the main reason parents participate in a church is for the sake of their children, if they themselves derive little if any spiritual benefit from the program, then a time bomb is ticking. For as soon as those children grow up and leave home, the parents will have no more need of the church. Once again, they can be expected to leave the institution.

Of course, there's a more positive way to look at this situation. In effect, the church has a twenty-year window of opportunity. Boomers may come for the sake of their kids, but there's no reason why churches can't help them identify their own needs and then offer ways to meet those needs. Issues such as mid-life, career decisions, parenting, and the care of elderly parents come to mind.

One thing is clear: if churches fail to ignite the spirituality of Boomer parents, they are liable to lose *two* generations of Americans. The Boomers will stop coming when their children leave home. And sooner or later their children will realize how little religion has meant to their parents and in all likelihood reject it themselves—repeating the pattern set by Boomers in the sixties and seventies.

At any rate, Tom's exposure to Sunday school was short-lived. His family relocated to another city during his elementary school years. "We just stopped going," he recalled, "and it wasn't until my sophomore year in high school that the only time I'd go to church was when I was over at my cousins' house or when I was visiting my grandmother."

"Church was something I wanted to do and enjoyed but didn't want to do too much. When I was with my cousins it was an interesting experience, but it wasn't what I'd call 'fun.' I can remember actually feeling sorry for people who had to go to church, because I got to sleep in on Sunday. They all had to get up and go to church. It seemed like an awful lot of work to give up the whole morning to go.

"It had some value. I mean, the environment of being in church and singing. Singing in particular helped me. I really enjoyed that. I always had some feeling of peace when I'd be in church singing and stuff. But I certainly didn't see the personal connections."

However, a number of events in Tom's early adolescence changed his outlook. They especially affected his self-image. "I really began to doubt my worth, in a sense. I got into trouble with the fire department for lighting a fire in a field. I remember standing in front of the fire chief and having him say to me that if he saw me again, he was going to throw me in juvenile hall.

"Also, I almost drowned in a boating accident. And then a couple of months later, there was a really important concert at school, and I'm still not sure exactly what happened, but my parents didn't come. They had a real good reason, but it really hurt. And shortly after that, my dad signed me up for a summer fitness program, and I ended up dropping out of that, kind of knowing as I did so that I was not living up to my dad's expectations.

"So through a combination of those things during junior high school, I think I was basically separating myself from my parents. I was saying, 'They don't love me,' or, 'I'm never going to find love there, or approval,' or something like that. And I started looking for it in other places.

"I felt like I was off on my own, making decisions by myself. Part of that, I'm sure, is kind of normal adolescent separation from parents, and part of it was emotional trouble.

"I finally got to high school and started looking at the world around me, trying to make sense out of it. I was feeling more and more like I was off on my own. I was really scared, because I considered myself to be very logical, and everything around me seemed to be totally illogical. I couldn't understand anything at all."

Alone. Afraid. Confused. Looking for love. Tom was in a very vulnerable position. He was also an ideal candidate to hear the gospel, especially since he thought about spiritual matters quite a bit. "My question every day was always, 'What is God doing in my life today?' In many ways, I was trying so hard [to find out].

"During this time I was in an English class that on some days met for half an hour and on other days for an hour and a half. On the hour and a half days, the English teacher didn't try to keep us interested for that long. She'd see what we wanted to talk about, and then we'd have a debate. We'd argue about whether there was a God or not, whether there was a plan to the world. Some people in the room were Christians. They were going to [a youth group sponsored by a parachurch ministry] and events like that.

"I would always argue that there wasn't a God, partly because I liked to argue and that was the other side, and partly because I had never seen God. You couldn't see Him, so you didn't know if there was a God. It didn't make sense to me. But it was just fun to go and argue— argue in my head, anyway."

Tom was outnumbered by the Christians in the room. At least, he felt outnumbered. "I remember one time asking a question. Everybody in the room just looked at me aghast like, you know, this was so contrary to where they were coming from. It almost scared me. Another time, one of us was trying to quote Genesis and everybody pulled out a Bible. It almost freaked me out! I couldn't imagine a world where everybody was carrying a Bible around."

Eventually some of Tom's Christian classmates invited him to go to a religious youth group in the community. He went and ended up becoming a fairly regular attender. Part of it was the whole dynamic of the group. "I could kind of sit on the edge and be a little bit involved. I was really feeling isolated at the time. I liked the singing. I liked the talk. I liked to sit there and listen and dissect the talk and figure out what they were saying 'wrong.' I liked arguing with people afterwards."

I could imagine that some of the other group members must have wondered who this skeptic was and why he kept coming. "That's right," Tom said. "I was told later that one of the group leaders told another leader that of all the people who were there, he was sure I would be the one who would become a Christian," because Tom was fighting so hard not to become one.

In the end, the leader was right. "It eventually got to the point where there was no reason to argue about what I believed versus what they believed. Then somebody gave me a book [on end-times prophecy]. I started reading it and saying, 'This isn't true, and this isn't true, and this isn't true.' And I got about half-way through the book when suddenly it hit me: if *any* of it was true, I was really out of my league. There was no way I was going to make it. I was already scared of life in general and people around me.

"So at that point when it hit me—I was in the shower at the time—I basically prayed, 'I don't believe there's a God, but if You are, then show me.'"

It may not have been the greatest prayer ever prayed, but there was no doubt Tom meant it. As best he knew how, he was reaching out to a God he could not see and scarcely believed existed.

"Some time later that evening, after I went to bed, I was overcome by a feeling of warmth and love and security. It was totally foreign to my experience at the time. And it was real clear to me that God had answered a prayer.

"The next morning I woke up, and the feeling was all gone. I didn't really know what to do from there. I let the youth group leaders know that I felt like I had basically become a Christian. I felt like I had made this decision, because I felt like God had answered me, and that was totally foreign. They kind of led me in some directions to get me started into group meetings and Bible study. I also got involved in some weekend work groups at [a Christian] camp and started getting involved in study groups."

And so Tom quickly became immersed in programs of spiritual development. There is some question as to whether he had yet crossed the line from unbelief to belief. If not, he was certainly well on the way. Before long, he joined a local church.

"I got involved in a church that the youth group leader was involved in. He made no big deal about going to his church, but he went there, so I went there. I met people there—the pastor, high school and college people, et cetera. Actually, for the first time in my life, I really had friends, which was quite significant. What's more, I had friends who were girls. A friend of mine said that was actually the reason I was involved in that church. I don't think it was quite true, but it certainly was healthy.

"Another aspect that had significance was that this was the first group that looked at me independently of my schoolwork. My whole self-image at that time was based on my academic standing. So it was kind of refreshing to be in a place where people could know *me*, where schoolwork didn't matter, and I had no fear to be who I was and experiment with who I was."

Having heard so many of my other interviewees describe groups that had been confining, rigid, and legalistic, it was very refreshing to hear about a church where a young person was free to "be who I was and experiment with who I was." That kind of freedom was especially important in Tom's case, because he was still at a delicate stage. His faith was still embryonic, emerging in two important ways that demanded a lot of compassion and latitude.

First, he was working out the intellectual implications of Christianity. "I began to reconstruct my view of the world based on the belief that God existed and was in my life. I was trying to figure out how involved is God, and in a sense who God was. I can remember asking who created the universe, who created God, questions like that. I can remember going around trying to figure out what did I believe and what was believable."

A second area of experimentation for Tom was relationships—particularly his relationship with God and his relationships with girls. The two seemed to go hand in hand. "During my junior year, I had several girlfriends for short periods of time—two girlfriends in three weeks! The spiritual part of that was trying to figure out how God was involved in those relationships. The big issues back then were Christians in relationships. People talked about the whole question of whether or not you'd marry some day, which way should you go, what does it mean, what does God want."

It all sounded rather normal to me. It also reminded me of my own experiences as a Christian in high school. As they were for Tom, dating and God's will seemed to be the two most important topics for people in my youth group. Discussion of one invariably seemed to bring about discussion of the other.

And I can recall countless lectures and seminars on relationships with the opposite sex. But I'm still not satisfied that Christians have paid nearly enough attention to what even as a teenager I called a "theology of dating." Many will laugh just thinking about it. Surely there are more important matters to occupy serious minds! But when one looks at my generation's appalling track record in marriage, with all of the related implications, a theology of dating is not really such a laughing matter.

Dating, after all, is our culture's way of getting into marriage. Is it the best way? Many would ask, is it the "biblical" way? But it's a pointless question, because dating as we know it was unknown in Bible times. How, then, might Christians think biblically about dating? We know that God cares a great deal about marriage. Does He have anything to say about how people—especially His people—get into marriages? The church would be well served if its theologians could speak to this universally problematic area.

So far, Tom had described a fairly typical scenario for a new Christian. I wondered what sort of expectations he had about what he was supposed to get out of Christianity and what God was supposed to do for him.

"Expectations were being formed," he explained. "I don't think I came into it with any expectations. I think just being in a group where people were going through the same questions, there were a lot of expectations that were kind of shared by the group. They were kind of absorbed by the Christians.

"For example, the idea that God would take care of you. You know, seek first the kingdom of God, and He'll take care of you.[2] That was definitely a teaching that people accepted. There were a lot of expectations like that that I was just picking up as I went along."

I asked whether that included expectations for what were appropriate Christian thinking and behavior. "Oh, definitely," he replied. And the obvious one that comes to mind is quiet times. I can remember one friend of mine talking about a group that she had been a part of. If you wanted to be a big disciple, you had to have a certain number of unbroken days when you had your quiet time. That was a requirement for being a disciple. And that just flipped me out. I couldn't believe it.

"The groups that I was involved in were not like that. However, there was a certain expectation that people were having regular quiet times and stuff. They were involved in certain activities. I remember later, when I was a senior in college, a friend of mine wasn't involved in Sunday evening service, and I kind of looked askance at him. I thought, 'You're really slipping up because you're not involved.' Now I look back on that and feel ashamed of myself for evaluating his spirituality based on whether he was attending Sunday evenings."

These patterns for Tom's spiritual life that were established during high school continued into college. Again, the two major issues for him were how involved God was in His life and relationships with girlfriends. Both questions confronted him as soon as he arrived on campus.

"I immediately met a girl on my floor of the dormitory. After about three days, we started going together. She wasn't a Christian, although she became a Christian subsequently. That relationship set off this huge conflict in me between what I believed to be true about not being unequally yoked and not marrying a nonbeliever,[3] not dating non-Christians, and the fact that she was offering me what I'd been searching for for years and years, and that was for somebody to love me.

"We ended up breaking up after three weeks. But we got back together again, and I basically just gave up at that point. I physically told God, 'I'm walking away. I know I'm walking away, but I'm going for this that I can see rather than for You that I can't.'"

I thought Tom's prayer of "rebellion" against God was interesting after all his agonizing over how his faith might apply to dating relationships. "It felt to me like making a choice," he explained, "in relationship to the here and now versus God."

Yet, ironically, religion turned out to be an important part of his relationship with his girlfriend. "We continued to go to [the campus church] that was basically geared towards college kids. It was very low-key, with guitars and songs and a form of [Catholic] Mass. Everything was real informal, and everybody wore blue jeans. We would go to that, which she was comfortable with, and I was comfortable with it.

"During that next year, one of the significant events happened, and that was that my girlfriend gave me a book by Ayn Rand called *Atlas Shrugged*. I read it at the time and found it really compelling, not knowing what it was. It was a book that I really liked, and I've read it three or four times since then.

"But during the course of that next year, I had become so emotionally dependent on her that my whole feeling of worth was tied up in my relationship to her. Any time she was unhappy, I felt responsible for it and needed to fix it somehow. I didn't know how to do that. She realized that this wasn't very healthy, so she broke up, which totally smashed me.

"I remember going through a period of time where I was feeling kind of OK, and then I'd go over and spend time with her, and she'd say something that was innocuous. One time, she was talking about the kind of guy that she wanted to marry someday, and I could tell that it wasn't me. So I'd crash and leave and go build myself up again, and then go back and see her some more.

"One night, she started listing things that she thought were wrong with me. Later she said her purpose was for me to stand up and say, 'No, that's not true. That's not accurate.' But I took them all. And I left that evening consciously feeling like I basically had no ego left in me. There was no low that I could go to that would possibly make me feel as bad as I felt at that point.

"It was that night that I felt I came to a point of realizing not only did God exist, but that I needed Him to forgive me. There were parts of me that I couldn't change on my own. There were areas of me that would hurt other people or do things that I didn't want to do. Later, I came to question whether I had really been a Christian in high school, because I only had an emotional experience of God, and I'm not sure whether I really had a knowledge that I needed His saving grace."

So it would appear that the "hound of heaven," as the pursuing God has been called, finally brought His quarry to bay at the foot of the cross. Yet I suppose a case could be made that this second "conversion" experience was still driven more by emotion than anything else. Moreover, some might see this episode as a perfect example of how people today are responding to a "gospel" that allows and even encourages them to become preoccupied and even obsessed with themselves: What has God done for *me*? Where is He in *my* life? Will He heal *my* hurts, bless *my* life, meet *my* needs?

This kind of *self*-oriented gospel is a legitimate concern and challenge for the church. Narcissism is the spirit of the age, and people have become "lovers of themselves"[4] Christians do well to resist that mind-set. Yet as long as there are young people and hormones, it's hard to see how Christianity can avoid a "personalized" gospel.

Youth, after all, is a period of narcissism (and idealism, too—a fact well worth taking into account while reading the stories in this book). We might wish that it were otherwise. But it seems that young people are destined to have their energies wrapped like a yo-yo string around whatever is going on in their inner life, which, as Tom's story illustrates, is so often dependent on one's "sweetheart *du jour.*"

So the question is not whether the church should promote a gospel of self-obsession, but what does the gospel have to say to people who are at a very self-absorbed stage in life? For Tom, rejection by a girlfriend led to self-examination that brought him back to God. The experience proved to be something of a turning point in his life.

"I got involved with a different group of Christians," he continued, "and I got involved in a different church and started back on track in the sense of where I was before. My main question at that time was basically, what difference does [Christianity] make?

"We had broken up over the winter of my sophomore year. By the time I was a senior in college, I was part of the core group in the youth group at church, and I was involved in Bible studies and helping the youth pastor. I spent a lot of time talking and praying. Sometimes I would read the Bible."

All the old questions persisted. "I was involved in other relationships and the whole question of marriage was still there. Who would I marry, and how would I know, and how would I go about establishing a relationship with somebody who was serious about Christ? A lot of questions like that."

Meanwhile, graduation was quickly approaching and Tom's thoughts turned to career decisions. In high school he had felt that he wanted to work with computers, so in college he became what he described as "quite a serious student" in that field. As with the issue of marriage, he thought about how his faith ought to affect his career choice. In the process, he began to wonder whether computers was the best career to pursue.

"I started to realize that the Bible was talking about all these things like the beast and the mark on the forehead, and it seemed obvious to me that things were coming to a point like that was describing. Computers were really coming into the forefront, and I realized that computers were going to be controlling everything. So I went through a real quandary as to whether I should stay involved in computers. Would I be contributing to the end of the world? Finally, I came to the conclusion that I did want to work on the inside and make my contribution there. But that was a major aspect of my life that I was trying to figure out."

Tom's story then fast-forwarded through a series of entry-level positions, promotions, job changes, and relocations, including this statement: "My company moved me to a city in the Rockies. I met a bunch of people there and got involved in Bible studies and stuff. I ended up meeting my wife there at a church. Got married, and very shortly thereafter, we moved to [where we live now]." I could not help but notice the passing reference to marriage. Given all of his anxiety about that issue over the years, he seemed almost casual in mentioning it. Perhaps he had resolved his previous concerns. Perhaps he had simply matured.

Whatever the case, the stability of a job, marriage, and a home only managed to precipitate a new crisis. "We had a house, I got a promotion, and we were basically clipping along," he recalled. "And I hit a point at which I had basically achieved all the goals that I had set for myself. And it was really a stupid thing to do, to run out of goals. I didn't know what to do with myself! I mean, I had been driven for years to get a good job and have a house and settle down and have a family. These were all the goals that I had. And I hit them.

"So then I decided that I didn't want the promotion that I had. I transferred to another job. Well, actually I went through a period where I was thinking about starting my own company. But I decided that the only reason I wanted to start my own company was to be rich, and I decided that wasn't a sufficient reason. So I went to work for somebody who was doing something similar to what I was interested in. The company turned out to make an extraordinary amount of money. And then I spent two years being miserable because [of the nature of the work]. I had to give my boss a monthly report, and a month later he'd tell me whether he liked it or not. I just couldn't take it. I wasn't enjoying what I was doing."

It sounded like a mid-life crisis, only about fifteen years too early. "That's what it felt like at the time," Tom agreed. "My wife and I were trying to have a baby, [but we weren't succeeding]. We went through lots of tests. And I was going through all this stuff at work, trying to figure out what I was going to do with my life.

"At some point, I asked the question, what would I do if I were independently wealthy? That seemed like a good test. I decided that maybe what I would do was research, and if I didn't have to worry about money, I would go back to school. So we ended up selling the house, quitting the job, and [going to graduate school]."

In retrospect, this period was a time in which Tom's church could have made a major difference. I don't know the details of his involvement. But it may be that no one realized what a strategic opportunity this was to affect Tom's spirituality. He was making a far more significant career decision than he had made at the end of college. Yet, based on what he told me, he had little to guide him in the process.

In fact, it sounded like his ability to integrate his faith with his decision making had developed very little in the years since graduation.

"At that point, we felt like all the indications we had were that we were supposed to go in this direction, so we decided to keep going. There were definitely some dry spells during those years, as far as being involved in Bible studies and quiet times.

"I wasn't seeing [God involved that much in my life]. Maybe it was the kinds of decisions I was making about what I wanted to do with my life and mundane things like what kind of research I wanted to do. I felt somewhat of a conflict, because my expectations were [based on the fact] that I had been a Christian for several years. I had been living my life for God. The expectation was that He had some special plan for me. When I was a brand new Christian, I had a very strong sense that I was somehow special to God and that He had big plans for me.

"Anyway, there were definitely some dry periods in there, and I was just trying to figure out, is God relevant, is He involved with my life? There were times when I consciously asked God for direction and really feel like there were some prayers answered and things happened. For example, we sold our house within a week, right at the beginning of this huge bust in the housing market, and a lot of people around us weren't selling at all. So we ended up in [my master's program] feeling like we were there because that's where God put us. But we were still trying to figure out what to do with our lives."

One thing that helped focus matters was the birth of the couple's first child. "I really had to grow up a lot faster than I expected," Tom commented. "Children will do that to you. I'd lived my whole life up until then based on convenience, not on sacrifice."

Tom quickly wrapped up his master's program and took a new job. He and his family also began looking around for a church home. They settled on a congregation that by no means offered everything they were seeking in a church, but they met some other couples there whom they liked, so they decided to stay.

Before long, Tom and his wife joined a mid-week "house church," a small group of church members that met in a home in their area. Meanwhile, Tom tolerated the things he didn't like in the larger congregation.

As far as his own spiritual life was concerned, "I started moving down this slope of reading the Bible with a different perspective. Rather than reading it as just instructions for how to live life morally, I was reading it from the perspective of how is God involved in my life, and what does He expect, and what does He want? Before that, by the way, I'd been going through periods of dryness, not really seeing the relevance of what I was doing in terms of quiet times and things like that. Just kind of sticking with it. Just trying to believe that [it would eventually make a difference]."

I was familiar with what he was describing. I had met others who carried out spiritual disciplines such as quiet times with the same desperate, "gut it out" approach. What they wanted was to experience God. Yet a genuine encounter proved elusive. They felt "dry," to use Tom's expression. Yet they felt that if they just kept at it, if they just maintained the discipline, sooner or later they might get over the hump and then somehow the life would kick in.

For Tom, it never did. "One of the things I learned about myself was that if I'm not interacting with another person or with a computer—which is one of the reasons why I work where I work—I'm not really thinking. It's hard for me to sit down and work through things without being able to talk through things. I need the interaction."

That was a profoundly important insight. It suggested that no matter how much time Tom spent on his own trying to have a "quiet time," it would benefit him very little. He *could not* move forward on his own. He required another human being beside him. Yet apparently he prayed and studied in isolation, perhaps hoping that somehow God would reveal Himself in a tangible, virtually beatific way. But it never happened.

"I never experienced that in prayer or Bible study," he continued. "I never felt like there was someone else there interacting with me, giving me this dynamic that I needed in order to process things. And I came to the conclusion that I was going to find out how to make this a real relationship, because it was just not working. I was staying where I was, essentially going nowhere.

"So I spent a period of time trying to figure out what does it mean to have a relationship with God, and what does He promise in that relationship? I was re-reading the Gospels, looking at the promises of His presence and the dynamics of His being here. At the same time, I was reading a variety of things about God and His relationship with people, and what that means. But during this time, what I believed was continually divergent from what I experienced. I was believing more and more that God was available and wanted a relationship. But that wasn't the case for me."

This was a sobering statement. When I put Tom's description of "dryness" together with his ambivalent feelings about his church, I could only conclude that he was slipping into the condition I described in chapter 12 as a spiritual version of chronic fatigue syndrome. He was committed to a local fellowship, his life was stable, and to all outward appearances he was the ideal layperson. But deep inside him lingered a low-grade virus of discontent. In a vague, undefined way, he was growing increasingly disillusioned with the faith. The only thing lacking was a crisis.

"Things get a little bit jumbled now," he went on, "but something that struck a chord was a report I heard on the radio. It was talking about some research that had been done about the psychology of how people interpret things. It was basically that people see what they want to see. If you have *n* events, they'll pick out the half of them that fit their theory, and they'll ignore everything else. It really struck me that I did that, that all the good things that happened, I attributed to God, and all the negative things that didn't fit my theory as to what God was doing in my life, I kind of tossed out.

"And I realized that I didn't have any theory at all that fit all the things that were going on in my life as far as, was God involved, and if He was, why was it always so hard to see how? Then one of the things that happened was that my wife and I found out that our son was deaf. He was ten months old at the time, and that was a severe blow. I mean, this kid was ten months! We went ten months thinking we had a perfect child and found out that we didn't.

"We didn't know what to do. My initial thought was, 'Well, medicine fixes everything these days. There must be some operation.' And I found out there really wasn't.[5] We went through a period of grief. Not much. I think I take most things rather stoically. In fact, I came to a conclusion during this time that I was too stoic. But we also went through some real questions about whether God was going to heal him. Does God heal? There were a lot of people around me who believed that He did.

"We prayed for healing. You know, we basically didn't know what to do. [The whole experience] turned out to be a real crisis point for me, because I really questioned, do I go with faith or do I go with science? Which way do I go? And I thought, twenty years from now, who is going to hand me more progress in dealing with my son: Christians and faith, or science and medicine? And it was clear to me that science and medicine were going to be much farther ahead. And that caused me to pause.

"Another question was, if you took a random sample of Christians and non-Christians in terms of their health, their well-being, their security, and their safety, would there be any difference? And the conclusion I came to was, probably not. And whenever I asked Christians that, they also said probably not. But all the Christians I know have constantly prayed for health, safety, security, safety for their families, not getting into car wrecks—the whole bit. But if there's no difference at all, why pray?

"From that point, I went through a period of trying to figure out what do I really believe, and what is really believable. And in the end I decided that I didn't have enough evidence anymore to believe that God existed."

It's hard to say exactly what sort of evidence might have proved convincing. But it seemed clear that Tom was not looking for the usual answers of apologetics—the argument from design, the moral argument, the resurrection, the historicity of Jesus. No, Tom's crisis was existential more than intellectual. He lacked any *experience* of God. The question was not so much is there a God, but *where is He—today, right here, right now, in my life?*

Of course, some readers will wonder whether Tom was ever a true believer in the first place. Otherwise, how could he be a member of God's family and not experience God's presence? For that matter, how could he be a true child of God and end up leaving the faith?

When I asked him about this question of his salvation, he told me, "It wasn't too many years ago that I would have assumed that that would have had to have been the case, because how could anybody go from the point of knowing forgiveness to denying it? Being basically from a Baptist background, my perspective on the whole question of whether somebody can lose their salvation was that they must not have ever known what that salvation was, or else how could they give it up? So I understand the concern.

"On the other hand, all I can say is that I was certainly convinced of my need for salvation and of my utter helplessness to do anything in my own strength or power or ability to acquire it. Somebody once said that they wanted to be at a place where when they stood before God and He said, 'Why should I let you into heaven?' that they would say, 'Because Christ died for me.' And if He said, 'That's not good enough; what else do you have?' then they would turn and walk away, because they didn't have anything else.

"And that was certainly my perspective. That's all that stood between me and God, and I thought, if that wasn't enough—and I believed that it was—then I didn't know what else to do. So I certainly believed that I was a Christian, and there wasn't anything else that I

needed to do in order to become one, other than to accept my utter
dependence on God's forgiveness."

This was a strong statement. But I wondered how Tom's church,
and especially his pastor, viewed the situation. That person would be in
as good a position as any to assess Tom's spiritual condition. So I asked
Tom whether he had discussed his doubts with leaders at his church.

"Yeah, one of the things I feel very good about is the fact that
people have been very accepting and encouraging. I've tried to make an
effort to let people know the process that I've been going through. My
pastor has said that he thinks what I'm going through is necessary,
even though he doesn't know where it's going to come out. And I've
been very fortunate. There have definitely been people who have kept
in touch, and people who have called me up."

One reason, of course, is that Tom's wife has continued in the fellowship. I asked him about the impact of his doubts on her and their
marriage. "It's been a real readjustment for us," he admitted. "To go
from what had always been an assumed part of our life that was a major
part of what we shared together, and having a common involvement and
commitment to the faith, to not having that . . . " His voice trailed off.

Had his disillusionment with Christianity caused her to doubt as
well? "No, I'd say that she's held onto her faith. It's been threatening,
because she kind of leaned on me. So when I basically fell apart, she
had to stand on her own. I guess it's been good in that sense."

I thought this response of Tom's wife was rather important. She
had gone through many of the same things he had, yet her faith apparently remained alive and growing, while his languished. Likewise, other
Christians have had to contend with far more trying circumstances than
Tom has, yet their spiritual lives have not only survived, but thrived. I
asked him whether he didn't find that a bit unsettling.

"To me, it's irrelevant," he replied. "Other people's experiences
are either true or they're not. If I can't find a way to [make my relationship with God work], then the fact that you do doesn't help me much.

"One thing that comes to mind is, I remember reading a story that
talked about God's love as a father's love. And it really struck me that
the person was basically talking about a secondhand thing. Rather than
describing how God actually does love us, and how we can experience
that love, he was talking about how to interpret how God would love us
if He was actually involved. I mean, it wasn't his intention at all to write
it that way. But it was all secondhand: we should look at God's love

being *like* a father's love, rather than this *is* how we experience God's love.

"I spent years looking at the events of my life [in the way this article talked about]—what I was thinking and feeling, what was going on around me, what other people were trying to say God was doing—that if you looked at things *as if* God loved you, *then* you could experience God's love. I don't know. Somehow that didn't seem quite right. It was this secondhand thing.

"I don't really have anything against God. I loved Him greatly. But I see a lot of 'I believe that God exists because I believe that God exists, and I interpret the things that are going on around me because I believe that the God who loves me has a purpose in it.' [People who say that] aren't at the place that I came to, which was, if we take all the information that we have, all the data—and not just the ones that fit my theorems—would we come to the same conclusion?

"And so my wife, who has been greatly grieved by this process that I've gone through—for personal reasons as well as fears for me—she'll basically interpret events according to her worldview, which is a natural thing to do. But I don't feel like she's any closer to really having a personal experience with God than I ever was. There are certainly experiences that people have had that I haven't pushed into yet. But in general, I think the people who have been around me over the last fifteen years have been in that same place of 'walking by faith' and interpreting events according to that faith, yet never really being any closer to an experience of God than I have."

NOTES

1. Translated by Eugene H. Peterson, *The Message: The New Testament in Contemporary English* (Colorado Springs: NavPress, 1993), 416.

2. An allusion to Matthew 6:33. The text actually reads: "But seek first his kingdom and his righteousness, and all these things will be given to you as well."

3. An allusion to 2 Corinthians 6:14.

4. 2 Timothy 3:2.

5. There wasn't at the time. Later, medical researchers developed the technology to do cochlear implants, an operation that made it possible for Tom's son to hear.

18

Seven and a Half Churches a Day

*If people are well served, they come back and tell their
friends, whether it be a Honda, a restaurant, or a church.*
George McCammon[1]

We have been standing, as it were, at the "back door" of the church, microphone in hand, asking people to tell us why they are leaving. We are not unlike reporters conducting an exit poll, trying to anticipate the outcome of an election. But having gathered our data, the time has come for some analysis. What have we heard? How accurate is it? What difference does it make? I want to address these kinds of questions in the final four chapters.

The place to begin is with context. Context plays a major role in how we interpret what we have heard. So it's worth asking, what is the context of the church today, in which these stories have been given?

Of course, it is difficult anymore to say anything intelligent about the church. "The church" is far from a monolithic institution. The number of denominations alone is estimated to be at least 20,800.[2] So it would be more accurate to speak of "the churches" as a reminder that whatever general comments we might wish to make, someone somewhere can find an exception.

Having made that disclaimer, though, we may ask where the statements made in the preceding chapters fit into the larger story of the church, especially the church in the United States. Are they in any way representative of what many people may be experiencing today?

Or have I managed to interview all two dozen disgruntled Christians in America?

The way some people talk, one might think that I have. As I mentioned in the first chapter, a great deal of noise is being made about the numbers of people coming through the "front door" of the church. Two trends that have received especially heavy press have been the return of Baby Boomers to religion and the rise of "megachurches."

To appreciate the Baby Boomer story, we have to go back to the late sixties and early seventies. It's no secret that countless young people were dropping out of organized religion during that turbulent era. In fact, by 1972, church attendance had declined so much that the National Council of Churches gave one of its officials a sabbatical to find out why.

His landmark book opened by asking, "Are the Churches Dying?" and then answered with a rather bleak report: "In the latter years of the 1960s something remarkable happened in the United States: for the first time in the nation's history most of the major church groups stopped growing and began to shrink. . . . At least ten of the largest Christian denominations in the country . . . in 1967, had fewer members the next year and fewer yet the year after. Most of these denominations had been growing uninterruptedly since colonial times. . . . [N]ow they have begun to diminish, reversing a trend of two centuries."[3]

Declining membership. Declining contributions. Declining influence. No wonder the book's second chapter went on to ask, "Is Religion Obsolete?" For countless Baby Boomers, the answer seemed to be *yes* as far as conventional Christianity was concerned.

Moreover, "new gods were being born in the most unexpected of places—the secular college campuses. At colleges and universities across the country, many new sects and cults emerged, with their members wearing strange garb, practicing ancient rituals, and speaking in esoteric tongues. . . . And the converts were disaffected middle-class youth who were looking for alternatives to the more established faiths."[4]

To be sure, only a minority of young people joined cults. Nevertheless, if you're a Baby Boomer and you more or less turned away from the faith in your teens or twenties, you had a lot of company. Millions of young people drifted away from church, seemingly disillusioned with American Christianity.

To be fair, not all Boomers left the faith, nor did all churches decline—as was clear from the title of the book just mentioned: *Why Con-*

servative Churches Are Growing. Dean Kelley, its author, documented the fact that "while most of the mainline Protestant denominations are trying to survive . . . other denominations are overflowing with vitality."[5]

In every case, these "other denominations"—some as large as the multi-million-member Roman Catholic Church or Southern Baptist Convention, and others so tiny as to be "hardly even visible to the other denominations"—were "conservative" churches. They offered authoritative, absolute answers to life's ultimate questions, and they demanded high commitment from their members. The more liberal churches tolerated theological experiments such as the "God is dead" movement, and they lost members by the millions. Meanwhile, the conservative groups skyrocketed in attendance, giving, and missionary activity.

Still, while their additions were impressive (and troubling to some in the liberal camp), conservative denominations did little to offset the widespread loss of the Baby Boomers. Many wrote that generation off as hopelessly mired in moral relativism ("do your own thing") and, in the eighties, Yuppie-led materialism.

But times changed. The Boomers grew up. They started getting married and having babies. Suddenly the "excesses of the eighties" went out of favor. It was no longer "cool" to do drugs, sleep around, or overwork. With middle-age rapidly approaching and their parents putting their own affairs in order, Boomers started taking a second look at religion.

Enter the megachurch. The megachurch is more than just a large church. There have been large churches throughout American history. What distinguishes today's megachurch is not size but *strategy*. Indeed, size is merely a function of strategy. In marked contrast to the traditional way of "doing church," the megachurch operates with a marketing mentality: who is our "customer" and how can we meet his or her needs?[6]

To ask that question and act on its answers at a time when a significantly large segment of the population is reexamining spiritual issues is one way to end up with a megachurch. That's why the idea that "worship in the 1990s must be made relevant to the culture of the Baby Boomer generation" is gaining rapid acceptance among denominational executives as they "grope for ways to stem the decline of mainline church membership."[7]

A dramatic example of how that translates into action was a recent plan by the Evangelical Lutheran Church in America to start a megachurch in Yorba Linda, California, designed to serve 3,000 to 5,000 members, using nontraditional approaches intended to appeal to Baby Boomers. To get the project started, leaders planned to hold high-visibility events fueled by a campaign of advertising, telemarketing, and direct mail. As for financing, Lutheran Brotherhood, an insurance company with strong links to the denomination, agreed to put up $200,000 toward the start-up; an additional $110,000 was coming from other Lutheran congregations in the Orange County area and $50,000 from the denomination's Division for Outreach.[8]

Is this sort of church a pipe dream? Not according to *Fortune* magazine: "Large interdenominational churches are the fastest-growing type in the U. S. In 1984, only 100 American churches averaged more than 2,000 worshipers on Sunday; that number has doubled, and some 10,000 churches now have an average attendance of 1,000 or more."[9]

Some pastors of these rapidly expanding congregations, where as many as 10,000 or 15,000 attend, are studying what the upper limits to growth are. Some experts predict that by the end of this decade, churches of 100,000 and even 300,000 will not be uncommon.[10]

Who in the sixties would have thought it could come to this? Common wisdom held that Baby Boomers were leaving the churches for good. They might pursue religion on their own, but never would they return to the institutional church. Yet ironically, the fastest growing churches today seem to be those that accommodate themselves to the needs, interests, and tastes of Baby Boomers.

So what does this scenario say about my interviewees? Perhaps they have chosen to leave too soon. Perhaps, as some to whom I have mentioned this project have suggested, they just haven't been exposed to the "right" church, one filled with "their" kind of people and sensitive to "their" kinds of needs.

I admit that as a possibility but remain skeptical about its accuracy. In the first place, not all my interviewees were Baby Boomers, nor are all Baby Boomers alike. Furthermore, recall that some to whom I spoke, such as Julia and Vince, attended megachurches for a while and were singularly unimpressed. Not to take anything away from the megachurches, but no one should see them as the ultimate answer. They appeal to some; they cannot appeal to everyone. Nor do they intend to.

However, there are far more significant reasons why we must not be overly optimistic about current trends among Baby Boomers and the large churches that go after them. For the fact is (speaking of context), church membership and attendance continue to decline and, more important, Christianity continues to have less and less influence on people's lives.

On any given Sunday you'll find four out of ten adults in church. But only half of those are likely to be returnees from the previous Sunday.[11] And don't expect significant numbers of the faithful to be Baby Boomers. According to one recent study, "the 'lost generation' of Baby Boomers who left mainline Protestantism in the 1970s and '80s is not coming back, and their churches will exert even less of a hold on their children."[12]

Sociologist Wade Clark Roof has found that 58 percent of Baby Boomers dropped out of church or synagogue for at least two years during their adolescence or young adulthood. Sixty percent of mainline Protestants dropped out, 57 percent of Catholics, and—a figure that many readers of this book may find surprising—54 percent of conservative Protestants. Only about one-third of those who left have resumed religious activities.[13]

However, activity and attendance do not translate into membership. Boomers especially demonstrate a "lack of felt commitment to any single congregation" and prefer to attend several different churches on an "as-needed" basis rather than establish a more traditional "church home."[14] As George Gallup puts it, "believing" is not the same as "belonging."[15]

Gallup should know. In his landmark study *The Unchurched American*, he found that 41 percent of the United States population has no church connection. Yet 45 percent of those "unchurched" pray every day, 64 percent claim to believe that Jesus is God or the Son of God, 68 percent believe in Christ's resurrection, and 77 percent had some religious training during childhood. At the same time, six out of ten agreed that "most churches and synagogues have lost the real spiritual part of religion," and about half agreed that "most churches and synagogues today are not effective in helping people find meaning in life."[16]

In other words, the unchurched are not necessarily unbelievers. As Canadian sociologist Reginald Bibby puts it, "Rather than readily losing people, the major religious groups in reality have extreme difficulty losing them. Over generations, religion has been fused with one's family, biography, and culture. The bond is not readily dissolved."[17] His research of Christians during more than twenty-five years offers strong evidence that most people have not necessarily given up on the faith; however, they do appear to be giving up on the institutional church.

Well, if the unchurched may be far more "spiritual" than they are usually given credit for, could the reverse also be true—that the "churched" are actually less "spiritual" than they are often assumed to be? Gallup suggests precisely that when he offers compelling evidence that "church attendance, it appears, makes little difference in people's ethical views and behaviors. . . . These findings will come as a shock to religious leaders and others, and underscore the need for religious educators and the clergy to channel religious interest in America not simply into religious involvement, but deep spiritual commitment."[18]

Church attendance makes little difference, Gallup says. Perhaps that explains why at least half of all adults now believe that religion is losing its influence on day-to-day life.[19] It certainly fits with what Chuck Colson recently told *Dallas Morning News* religion editor Daniel Cattau just prior to the Clinton-Bush election: "[Evangelicals] have won the political battles but lost the cultural war. Ultimately we're going to lose the political battle."[20] (In the eyes of many, that prediction was fulfilled ten days later when Bill Clinton defeated George Bush.)

Colson went on to paint a rather bleak picture of the conservative Christianity of which he has been a part since his conversion in the mid-seventies. He noted that 1976 was declared "the year of the Evangelical" (by *Time* magazine), when evangelicals helped send Jimmy Carter to the White House. Four years later, they rallied around Ronald Reagan. Yet for the last decade and a half, the public's opinion of "born-again" Christians has plummeted. The future, he predicted, will see "the coming eclipse of Evangelicals," and our culture will continue to slip into a "post-Christian age."[21]

Colson had offered a prelude to these somber remarks in a 1990 *Christianity Today* column entitled "From a Moral Majority to a Persecuted Minority." After gathering with a hundred evangelical leaders and political activists, he concluded, "This Washington meeting was symptomatic of a growing sense of despair and defeatism in Evangelical ranks that I've witnessed around the country."

One leader, whom Colson identified as a "prominent Evangelical" and a "veteran of the battles of the Eighties," confided to him that he was through. "Why bother?" the man lamented.[22] What a telling remark! Apparently it is not just the "little people" walking out the back door of the church who are disillusioned. Even some of those who stand at the front door are equally inclined to throw in the towel.

But as disturbing as these developments might be, the most troubling statistic by far for conservative Christianity relates to evangelism:

"Since 1980, there has been *no growth* in the proportion of the adult population that classify themselves as 'born again' Christians." The number remains fixed at 32 percent.[23]

This is a truly distressing piece of news if you're a conservative, "born again" Christian. It is particularly exasperating in light of the *billions* of dollars raised to accomplish evangelistic purposes in this country, let alone for foreign missions. And it forces us to ask how Kelley could write *Why Conservative Churches Are Growing*. The answer is that those churches were "growing" all right—but not through conversion growth. Most of it was babies and transfers.

At the very time that Kelley was writing, a five-year study was underway, analyzing the growth of twenty randomly selected evangelical churches in the "Canadian Bible belt." The researchers found that 72 percent of the new arrivals were already evangelical Christians when they walked in the door. Another 18 percent were children of evangelicals. Less than 10 percent had come from outside the evangelical community, and even those were primarily recruited from other churches or became members through intermarriage.[24]

So it turns out that "while many churches across [North America] receive attention for their explosive growth, relatively few of those churches are attracting adults who are [bona fide] newcomers to the faith."[25]

There are, of course, numerous responses to numbers like these. One of the most popular is that while it may be true that Christianity isn't making much headway in the United States, it is racking up impressive gains overseas—in South America, for example, or Indonesia and other parts of East Asia. Likewise, I've heard more than one mission leader state publicly that so many people are coming into the faith in Africa that that continent may become "Christian" by the end of the century.

Conversion growth, especially in the Southern Hemisphere, cannot be denied and certainly ought to be celebrated. But I'm afraid it may be a case on a global scale of the very thing this book has been suggesting: that while many people are coming through the front door of the church, to great fanfare, many others are quietly walking out the back.

This would seem to be the conclusion of a massive, twelve-year research project overseen by British demographer David Barrett. Employing a small army of researchers who gathered data from churches and denominations in every corner of the world, Barrett put together a composite picture of the worldwide church for Oxford University Press.

Here's what that picture reveals: "Christianity has experienced massive losses in the Western and Communist worlds over the last 60 years. . . . In Europe and North America, nett [sic] defections from Christianity—converts to other religions or to irreligion—are now running at 1,820,500 former Christians a year. This loss is much higher if we consider only church members: 2,224,800 a year (6,000 a day). It is even higher if we are speaking of only church attenders: every year, some 2,765,100 church attenders in Europe and North America cease to be practising Christians within the 12-month period, an average loss of 7,600 every day.

"At the global level, these losses from Christianity in the Western and Communist worlds slightly outweigh the gains in the Third World. . . . Practising Christians have fallen from 29.0 percent of the world's population in 1900 to 23.3 percent today."[26]

Reading these numbers, I was reminded of another comment that Chuck Colson made to the *Dallas Morning News*. He was referring to evangelicals, but the remark applies to the church in general: "If this were a business, you'd be contemplating Chapter 11 [bankruptcy]."[27] That's because it's hard to sustain a business when you're losing more customers than you're gaining.

The church is losing 7,600 customers *a day* in Europe and North America, according to Barrett. That means that every week, more than 53,000 people leave church and never come back. To put that in perspective, consider that the United States lost about 57,500 people in the Vietnam War. In a different sense—though strangely appropriate—the church "loses" almost that many *every week.*

Or look at it another way: a "large" church is said to be one that has 1,000 people attending each Sunday. We would have to plant at least seven and a half large churches *every day of the year* to offset the number of people walking away from the churches we already have.

I'm not a professional demographer, so I can't pass judgment on the accuracy of Barrett's research.[28] But even if he is off by *half*, the implications remain the same: in general, the church as we know it today doesn't seem to be doing a very good job of holding onto people. So when my interviewees talk about leaving, they apparently have plenty of company.

In the end, however, what matters when it comes to the church is neither membership nor attendance but *spirituality*—one's relationship with God and the implications of that relationship for day-to-day life. The real question, and one that is always hard to answer, is whether our churches and parachurch structures are helping people meet God. But should that be so hard to answer? The fact that it is may explain why people have grown skeptical about the usefulness and need to be part of a church.

It seems that more and more people today feel about their religious institutions the way they feel about the institutions of government. Just as church membership and attendance are languishing, so voter participation is low and cynicism runs high. The *Wall Street Journal* reports that during the past two decades, the number of people who have expressed confidence in the federal government's ability to do its job has dropped from 74 percent to only 42 percent.[29]

Yet notice: Americans by and large have not lost faith in the ideals of democracy and freedom. We believe in those as strongly as ever. But there is real doubt as to whether the current system is living up to anywhere near those ideals.

In the same way, both the churched and the unchurched in this country seem to be holding onto some bedrock beliefs, such as the existence of God, the deity of Christ, the authority of Scripture, and the relevance for today of teaching such as the Ten Commandments and the Golden Rule. But there is growing doubt as to whether organized religion is the place to go if one wants to build on those beliefs. People crave spirituality, but for many, the search for it seems to lead them outside the programs and away from the structures.

Is there hope, then, for the church? Of course there's hope—the very sure hope of Jesus' promise that He would build His church and nothing, not even hell itself, would overcome it.[30] However, nothing in that promise obligates Christ to maintain "our" church. He has committed Himself only to building *a* church, *His* church.

So the issue is not how to get people back into churches, but how to make our churches into His church. Ironically, one of our best sources for how to do that are the very people who have left. Not that what they have to say is gospel. Far from it. But if we listen carefully, I believe we may hear the Lord's voice speaking to the churches. It would not be the first time that God has spoken to His people from outside the system.

NOTES

1. As quoted by Doug Cumming, "God Is *Not* Dead," *Southpoint*, December 1989, 39. The Rev. McCammon is the rector of the Church of the Resurrection in Longwood, a suburb of Orlando, Florida.

2. David B. Barrett, ed., *World Christian Encyclopedia: A Comparative Study of Churches and Religions in the Modern World, A.D. 1900–2000* (Nairobi, Kenya: Oxford Univ., 1982), v.

3. Dean M. Kelley, *Why Conservative Churches Are Growing* (New York: Harper and Row, 1972), 1.

4. Wade Clark Roof and William McKinney, *American Mainline Religion: Its Changing Shape and Future* (New Brunswick, N.J.: Rutgers Univ., 1987), 12. Roof and McKinney's analysis shows that it was widespread disillusionment among the young that created such massive losses for the churches. "There was no massive exodus of old members from these institutions. Rather, after the midsixties fewer young persons were joining the mainline churches, and fewer still chose to become active participants and faithful supporters. Youth growing up in church families were not remaining within the fold as they once did. There were simply too few recruits to keep the membership rolls of the old established churches constant, much less growing" (22).

5. Kelley, 21.

6. See James Mellado, "WillowCreek Community Church," Harvard Business School Case Study No. 9–691–102, 1991, 1. WillowCreek has become the quintessential model of the megachurch.

7. Gustav Spohn, "'Church Growth' Movement Gains Favor," *Dallas Morning News* (April 18, 1992): 30A.

8. Ibid.

9. Thomas A. Stewart, "Turning Around the Lord's Business," *Fortune* (September 25, 1989): 128.

10. Russell Chandler, *Racing Toward 2001: The Forces Shaping America's Religious Future* (Grand Rapids: Zondervan, 1992), 163–64. Churches of 100,000 participants are certainly not impossible. Dr. Paul Yonggi Cho pastors a church in Seoul, Korea, of 600,000 people—and it continues to grow.

11. George Barna, *The Frog in the Kettle* (Ventura, Calif.: Regal Books, 1990, 132).

12. David Briggs, "Study: Ex-Protestants Not Returning to the Fold," *Dallas Morning News* (June 5, 1992): 6A. The article reports on a 1989–91 study, financed by the Lilly Foundation, by Dean Hoge, Benton Johnson, and Donald Luidens.

13. Wade Clark Roof, "The Baby Boom's Search for God," *American Demographics* (December 1992): 54.

14. *National and International Religion Report,* September 25, 1989, reporting on research by the Barna Research Group.

15. Interview, Reformed Theological Seminary newsletter, 10–11, n.d.

16. As reported in "The Outsiders," *Eternity Magazine,* n.d.

17. Reginald. W. Bibby, *Fragmented Gods: The Poverty and Potential of Religion in Canada* (Toronto: Irwin Publishing, 1987), 51.

18. George Gallup, "Secularism and Religion: Trends in Contemporary America," *PRRC Emerging Trends* 9, no. 10 (December 1987): 3.

19. "Many More Today Than in 1986 See Religion Losing Impact on U.S. Life," *PRRC Emerging Trends* 10, no. 3 (March 1988): 1.

20. Daniel Cattau, "Evangelical Movement in Trouble, Colson Says," *Dallas Morning News* (October 24, 1992): 33A.

21. Ibid.

22. *Christianity Today* (May 14, 1990): 80.

23. George Barna, *Marketing the Church* (Colorado Springs: NavPress, 1988), 21–22.

24. See Reginald W. Bibby and Merlin B. Brinkerhoff, "The Circulation of the Saints: A Study of People Who Join Conservative Churches," *Journal of the Scientific Study of Religion*, 1973, 12:273–83. Bibby confirmed his findings in a follow-up study in 1978 entitled "Why Conservative Churches *Really* Are Growing: Kelley Revisited," *Journal of the Scientific Study of Religion*, 1978, 17:129–37. A related study with Brinkerhoff in 1983 was "Circulation of the Saints Revisited: A Longitudinal Look at Conservative Church Growth," *Journal of the Scientific Study of Religion*, 1983, 22:253–62. On the applicability of Canadian research to the United States, see *Fragmented Gods*, 214–22.

25. Barna, *The Frog in the Kettle*, 135.

26. Barrett, 7.

27. Cattau, op. cit.

28. I have to admit, Barrett's numbers are so staggering as to sound suspect. According to the *Encyclopedia*, he and his team collected them by visiting every country in the world, through extensive correspondence with religious leaders, and by "part-time investigations of a modest network of specialists in every country. . . . Christians of every persuasion willingly co-operated in collecting accurate data about their own co-religionists" (v).

    He also writes that the researchers arrived at their conclusions using "existing data collected by the churches for their own purposes." He adds that "all statistics resulting have been checked and counter-checked, sources investigated, and documents verified." This included computerizing the data in order to run "a large number of checks . . . for consistency, plausibility, probability, and so on" (xiv).

    Among the many editors and consultants listed for the project were Malcolm McVeigh of the United Methodist Church, Ed Dayton of the Missions Advanced Research and Communications Center (MARC), missiologist Donald McGavran of Fuller Seminary, Donald Tinder of *Christianity Today*, Francois Houtart of the Catholic University of Louvain, and Bryan Wilson of All Saints College, Oxford.

29. Jill Abramson and Gerald F. Seib, "Paths of RFK Aides Reflect the Divisions Among Democrats," *Wall Street Journal* (June 4, 1993): A1.

30. Matthew 16:18.

19

What Have
We Heard?

Keep your eyes open and your mouth shut!
Davy Crockett

During the past few years, I have been privileged to work with Pete Hammond of Marketplace Networks and a team of highly dedicated people to produce something called the *Word in Life Study Bible*. As part of my responsibilities, I was asked to observe several focus groups that Thomas Nelson, the publisher, brought together to comment on the material. Those focus groups turned out to be one of the most educational experiences of my life.

A focus group is a carefully selected panel of people who are asked to sample a product and then meet with a researcher to offer honest, critical feedback. The idea is to get unbiased reaction from potential customers before committing money to manufacturing, marketing, and distribution.

In the case of the *Word in Life* project, the comments of the focus groups were eye-opening indeed. The team of which I was managing editor had spent thousands of man-hours producing a prototype. Now we were sitting behind a one-way mirror, listening to people react to our work in the most dispassionate terms, caring not a whit for our feelings or welfare. It was a humbling experience, I can assure you.

But . . . it was *honest*, at points brutally so. And therein lies the value of a focus group: it gives one the unvarnished truth. Flattery you can buy elsewhere; if you really want to know what customers think and feel about your product or service, you have to figure out ways for them to tell you, with no strings attached. The focus group is one of those ways.

I wish that every pastor, Sunday school teacher, seminary professor, parachurch worker, missionary, or other person associated with the church and its work could have the experience of hearing a focus group related to his or her assignment. Who can say what changes in Christianity might be made as a result? I feel certain they would be for the better.

In the preceding chapters, we have something approaching a focus group. Rather than pull together a panel in a conference room, I have gone out and polled a number of the church's former "customers." This book serves as a one-way mirror and microphone through which anyone can hear these people's honest feedback.[1]

In this chapter I want to summarize what I hear them saying and what we need to hear. But let's start by pointing out what they are *not* saying:

They are not saying that they want to leave the faith. With the exception of one or two people, I heard again and again that they very much want to remain Christians and nurture their spiritual lives. They may have met with disappointments and setbacks in their spiritual pilgrimage, especially in relation to the institutions set up supposedly to help them along the way. But none expressed avid interest in leaving Christianity for a different religion or worldview.

They are not saying that they want to leave the church. I did not talk with one person who had been *trying* to leave the church; on the contrary, all of them had been trying to stay. They *wanted* things to work out. Indeed, much of their frustration was that things had not.

This surprising attitude recalled Bill Moyers' observation about the stubbornness of people's search for meaning and longing for spirituality. My interviewees did not seem to be fundamentally antichurch or antiparachurch; they still believed in the value of Christian community, at least in the ideal. Nor did any of them rule out the possibility of ever coming back.

They are not saying that the church is full of hypocrites. Popular opinion often holds this up as one of the main reasons why people reject Christianity or leave the church. My conversations did not bear this out.

To be sure, I heard plenty of tales of churchgoers acting in direct contradiction to Christian teaching. But my interviewees seemed to put these wrongdoings in perspective. They accepted that people are sinful. They also seemed to imply that hypocrisy is in one sense confined to a minority of so-called Christians, and in another sense is so widespread that no one, either inside or outside the church, is in a position to judge.

They are not saying that all clergy are dishonest. Another popular notion is that the church today is led by a corrupted clergy. Media reports of scandals involving religious figures have helped to fuel this perception. Perhaps that's why only 54 percent of Americans now view the honesty and ethics of clergy as "high" or "very high," according to the Princeton Religious Research Center. That's an all-time low, down from 67 percent in 1987. [2]

Again, however, my interviewees did not characterize ministry leaders as fundamentally crooked. I did hear several cases of scandal, one of which was rather severe. But even these were seen as exceptions, rather than the rule.

They have said very little about the social implications of the gospel. For the most part, there was a deafening silence when it came to making a connection between spirituality and matters of social concern— the poor, justice, human rights, the environment, issues of public policy, and so on. I found that most disturbing. But it's hard to know how to evaluate the omission. It may be that my selection process—which hardly yielded a representative sample of Christians—failed to include enough "socially minded" believers. It could also be that I failed to ask the right questions.

I wonder, though, if the silence does not also reflect a view of spirituality that has prevailed in the United States during this century, especially among conservative Christians—that is, a privatized religion that emphasizes piety, the devotional life, and the personal benefits of the gospel. Not to take anything away from these, but what about the public side of the faith? There were a handful of socially-minded comments made; for example, Ralph criticized his church's use of money in light of basic needs that he saw going unmet. But overall, the public side of the gospel was a non-issue. That's troubling.

Those are some of the things that my interviewees were not saying. What, then, were they saying? What do we need to hear?

Perhaps the most important thing to hear is this: *There is no one, overriding reason why people are leaving the church today.* As I've discussed this project with people, the most commonly asked question has been, what's the common thread? Why are people leaving the church? The answer is, there is no one reason; there are many reasons—perhaps as many reasons as there are people leaving the church. If I had interviewed two dozen different people, I feel certain I would have heard two dozen different stories.

Of course, that's not particularly comforting. There are sixteen chapters of interviews here, each one very different. That means there are at least that many ways to become dissatisfied enough to leave a church or ministry organization.

However, some common themes do recur throughout these interviews. I want to point out several, though I cannot discuss them in detail here. So I encourage readers to investigate, reflect on, and discuss the following issues on their own:

An initial trust in churches and ministries. Almost all of my interviewees brought high hopes to the church or parachurch ministry that they eventually left. They assumed that the institution existed for their good. Group psychology and attractive leaders helped them to feel trusting. In my view, they had a right to trust those organizations. Unfortunately, the groups did not always honor the people's confidence, and they left.

A longing for community. Even though most of those interviewed are now nurturing their faith pretty much on their own, they still dream of being part of an intimate group of believers. They want to share life together with a handful of others where they can know and be known. To them, the church *should* be about camaraderie, belonging, commitment, honesty, and forgiveness. They'll know it when they see it. But where can they find it (they ask)?

Boredom with church services. Sermons were not very popular among this crowd. At best, sermons were tolerated; at worst, they infuriated. Perhaps the most common complaint was that worship services were boring. It was not just that these gatherings were not interesting; they were not *worshipful.* They did little to help people meet God. However, I did not hear this as a call for more entertainment, but for more participation. Altar calls and missionary calls fared poorly. And the singles I interviewed all had disparaging remarks to make about singles groups.

A craving for "truth" and "reality." There seemed to be a feeling that religious situations too often lack authenticity. The truth is not told; people are not "real." Christian sermons, books, and conversations too often seemed to avoid the "bad stuff." Indeed, religion sometimes seems off in a world of its own. Yet my interviewees felt that if the faith is to make any difference in people's lives, it has to face cold, hard reality. It also has to get under the surface to a person's real self, to one's sin and pain and the things one wants to hide. We'll revisit this point below.

The importance of psychology as a resource. Over and over I heard people describe the "garbage" they had brought with them into the faith. In some cases they came expecting help with cleaning it out. In other cases they discovered their need after being in the faith for a while. Either way, many of them turned to psychotherapy to deal with those issues. Rarely did churches or ministries encourage that "outside" help, despite the benefits to people's spiritual life.

Growing resentment among women. If some of the comments from the women I spoke with are any indication, the church has a time bomb on its hands. Women are angry and getting angrier. I would not presume to characterize all women in the church this way. But the message is loud and clear: when it comes to issues like language, opportunities, praise and rewards, authority, staffing, expectations, marriage and sexuality, and justice, women increasingly see the church as dominated by a male perspective. Many feel that Christianity, as represented by its institutions and leaders, comes across as insensitive. Certainly they would say there are exceptions, but overall it feels like a system that doesn't respect women.

No easy path to spirituality. The people I spoke with showed extreme antipathy toward formulas and "packaged" Christianity. In their experience, it was downright misleading to try to reduce spiritual growth to a handful of steps. Likewise, they rejected as simplistic any attempts to explain complex truths through proof-texts and clever diagrams. Almost every time they spoke about the various prescriptions they had been given, their voices lapsed into sarcasm. They had tried what they regarded as "cookbook Christianity," and it failed miserably.

False advertising. In several cases there was a feeling that Christian institutions and their leaders sometimes promise more than they deliver or that the faith was perhaps ever intended to deliver. However, the problem was not seen as outright deception so much as overblown optimism and hype. Even so, it amounted to false advertising, and the people I spoke with deeply resented it.

The red herring of busyness. A number of interviewees pointed out that heavy involvement in programs and church- or ministry-related activities is neither a sign of spirituality nor a means toward it. Like Martha,[3] one could be busy serving the Lord, yet starving inside due to a lack of intimacy with God. Nevertheless, they implied that religious leaders had encouraged program commitments as a way to grow in the faith and to show one's dedication to the Lord and the body.

A desire to express spiritual gifts. Anthony in particular discussed this at length, but several others alluded to it. They seemed to feel the most alive and connected with God and the community of faith when they were able to employ their God-given abilities in meaningful ways. Yet few churches seemed to identify or make use of these valuable human resources. I'll have more to say on this point in the next chapter.

Wholesale rejection of prosperity theology. My interviewees took a dim view of the teaching that God will bless people—with health, wealth, or even spiritual rewards—in exchange for certain behaviors. Not only had they not experienced the faith that way, they were skeptical that the "prosperity gospel" is a biblical doctrine.

Who is the enemy? Who is a friend? "When I look back over the years, the hurt and the pain, do you know where it's come from? It's come from the family of God. It hasn't been from unbelievers." This comment from Jennifer was echoed by many of the others. Tragically, almost all the casualties recorded here were from "friendly fire."

Mixed attitudes about Christian homes. A number of the people I spoke with had been brought up by Christian parents who attended church regularly. The interviewees' feelings about that were ambivalent, to say the least. While they would not necessarily have wanted to be raised by non-Christians, they found that many of their later problems could be traced back to their upbringing. I'll have more to say about this in the next chapter.

Warnings about "ministry." Based on the interviews with Elaine, Jennifer, Chris, John, and Norman and Judy—all of whom were involved in "full-time" Christian work—it would appear that people in ministry suffer the hardest falls. Perhaps their expectations are higher. Whatever the case, these good people have had to endure a crisis not only in their faith, but in their vocation as well. It's a one-two combination that has left them reeling.

Theology makes a difference. In almost every case, teaching about God, the body of Christ, the nature of humanity, sin, salvation, spiritual growth, and other theological issues made a profound difference in people's thinking, attitudes, and behavior. For better or for worse, doctrine colored their perceptions and influenced their responses. However, as Diana pointed out so eloquently, theology was more than an intellectual exercise; theology must affect people's lives by being "felt out" as well as thought out. Furthermore, many expressed that spiritual growth involved "unlearning" bad ideas and falsehoods that had been taught early in their Christian experience.

Let me dwell on the following points in more detail:

Spirituality is a process. If my interviewees revealed anything, it was that cultivating a relationship with God, becoming like Christ, reaching spiritual maturity, or otherwise nurturing one's spirituality is a life-long process. Conversion is merely the first step in the journey.

Or, to return to the metaphor I mentioned at the end of the first chapter, which is perhaps more helpful and, I believe, more accurate, the life of every person is a story. Coming to faith is not the beginning of the tale but rather a key development in an ongoing plot. That means that all that has preceded conversion has meaning. Indeed, it often proves decisive for later events in the narrative. Likewise, whatever happens after salvation ought not to be seen as anticlimactic, but just the opposite: the building of plot and character toward their final resolution *in Christ.*[4]

At any rate, spirituality is a process, and people come to the church and its related institutions expecting help with that process. "Help," however, does not necessarily mean a program. As mentioned above, my interviewees came to look upon structured approaches to spiritual growth with suspicion and even scorn.

It is easy to see why. Programs designed to aid spiritual development tend to treat people as if they were all the same. The reality is, everybody is different; in fact, each of us is unique. Nowhere is that uniqueness more significant than in our relationship with God, the very heart of our spiritual life. God relates to us according to the way He has made us. His hands, which "knit me together in my mother's womb,"[5] wove a tapestry in me that looks very different from the one crafted into you. No two stories are quite the same.

Spirituality, then, is a function of how God has designed individuals. So why expect people to grow in the same way, through the same means, at the same rate?

Educators are beginning to appreciate the implications of individual differences in the classroom. One researcher has found evidence of at least seven kinds of intelligence.[6] Yet schools typically favor only two—language and logic—with the result that some children look "dull," when in fact they are very bright. They are just not given a chance to demonstrate their aptitude in the academic setting.

A similar situation exists in the church and parachurch, where the approach to spiritual formation is often the religious equivalent of a traditional schoolroom. Some "students"—or, as the New Testament calls them, *disciples*, or "learners"—do quite well in the prescribed regimen. Others fare poorly. But is their poor showing really the result of sin, or a lack of "spiritual discipline," or a "rebellious spirit," or apathy, as they are frequently told? My hunch is that they have been placed in a situation that makes little if any use of the good things God put in them when He created them.

Much more could be said. The point is that the church is in the people-development business.[7] One reason people leave is dissatisfaction with the results. Having worked the program, they are frustrated because they still feel spiritually illiterate, and the God they wanted to get close to still seems as distant as ever.

A two-story church. The people I interviewed frequently alluded to the gap between the ideals taught by churches and the reality people face in the day-to-day. It was a gap they perceived as widening. More and more they felt as if they were living in two worlds—the world of religion, with its own language, rituals, and code of behavior, and the "real" world of everyday life.

I suggest that they felt as if they were straddling two worlds because, in fact, the church has convinced them that they have a foot in two worlds. Modern-day Christianity's worldview is very dualistic.

Doug Sherman and I described this "two-story" view in *Your Work Matters to God.*[8] It's a view that promotes ideas such as: the soul is superior to the body, and therefore more important to God; the things of eternity have value, while the things of time are inconsequential; some things are "sacred" (prayer, worship, church activities, ministry) and some things are "secular" (work, politics, sports); and clergy have a "higher calling" and do the "Lord's work," whereas laity pursue "secular" tasks, except occasionally when they come to church and volunteer for "ministry."

Can you see the hierarchy here? That's why we call it a two-story view. It carves up the world into two categories, assigns one category (the "spiritual") importance over the other, and suggests that God is only concerned with the "upper story." I've already gone on record as rejecting this view as "wholly inadequate. It rests on sub-biblical assumptions and produces sub-biblical results."[9]

Yet we meet it again and again in the experience of people leaving the church. They struggle with the issue of "calling." They complain of

a lack of authenticity among believers. They find it hard to be "real"—
that is, honest about their sin as well as normal in their humanity—in a
church or religious setting. They find little appreciation for "nonspiritual" categories such as the arts. They feel a lack of significance when it
comes to career choices. They're convinced that Christianity is true;
but how do you make it work?

These are complex matters, to be sure. But they might prove a
lot less problematic if the church could ever abandon its two-story view
of life in favor of a more unified, biblical approach. Unless it does, it is
hard to see how the church can keep holding onto people in the "real"
world.

Where is God? In 1977, writer Philip Yancey produced a book that
asked the poignant question, *Where Is God When It Hurts?* Apparently
a lot of people were wondering the same thing, because the title quickly
became an award-winning best-seller. Soon Yancey began to receive
letters from people all across the country driven to the edge of doubt
and despair. Yet their stories raised even more troubling questions.
Before long, Yancey felt compelled to write a follow-up entitled *Disappointment with God.* It proved to be even more popular than the first
book.

Disappointment with God addressed "three large questions about
God that . . . are lodged somewhere inside all of us. Yet few people
ask them aloud, for they seem at best impolite, at worst heretical": Is
God unfair? Is God silent? Is God hidden?[10]

Many of the people I interviewed were asking these questions.
They were not terribly impressed with the answers they had received
from Christian teachers. And no wonder. These are tough questions to
which, as Yancey and others rightly point out, there are no simple answers.

Yet people like Diana, Robert, Daniel, and Sheila felt that they had
been led to believe otherwise. The authorities they followed raised high
expectations that if they practiced certain spiritual disciplines, they
would enter into intimacy with God in which they would enjoy the
steady confidence of His presence and the sure anchor of His help. But
that didn't happen. As a result, these hapless believers may have been
disappointed with God, but they were even more disappointed with the
church.

It's a serious matter, because the question, *Where is God?*—the
doctrine of God's imminence—lies at the heart of why people come to
church. They expect to find God there. And why not? If you can't find

God in a church, or by extension through the programs and practices prescribed by the church, then where can you find Him?

My interviewees had a longing to see God in the day-to-day. How involved is He, for instance, in one's decision making, work, or family life? Christian teaching says He is lord of everything. How does He express that sovereignty in the affairs of life in any practical, tangible way? Or is He like an absentee landlord who inserts Himself only when there's a problem?

On a more global scale, where is God on the turbulent sea of world events? Things look pretty chaotic at times. Is God involved to any degree? Should we see His hand behind the movement of peoples and the changing fortunes of corporations and governments? Or is He the ultimate poker player, holding His cards close to His vest, biding His time until He finally lays down all the aces?

The question *Where is God?* is no essay question for a seminary exam in theology proper. It's the kind of simple but profound question people are led to ask when they sing hymns such as "What a Friend We Have in Jesus" and "He's Got the Whole World in His Hands." It's not that anyone disagrees; they would just like the church to clarify in what sense Jesus is a friend and God has things under control.

Grace and guilt. "We have to be careful with what we teach about grace because people tend to take advantage of it." The first time I heard one of my interviewees tell me that that, in effect, was what he had been told by a church leader, I felt sad but figured it was just one person's experience. In a way, I could see the leader's point.

The second time I heard it, I thought it coincidental. The third time I heard it, I stopped to consider whether I was being set up. The fourth time I heard it—in the space of three days—and then when I continued to hear it in later interviews, I realized that modern-day American Protestantism has given back a lot of theological ground that Luther, Calvin, and the other Reformers in its heritage paid for in tears, and that Christ paid for in blood.

The retreat is not from whether we are saved by grace. As John pointed out, "Almost any evangelical church worth anything will teach that salvation is by grace. But after somebody accepts grace, then grace is virtually forgotten, and the Christian life becomes some combination of faith and works. Most churches preach grace and live works."

Story after story bore this out. The results were invariably tragic. Perhaps the greatest tragedy was that a system promising forgiveness to people and freedom from guilt ended up making so many of them feel guilty.

That, in turn, led to chronic legalism. At every turn, they staggered under massive expectations that they never could quite fulfill. Virtually every detail relating to spirituality—Bible reading, prayer, evangelism, church attendance, ministry, missions, financial contributions, even academic studies—was freighted with demands. And failure! They could never do enough. Try as they might, they could never rest in the confidence that God was pleased with them.

Thus grace became a theological fiction. Yet rumors of a gracious God persisted. And once people discovered what for so long they had been denied, they felt cheated and outraged and made a beeline for the exit.

Overall, the Christianity that my interviewees left had a negative face on it. It often felt like a religion that was constantly trying to get people to believe what they didn't really want to believe, do what they didn't really want to do, and not do what they really did want to do. There was rarely an appeal to the positive. It was as if there was no thought to motivating and helping people do what they genuinely, sincerely, and willfully *wanted* to do. In fact, efforts at nurturing spiritual growth in ways that felt good and affirming were often dismissed as dangerous.

The fear seems to be that Christian people will settle for "cheap grace," the idea that "the account has been paid in advance; and, because it has been paid, everything can be had for nothing."[11] That seems like a legitimate concern. Yet listening to my interviewees, I heard about a form of "grace" that was at least as perverted: *nothing* could be had, yet even that might cost them everything—their freedom, their emotional health, even their personhood.

As I say, it appears that the church has a lot of theological ground to reclaim.

A respect for feelings. As I reflected on my conversations with "back-door believers," I noticed an interesting phenomenon: there seemed to be a correlation between people coming alive to their emotions and their exit from the church. This was not always true, nor is it universally true of those who leave churches. John Savage, a consultant to parishes in the areas of conflict management and attendance dropouts, has found that a person's *inability* to deal with negative emotions often propels him or her out of a congregation.[12]

Either way, though, I was struck with the way that feelings are treated—or, as many of my interviewees seemed to feel, *mistreated*—by churches and ministries. In the main, there seemed to be a conflict between emotions and spirituality. I mentioned one example of this problem in chapter 14, the popular formula, FACT-FAITH-FEELING. There were many others that I did not point out.

Now obviously Christendom today is increasingly aware of psychology. In fact, a burgeoning industry has sprung up to service the Christian community's psychotherapeutic needs. Still, based on the conversations recorded here, it would appear that the tension between faith and feelings persists. Once people allowed themselves to experience their emotions and own what was really going on inside, they ran into countless questions about how to integrate that self-knowledge with the Christian teaching to which they had been exposed. Quite often, they described themselves as moving closer to God *but further away from the church!*

These are deep waters, and they're about to get deeper. As I mentioned in chapter 13, a vast number of Baby Boomers are reentering the church. I view this as a good-news, bad-news scenario. The good news is that the church is getting a second chance with this generation; the bad news is, it may not want that chance.

Think about it: the Boomers may be remembered as one of the most dysfunctional generations the world has ever seen. My generation probably has had a higher incidence of drug abuse, alcoholism, divorce, crime, and other social, moral, and spiritual problems than any other group in history. We are at least as materialistic today as we said our parents were in the sixties, probably more so. And the jury is still out on our own effectiveness in parenting. So far, things aren't looking good.

So in light of the challenge, I think it's fair to ask, is the church up to it? Is it prepared to handle such an influx of need—on top of what it already has? Not unless it respects the emotional side of people, for, as my interviewees have discovered, that is a doorway to the soul.

Disillusionment is a process. C. S. Lewis said that "if you examined a hundred people who had lost their faith in Christianity, I wonder how many of them would turn out to have been reasoned out of it by honest argument? Do not most people simply drift away?"[13] Well, we haven't examined a hundred people, but we have talked to a couple dozen. And most of the people we've interviewed haven't exactly lost their faith, but they have pulled out of various faith communities.

So, having gone through that exercise, I think we can say with some confidence that the answer to Lewis's conjecture is yes, people do drift away (though I'm not sure how "simply"). Just as spirituality is a process, disillusionment with the church—or the faith—is a process, too. It doesn't happen overnight.

I think this is evident in the stories. Each one is different, but a general pattern seems to emerge. A person enters the faith and, sooner or later, the church (or parachurch or some other Christian institution). For a while things seem fine. The person grows spiritually. Perhaps he carries out some task related to ministry.

Over time, however, questions and doubts begin to emerge, especially doubts related to spirituality, to how he applies the faith to life. Any number of things can create those doubts. In fact, it's usually not one big thing, but a lot of little things over time. Taken together, they point to a gap between the way things are "supposed" to be (according to the teaching) and the way things actually are (according to his experience). He slowly wakes up to the fact that his faith isn't "working," at least not the way he expected—or was led to believe.

At first, and sometimes for quite a while, the person assumes that the problem must be with him. After all, it can't be with Christianity, can it? (In most people's minds, the faith is equivalent to whatever teaching they are getting.) Perhaps he has misunderstood the teaching. Perhaps he is misapplying it. So, if the person is serious about the faith, he redoubles his efforts, perhaps even trying some new strategies. In any case, he hopes to close the gap between the ideal and the real.

The person may actually make progress toward that. Or he may not but convince himself that he has. Quite possibly, though, he may continue to meet with failure. In that case, he may eventually give up trying and conclude that the advertised benefits of the faith are for a special breed of person with superior spiritual acumen; *he* must settle for mediocrity. Having run the race of faith, he qualifies merely as an also-ran. It's a very disappointing outcome.

Countless people in the church today probably fit that profile. They attend, they support the church financially, they may occasionally volunteer. But they are dissatisfied with "church." They feel like spiritual also-rans. And as they listen to the teaching week in and week out, they develop that low-grade virus of discontent that I described in chapter 12. Dr. Savage, the consultant, estimates that what he terms "apathetic and bored church members" number about one-third of the membership of most congregations.[14]

So what keeps them hanging onto churches and ministries? Very little. They don't leave right away, because where else are they supposed to go? And there's always a remote chance that things will change for the better. But if they feel enough dissatisfaction, it doesn't take much to trigger an exit—the infidelity of a pastor, a conflict with another church member that is not resolved satisfactorily, an incident in the family to which the church turns a deaf ear, an alternative that somehow looks more promising.

Can these dropouts be prevented? In most cases, yes. In fact, knowing that disillusionment is a process is a valuable piece of information. It tells us that there are points for intervention all along the way. By recognizing the signs of trouble, churches that care can actually turn the process around.

Indeed, they can turn it into a process of growth. For it turns out that disillusionment and spirituality are in many ways the same process! I'll say more about this in chapter 21. For now, it is enough to point out that when someone finds a gap between the real and the ideal, he has the wonderful opportunity of learning a truth. Maybe it will be a truth about himself, maybe it will be a truth about what he has been told. Almost certainly it will be the truth that human life "is a pilgrimage from appearance to reality."[15]

It remains to be said what part the church plays in that pilgrimage. What can the body of Christ do to fulfill its mission of developing people and bringing them to maturity in Christ? I invite you to consider that with me in the next chapter.

NOTES

1. Let there be no misunderstanding. This book does not present the findings of a scientifically constructed sample of former churchgoers. For that, one would need to consult works such as Dean R. Hoge's *Converts, Dropouts, Returnees: A Study of Religious Change Among Catholics* (New York: The Pilgrim Press, 1981).

2. New York Times News Service, "Public Opinion of Clergy Reaches All-Time Low, Poll Finds," *Dallas Morning News* (November 28, 1992): 49A; *PRRC Emerging Trends* 9, no. 10 (December 1987): 3.

3. Luke 10:38–42.

4. This, at any rate, is one way to understand passages such as Romans 8:28–30 and Ephesians 2:1–7.

5. Psalm 139:13.

6. See Howard Gardner, *Frames of Mind: The Theory of Multiple Intelligences* (New York: Basic Books, 1983) and *The Unschooled Mind: How Children Think and How Schools Should Teach* (New York: Basic Books, 1991).

7. Ephesians 4:12–13.

8. NavPress, 1987. See especially chapter 3, "Ye Cannot Serve God and Mammon."

9. Ibid., 60. There's no secret why dualism is flawed: it does not come from Scripture but from a number of ancient Greek philosophers such as Plato, Aristotle, and Plotinus, among others. This pagan worldview entered the church after the time of the apostles and has plagued Christianity ever since.

10. Philip Yancey, *Disappointment with God* (New York: Harper Paperbacks, 1988), 29–30.

11. Dietrich Bonhoeffer, *The Cost of Discipleship*, 2d ed. (New York: Macmillan, 1959), 45.

12. For more on Dr. Savage's research, see p. 24 (chapter 1, endnote 10).

13. *Mere Christianity* (New York: Macmillan, 1943), 124.

14. John S. Savage, *The Apathetic and Bored Church Member: Psychological and Theological Implications* (Reynoldsburg, Ohio: L.E.A.D. Consultants, 1976), 79.

15. Dame Iris Murdoch, *Metaphysics as a Guide to Morals* (London: Allen Lane/Penguin, 1993).

20

What Churches Can Do

*As I was about to cross the stream
the usual sign was given to me,—
that sign which always forbids, but never bids.*

Socrates

I come to a chapter that I would be just as happy not to write. Personally I would be satisfied to let these interviews stand on their own and let readers make of them what they will. But that would be irresponsible. Pascal said that everything that is written merely to please the author is worthless. So, having provided an "open microphone" to people leaving the church, I feel an obligation to say a few words to and on behalf of the church they are leaving.

In doing so, let me remind the reader that I am a layperson. That's been a tremendous advantage in gathering material for this book. Likewise it affords me some objectivity in making suggestions for how the church might improve its level of services. Of course, it also means that pastors and others who actually deliver those services day in and day out know a lot more about how to do that than I.

But the stories in this book can help them do their job better. In effect, I've written sixteen case studies of disillusioned Christians. Even if one dispensed with the rest of what I have to say in this chapter, that would still leave the statements themselves as useful tools for reflection, discussion, and evaluation. I would be delighted if church leaders used the material in those ways. After all, those are the words of the "customer"; therefore, those are the words that matter.

But now let me add some words of my own, beginning with some words of explanation. Throughout this book, I've used the word "church" in a variety of ways. What exactly do I mean? Keeping in mind that I am not a theologian and that this is not the place for a full-blown ecclesiology, as well as my disclaimer from chapter 18—that it is difficult anymore to say anything intelligent about the church—one way to describe my understanding would be to say that I hold a "high" view of the church as universal and organic and a "low" view of the church as local and institutional.

The church is universal and organic in that it comprises all believers in Jesus Christ. Thus I adhere to what the major orthodox creeds describe as the "holy catholic church." That means that whenever I meet someone who is a follower of Christ, I am dealing with a fellow member of the church, a fellow Christian. We stand in relationship to each other because of our relationship to Christ. Together with all other Christ-followers, we make up the body of Christ, the universal body of believers that Christ committed Himself to building.

As a practical matter, however, it is not enough to talk about the church as an amorphous body of believers everywhere; one needs to relate to actual believers somewhere. That sounds easy enough, but over the centuries we Christians have made it complex. Jesus said He would be present when even two or three of His people gather together in His name. But the greater the number of believers gathered together and the more they wish to accomplish, the greater the need and urge for organization and structure. Thus we have inherited and created the vast institutions of Christendom.

There is nothing intrinsically wrong with institutions. But how easily they become the enemy of spiritual life! In some cases we even have ecclesiastical structures with no spiritual life. I view structure as a means to an end, not the end itself. There is nothing sacred about structure. It is always negotiable. It varies from culture to culture. As a result, God gives us great latitude in how we set up churches and how we "do church." (At least we should hope that He does, given the incredible variety today of churches and their related organizations!)

In that spirit of flexibility, I believe God wants Christians to gather together for purposes of worship, instruction, fellowship, service, community, accountability, mission and evangelism, and whatever else brings glory to Him, meets the needs of the body, and proclaims Christ to the world. Christians do that through a variety of structures. The most common among them is the "local church."

I think it is crucial to observe that the distinction between the "universal church" and the "local church" is purely our own. The terms do not appear in the New Testament. This does not invalidate the idea of the local church. As I say, believers need to relate to and be committed to other believers somewhere, and the reality is that most will end up (and probably should end up) in what has been described as a "local" congregation.

But I do object to the preeminence that many local churches assume for themselves by declaring that they are God's *ordained and primary* means of helping people grow spiritually. That strikes me as an overstatement. Churches certainly ought to be means for the development of people's spiritual lives, as I have stated repeatedly. But one is on thin ice to insist that local churches enjoy a role of institutional superiority, especially when no one can define with precision what a local church is, given that there is no term for it in Scripture.

To be honest, the question of what is a local church and what is its authority is a battle I have no interest in fighting. Every pastor, church leader, and layperson reading this chapter probably has his or her own convictions on these matters, and I'm satisfied to leave those unchallenged. But I cannot completely avoid the issue, because it bears directly on the subject of this book. It is from local churches, after all, that many of my interviewees and countless others like them have disassociated themselves.

The question for many readers is, were they wrong to do so? And are they outside God's will if they remain apart from a local congregation? And can they grow spiritually on their own? How one answers depends largely on whether one holds a high or low view of the local church. The high view would tend to see church dropouts as being in grievous error. The low view would tend to back away from any fast judgments.

For my own part, I view people who leave churches but do not leave the faith as continuing members of the universal body of Christ. I think it is very possible, though neither preferable nor easy, to grow in the faith apart from an organized local church. But it is virtually impossible to grow without at least some relationships with other believers in which life in Christ is celebrated.

For that reason, we need the local church. And we especially need pastors, because we have explicit New Testament teaching on the role of pastors in developing spiritually mature people. I believe that pastoring a church may be the toughest job in the world today. I know many people who do it well, some extremely well. I know none for whom the work is easy.

This book illustrates one reason why. On the one hand, the pastor is expected to attract new people to the faith and to the church. On the other, he is expected to meet the needs of regular attenders.

Attracting new customers and holding onto old ones are extraordinarily different tasks, especially for the church. These are two distinct groups of people, with very different needs, or at least with different approaches to meeting their needs. Reaching out to the unsaved and the unchurched while at the same time meeting the needs and satisfying the demands of people who have been in the program for a while taxes the skills of pastors and church leaders beyond imagining. In fact, some churches have decided to concentrate on one group or the other, but not both, because to try and meet the needs of both is just too much.

Now along comes *Exit Interviews,* raising the issue of disgruntled people who are leaving. If I were a pastor, I have to admit I might be inclined to just let them go. After all, I've probably got other fires to put out, so losing a few "malcontents" would be doing me a favor. Besides, there are plenty of other churches around. Maybe those people will be happier somewhere else. (You can see why I'm not a pastor!)

I have no suggestions for any pastor or church leader who is satisfied to see people walking out the back door of his or her church or ministry. But for those who find it unacceptable, let me encourage two levels of interdiction. The first calls for some strategic work theologically. The other involves a more tactical assault on what admittedly is a very complex problem.

On the theological side, I believe the church is seriously in need of work on four issues:

A theology of spirituality and spiritual growth. Over the course of the church's history, some brilliant thinking has been put forward on the nature and process of salvation, or justification. Likewise, good work has been done on the question of our future hope in Christ, or glorification. But there's a gap in our theology when it comes to sanctification. What happens between coming to faith and meeting Christ?

For example, in the last chapter, I noted that spirituality is a process. What is that process? Can its steps or stages be discerned? In 1 John, the writer says that he is writing to "little children," "young men," and "fathers."[1] Are these phases of spiritual development? If so, what are their characteristics?

Likewise, what is the relationship between spirituality and biological age? At twenty, I had been a believer for sixteen years. What should I have been able to expect by that point, as opposed to a man of fifty who might have been in the faith for, say, five years? This seems like a crucial point in light of my interviews: notice that all of those with whom I spoke were adult veterans of the church, not new converts. None had been Christians for less than ten years, some for two or three times that long. Yet they were dissatisfied with their spiritual progress.

Along these lines, we tell people that the goal is "spiritual maturity." What is that? What are its characteristics? Is spirituality a destination or a direction? How long should it reasonably take to arrive at "maturity," whatever it is? Or do we ever get there? If not, how do we stay motivated? How do we mark our milestones? How do we even know if we're making progress?

In the next chapter I'm going to speak to the responsibility of the individual for his or her spiritual life. But how much responsibility does a person bear? What part of spirituality is God's responsibility? And what is the church's role in all of this?

I know of no single body of work that has thoroughly explored these issues and others like them. Yet spirituality is probably the foremost theological category in people's minds today. As long as the church lacks a cogent doctrine in this area, it will keep losing credibility—which is to say it will keep losing people. Why? Because people no longer evaluate Christianity on the basis of whether it is true, but *how* it is true. As my friend Doug Sherman says, today's question is not whether God exists, but what difference does He make?

A theology of persons. Hand in hand with a theology of spiritual formation, the church needs to develop a theology of persons. This is not quite the same as the theological category known as anthropology, which addresses the nature of human beings. A theology of persons deals with *personhood*. Its subject is not the human race, but the individual. It considers the question of identity, the essence of who someone is.

Why is that important? Because as I have stressed throughout this book, the church is in the people-development business. Ironically, the people to be developed are both the "customers" and the "products." So on both counts, we can't know enough about how God has made people. When the church takes someone from conversion to spiritual maturity, it is developing a human life. So what is a human life? What does God see when He looks at a person? *Who* does He see? Who should the church see? How can we know the essence of the individual?

To a large extent, theologians have looked to psychologists for answers to these questions. But in doing so, they may be giving away the keys to the kingdom. Not that psychology doesn't have much to contribute to our understanding of persons. But as psychologist William Kirk Kilpatrick says, psychology is not enough. "It offers plausible explanations, good insights, good techniques. It offers very good pills. But it doesn't offer the one thing that people require most: a sense of meaning. . . . One comes away from the psychology textbooks with the feeling that though life now seems more explainable, it somehow seems less meaningful."[2]

A theology of spiritual gifts. This book is about unfulfilled expectations. Perhaps in nothing does Christian teaching today raise more expectations that for the most part go unfulfilled than in the matter of spiritual gifts.

The doctrine is that God has given a special gift or ability to each believer so that he or she can contribute meaningfully to the work of the body. What incredibly good news! It's like telling people that there's a job in the want-ads with their name on it.

Naturally they want to find out what that job is. But that's when things start to fall apart. First of all, how many churches have a "technology" for helping people discover their abilities? For that matter, what exactly are the gifts mentioned in the New Testament?[3] How does each one serve the body? Are the lists exhaustive? Why do some letters, such as 1 Corinthians and Ephesians, stress them, while others, such as 1 Timothy and Titus, neglect even to mention them?

Of course, most people couldn't care less about questions like these; they just want someone to tell them what their gift is and how they can use it in the body. But again, how often does that happen? Some gifts seem fairly evident—teaching, for example. But what about the less obvious ones? If someone has a lot of money, she may be gently told that God wants her to express the gift of liberality (a gift she may or may not have). But for the rest, they are liable to end up in the catch-all category of "helps."

This inability to pinpoint people's giftedness only acts to dash people's hopes. Think what a letdown it is to be told that you have a "significant" role to play in the body of Christ, only to discover that you'll be handling a minor chore that, frankly, anyone could do—when what you were hoping for was a task that *only you* could do, one that you were uniquely created and gifted by God to do. It's like answering the afore-mentioned want-ad, which promised you a position "vital to the future of our company," only to find that your assignment will be the spiritual equivalent of flipping burgers.

I've heard countless pastors and church leaders cry that they can-not find enough volunteers, and therefore the work of the church goes undone. Their tendency is to blame the people. But could it be that the people are merely responding to a woefully inadequate theology of spir-itual gifts?

The keys to that theology, by the way, lie in the theologies of spirituality and persons mentioned above. It's not too hard to see that spiritual gifts and spiritual formation are related ("God is in my gift!" as Anthony put it), or that spiritual gifts and personhood go hand in hand ("When I run, I feel His pleasure!" Olympic runner and missionary to China Eric Liddell said).

As for detecting people's spiritual gifts, the tell-tale sign is pas-sion, as was so evident in Anthony's story. What is this person passion-ate about doing? What motivates him or her? If we get out of the way, how will the person *instinctively* serve God and other people?[4]

A theology of grace. As I suggested in the last chapter, the church has some remedial work to do in its doctrine of grace. And yet there's new ground to plow as well. What is the place of grace in today's world?

Here's the situation. Never have the expectations on believers been higher. We know too much. For example, think how much we now understand about family relationships and the development of chil-dren. For parents, that knowledge translates into a laundry list of shoulds and ideals at which past generations would have gasped. There are so many of them, and they're so high!

And the family is just one area of responsibility. Similar lists of "what committed Christians ought to do" could be generated for the believer's work, participation in the church, involvement in the commu-nity, responsibility to the world, and so on. Add it all up, and it's a crushing burden—absolutely staggering!

Yet never have people been less able to live up to those expecta-tions, biblically based though they may be. For one thing, we are not a morally or spiritually robust generation. It's not that we wouldn't love to live up to the high ideals with which we're challenged. But the fact is, we can't. We simply *can't*. They are so high and so many, and we are not only weak but in many cases wounded as well.

The standard response to this fact is that of course we're weak as human beings, but with Christ's strength we can do "all things."[5] With all due respect to that point of view, let me state plainly that it's not going to happen that way. People are not going to become super-saints. They're going to live less than ideal lives, and lots of times they're going to fail. They're certainly not going to live up to anywhere near the heightened expectations of well-intentioned Christian teaching. Spirituality is a process that includes failure.

So what does the church say to them? What is our "theology of failure," our "theology of Plan B"? It seems to me that the words we need at this point can be found in the language of grace. But, like the King James English, we need to update that language so that the good news of grace is intelligible to modern ears.

However, not everyone who claims to speak for Christ speaks in that language, new or old. And therein lies a crisis, especially for the conservative side of the church. Based on the stories presented here, I believe that the church needs to decide how long it is going to coddle legalists in its ranks. By legalists I mean people who preach grace but practice works. People who inflict guilt on others for being human, let alone sinful. People who say, "Well, we don't want to go overboard on this grace thing because people will take advantage of it."

The church has made it comfortable for those who hold that position. But at what cost! Legalism is keeping people out of the church, it is driving people away from the church, and it is poisoning the lives of those who remain in the church. So why permit it? Why even tolerate it, especially when Jesus and Paul, among others, reserved their harshest words for those who compromised grace?

On that note, it seems appropriate to recall the words of Luther that theology comes from living rather than thinking, reading, or speculating. An overstatement, to be sure—or is it? I have mentioned four theological issues that pertain to people leaving the church. Perhaps the best way to come to terms with those issues is to deal with the practical side of the problem.

The people responsible for that practical side are pastors and ministry leaders. Perhaps that describes you. If so, let me repeat what I said earlier, that I respect the difficulty of your job. I suspect that, like Socrates, you may have a voice in your head that always tells you what *not* to do, but never tells you what *to* do. So let me suggest a number of things *to* do with respect to disillusioned Christians:

Listen. I always asked my interviewees whether anyone had ever debriefed them on why they were leaving the church. Most of them said no one had. In fact, a number of them told me that I was the first person who had ever actively sought them out to hear whatever they might have to say. I wonder: might things have come out differently if someone had simply listened to them as they were heading toward dropout?

For that reason, I suggest that you put into place a *system* for listening to your people—not just the people who are pleased with the program, and not just the potential recruits, but the people on the fringe who are making up their minds whether to stay or leave.

That system can be as simple or as complex as your situation demands. A lot will depend on your style and the "culture" of your congregation. But take a clue from the business world, especially from companies where service is an obsession. I know of a CEO who publishes his phone number and invites irate customers to call him directly. He spends most of his time putting out fires—and building customer loyalty. If you're that type, maybe you'll want to personally visit with people who look like they're on their way out.

However, you may prefer to dispatch a neutral representative. In fact, if your church is large enough, consider a team of laypeople with the right skills whose job would be to scout out and listen to those who are disaffected. Then the team can report back to the leadership with suggestions for further action.

The point is to make listening a way of life at your church or organization. One intentional way to do that is to . . .

Initiate a technology of intervention. If your church or ministry experiences a chronic pattern of dropouts or faces a crisis of defections, I strongly suggest bringing in an expert to help you analyze the problem and set up a program for turning things around. Perhaps your denomination can provide someone.

The leading authority in the field is Dr. John Savage of L.E.A.D. Consultants, in Reynoldsburg, Ohio.[6] During the past seventeen years, he and his team have worked with thousands of churches across the country. On the average, those churches have reclaimed 70 percent of the people who had left. Dr. Savage has seen the percentage go as high as 80 percent.

He has found that churches typically divide into three classes of members: an active core group, a less active peripheral group, and an inactive dropout group. As mentioned before, apathetic and bored church members number about one-third of the membership of most congregations—a pretty strong argument for setting up systems of listening and intervention.

But there's an even stronger reason. One of the most disturbing patterns that Dr. Savage's research shows is that the inner core group is unlikely to care much about people who are dropping out. In one study, he says, the actives "felt that they were 'in,' and that kind of security produces a major problem. The 'in' (active) group was not sensitive to the need of those persons who were aching and leaving the church. That is why 100 percent of the [inactive] group could say, 'No one ever came to visit me.' The implication of that statement is that the [active] group did not sense the needs of those persons who were drifting away; who were, in fact, crying for help."

L.E.A.D. helps churches recognize problems such as these and initiate changes. It also trains laypeople to visit the inactives and reverse their movement away from the church.

Rethink your sermons. Sermons were not especially popular among the people I interviewed. In light of the boredom they felt, I think it's worth asking: What should be the function and value of the sermon today? There are no easy answers to that question. But let me offer one perspective worth considering.

I once talked about preaching with a friend of mine who was a great preacher. People came back week after week to hear his messages, which was ironic because he was not what I would call an outstanding communicator. Neither would he. But no one found him boring, and his sermons produced noticeable changes in people's lives.

I asked him what he thought a preacher's objective should be. I assumed he would say something about teaching and instruction, as his sermons were known for that. But he surprised me with something very unexpected: "I think the point of the sermon is to help people meet God, to have an encounter with God. Somewhere during that message, I want every person to have the experience of hearing God saying something to him or her personally. I'm not even that interested in what happens later, after they leave. As long as they meet God in that moment."

It was a novel approach, and I was reminded of it as my interviewees described their experiences with sermons. They were bored, but not necessarily because the preachers they had heard were boring communicators. Some were rather brilliant. No, they were bored *spiritually*; they had no experience of God. The church service was just another meeting, the sermon just another harangue, no matter how well delivered.

I don't know what you hope to accomplish with your preaching, but I do know why people ultimately go to church: they hope to find God there. They go for other reasons, too. But in the end, they're looking for God. So do they find Him in your sermons?

By now, the memo tacked up in the victorious Clinton presidential campaign headquarters is legendary: "It's the economy, stupid!" I think if I had to preach week in and week out, especially in a culture saturated with entertainment, I would tack a reminder to myself in the pulpit: "It's about God, stupid!"

Work at building community. Elizabeth O'Connor points out that the church is the only place where a person is received into the membership *solely* because he can say that Christ is Lord. "We do not do the calling. Christ does the calling, and this is very threatening if we belong to his Church, because the people he calls are the people with whom we are to have intimate belonging. This gives us a strange assortment of people to be with. They are often not our idea of the ones God should be using to proclaim his Kingdom." For that reason, she says, there is very little genuine Christian community in the world.[7]

My interviewees echoed this sentiment. What can you as a pastor do to make community possible? The short answer is, anything that encourages personal relationships and shared experiences.

Most people can only relate personally to a handful of others. Yet churches tend to emphasize large group programs. Moreover, whatever small groups or clusters there are tend to be organized in a way that works against intimacy. For example, groups may be task-oriented rather than relational. Yet it's interesting that often these work groups get little work done precisely because the people, who are starving to know and to be known, end up schmoozing about personal matters. So why not be more intentional about encouraging face-to-face interaction?

Here is where the small congregation (250 people or less) has a decided advantage. Diana, for example, found it far easier to experience and participate in community life in the small Methodist congregation she attended than in the large Presbyterian church with its huge singles ministry. So if you're the pastor of a small fellowship of believers, take heart! Potentially, you have a lot to offer in terms of intimacy and people getting to know each other.

Yet, ironically, some of the largest churches in the world feature that same closeness and community life. They do so by organizing their members into cell groups or small "house churches" in which people can relate to each other on a more intimate and ongoing basis.

One other suggestion for building community: help the generations talk to each other. One reason people feel such a lack of community today is generational segregation. The kids go off to school, where they are divided by grades. The parents work in separate settings, most often outside the home. The grandparents may be seen infrequently, especially if they live in a distant city. And if there are great-grandparents, they may be completely segregated in a nursing home somewhere.

Is it any wonder that people feel a lack of connection, of rootedness? As the generations in my own family turn over, I'm becoming increasingly aware of how much each generation needs the others—especially those who are one generation removed, that is, grandparents and grandchildren.

So I suggest that you find ways to get people together who have an age difference of forty-five to sixty years. In the case of my interviewees, things might have gone differently for a number of them had they had someone older to help them gain perspective, make choices, and, most important, be a friend or even surrogate parent or grandparent. Youth needs the wisdom of age. On the other hand, age needs the hope of youth.

Teach people theology. As I conducted these interviews, and as I listen to people talk about spiritual issues today, I was stunned by how much "folk religion" there is on the street. By folk religion I mean popular but inaccurate ideas about what our faith is and how it applies. Folk religion is marked by simplistic formulations of supposedly biblical truths. It is essentially "McDoctrine"—spiritual fast-food of proof-texts and clichés that are filling and fattening, but not particularly nourishing.

Yet I can understand why it appeals. "Real" theology has become so arcane today, so filled with abstractions, speculations, and departures from logic, that most of us in the pew are more than happy to leave it to the professionals. Even traditional, orthodox theology is now out of our league. Most of us just want to know what time it is; instead we get a Ph.D. lecture in quantum physics!

People don't trust what they can't understand. So even though folk religion may not answer every question, at least it "puts the cookies on the lower shelf," as they say. Perhaps that's better than nothing.

But not much. People whose understanding of truth is fed on what amounts to spiritual donut holes have little spiritual strength. All it takes is a good crisis and their faith may faint dead away.

They also become victims of heresy. I have not included in this book any interviews with people who have ended up in or come back from the cults. But as I pointed out in chapter 18, recruits to these groups have been shown to be primarily transplants from the more established faiths, especially young people looking for alternatives.[8]

The best prevention against these outcomes is to feed people solid food. If you're a pastor, that's your job—to make sure that your church offers a balanced spiritual diet and instructs people in good principles of spiritual nutrition.

In other words, teach people theology. But don't teach theology, teach *people*. Teach them how to think theologically. That way you'll develop people rather than just dumping theological information on them.

Two specific themes I suggest you visit frequently are . . .

Preach sin and then preach grace. Some readers may misunderstand my (and my interviewees') repeated calls for more grace. They may interpret it as an encouragement to "go easy" on sin. Actually, I advise just the opposite.

There's no need for grace if there's no such thing as sin. That's why I view churches that never mention sin, or that downplay sin, or that try to get people to focus exclusively on the "positive" as not merely heretical but dysfunctional. They are heretical because they willfully ignore the plain teaching of Scripture. They are dysfunctional because they ask people to practice denial about what is staring them in the face—their own sin.

There's only one remedy for sin: the forgiveness that is found in Christ. We need to call sin sin. But then let's also call grace grace. That's why I say, preach sin and then preach grace.

Help people discover their giftedness. This may be a somewhat unfair suggestion, given that earlier I said the church lacks a credible theology of spiritual gifts. Still, we can all agree that God has given gifts to His people. So your challenge as a pastor is to help people assess what their gifts are and then find opportunities that make use of those gifts.

That's easier said than done, but fortunately you have some help on the way. Within the next three to five years you can expect a number of tools and resources currently in development to come on the market that will help your church with gift assessment and placement. I encourage you to look for them. They represent a quantum leap forward for the church.

Do whatever it takes to promote emotionally healthy families. There's an important message for Christian parents from the stories in this book: Pay *at least* as much attention to the emotional climate of your home as to the spiritual.

That may sound like a complete repudiation of traditional thinking. I prefer to see it as a welcome correction. For the fact is, you can't say that Christ is the lord of your home if the relationships aren't working, if feelings are not being expressed, if conflicts and problems are not being resolved, and if family members are not in possession of their own selves. Christ's lordship doesn't produce that kind of pathological system.

Let me take it a step further. Based on my conversations with the people who grew up in Christian homes, I would say that feelings are the key to a child's spirituality. The point is not to try and make children feel good, but to allow them to feel *real*—to really feel whatever they happen to feel. Otherwise, they never develop a sense of who they are. Then how will they relate to God?

As a pastor, you can help parents and, by extension, do an invaluable service to children by presenting a view of the Christian home that is based on grace, not control. That's a new message for many people. But it's sorely needed.

Somewhere along the way, Christian teaching began interpreting biblical passages on the family through an authoritarian grid. Authority in the family is an issue, no question about it. But I wouldn't start there, especially with unhealthy, sinful people. Here's a father who has a high need for control; all he needs to hear is that God has put him in charge of his family! Here's a mother who has spent her life trying to please people; all she needs to hear is that she is supposed to submit to her husband! Look out!

But never mind what I would do. Is authority really the place where Scripture begins its discussion of the family? No. If you examine the context of such well-known texts as Ephesians 5:22–6:4 and Colossians 3:18–4:1, you find that they follow in the wake of instructions on the relational life of believers (Ephesians 5:15–21 and Colossians

3:12–17, respectively). Those relationships are always to be based on grace, not control, as the passages plainly show. So if we're to treat other believers with grace, how much more the members of our own families![9]

You may disagree with me on that interpretation, and that's fine. But let there be no disagreement over the effects on Christian homes where emotional unhealth goes unchecked. I suggest rereading the stories of Diana, Jennifer, Jeff (chapter 10), Mark, and Judy if you doubt the tragic impact of that on the second generation of Christians.

In thinking about that next generation, you may wonder what prospects I hold out for the future of the church. I have every confidence that Christ will continue to build His body. To me that means that He will always preserve a people for Himself.

But what about our Christian institutions? What will they be like in twenty years? That's impossible to answer: what will the world be like in twenty days? We now live in a time when even change itself is not what it used to be. It used to be fast. Now it is unpredictable. In fact, change has become so discontinuous, random, and out of anyone's control that we have entered what Charles Handy of the London Business School calls the age of unreason. Management guru Tom Peters has a similar word for it—chaos.

The institutional church in such a world has no choice but to change, which is to say that it will either grow and adapt or die and be discarded, to be replaced by something else. Clearly, some of the church is already growing, and some of it seems determined to die.

But even if we have no control over change, we have control over our choices. To that extent, we *can* choose our future. I think the stories in this book tell us a lot about what is worth choosing and what is worth discarding.

NOTES

1. 1 John 2:12–14.
2. William Kirk Kilpatrick, "Why Secular Psychology Is Not Enough," Hillsdale College *Imprimis* 15, no. 4 (April 1986): 2.
3. Several lists are given, among them Romans 12:3–8; 1 Corinthians 12:4–11, 28–31; Ephesians 4:11; and 1 Peter 4:10–11.
4. By paying attention to passion, people such as Art Miller, Jr., of People Management, Inc., have come up with remarkably powerful tools that can pinpoint giftedness.
5. Philippians 4:13 is frequently made to imply that nothing is impossible. The context suggests only that Christ helps us handle what comes our way.

6. See p. 24 for information on how to contact L.E.A.D. The information in this section is based on a phone conversation with Dr. Savage and a review of his materials, including his book, *The Apathetic and Bored Church Member: Psychological and Theological Implications* (Reynoldsburg, Ohio: L.E.A.D. Consultants, 1976).

7. *Journey Inward, Journey Outward* (San Francisco: Harper San Francisco, 1968), 24–25.

8. Wade Clark Roof and William McKinney, *American Mainline Religion: Its Changing Shape and Future* (New Brunswick, N.J.: Rutgers Univ., 1987), 12.

9. In this connection, I recommend reading Donald E. Sloat, *Growing Up Holy and Wholly* (Brentwood, Tenn.: Wolgemuth and Hyatt, 1990), especially chapter 16, "Wholeness Is an Option."

21

"You'll Never Find the Perfect Church"

*Their story, yours, mine—it's what we all carry with
us on this trip we take, and we owe it to each other
to respect our stories and learn from them.*
William Carlos Williams[1]

I t remains to say something to the people about whom and to a large
extent for whom this book has been written, those I have called "disillusioned Christians." And if in the previous chapter I felt reluctant to
address pastors and church leaders, here I feel even more wary
about what I should say to you who are leaving the church.

The last thing you need is another sermon. If your story is anything like the ones collected here, you probably turn away at the first
sign that someone is about to start telling you What To Do. But make
no mistake, there are many who are quite certain that a good harangue
is exactly what you need.

I am not among them. In the first place, it is not my way, and in
the second, it is pointless. If ten, twenty, or even thirty years of spiritual prescriptions have not "cured" you, then there is no elixir I can
dispense that will do the trick.

Moreover, I am extremely reluctant to shake my finger in your
face and say, "You turn right around and get yourself back in a church!"
I don't know your circumstances. It may be that there are lots of alternatives around you, in which case I certainly would encourage you to
explore them diligently until you find something that works.

But that may not be your situation. You may be like Jennifer or L. J., for whom there was only one (very unhealthy) fellowship in town. Hearing their stories, I have to wonder which is worse—no church or an abusive church? Or perhaps you're like Chris, or Mark, or Norman and Judy—too banged up right now to have much energy or enthusiasm to jump right back into a program.

In this connection, I suppose some readers will feel that I have gone "far too easy" on my interviewees. I've only given their side of the story, and I haven't challenged their statements. I also haven't pointed out things that they could or should have done differently, things that might have changed the course of events.

But what else could I do, really? Having asked these people to reveal some of the most intimate and sensitive parts of their lives to me, a total stranger, would it have been fair to turn around and tell the whole world where I think they were out of line? No, I've intentionally tried to avoid making judgments.

Another concern has been whether I am not implicitly sanctioning departure from the church. Suppose someone is contemplating quitting. Won't a book like this help to push him over the edge? Not really. In the first place, I am not advocating that anyone leave his or her church. Nor were my interviewees, as I pointed out in chapter 19.

In addition, I doubt that these stories will plant in anyone's mind the idea of dropping out. If you're determined to leave the church, you're going to find a reason to leave, whether it's this book or something else. You will make your decision. You have responsibility for how you nurture your spiritual life.

One thing seems certain: preaching at people and insisting that they not leave will do little to change their minds. Indeed, rather than keeping them in the church, it is more likely to hasten their exit. It will only confirm their suspicions that they cannot get a fair hearing and that no one wants to understand how they are experiencing this phenomenon called "church."

I'm going to argue that *Exit Interviews* actually may encourage disillusioned Christians *not* to leave. For it demonstrates that they are not alone. And here let me address my interviewees and every reader like them by stating emphatically: you are *not* alone! There are countless others in the body of Christ who are experiencing and feeling as you do. In this book we've had the privilege of hearing from a handful of them. Hopefully, at least one of these interviews has articulated something very like your own story.

Of course, I have not included all the stories that were available to me. For example, I have not told about the tortured journey of the person who left the traditional church for a cult and, after going through a nightmare of mind control, broke free. Now she distrusts all religion. I have not presented the anguished narrative of the African-American who finds himself slipping into Islam because of racism in a white church and improprieties in a black church. I have not included the tragic case of the divorcée who sought out a Christian counselor, only to be sexually abused. Nor have I described the very problematic situation of the gay believer who is struggling with whether his spiritual needs will best be served by attending a "straight" church. And there were many others.

The point is, even though your pilgrimage in the faith will not be exactly like mine or anyone else's, we all have something in common—the search for spirituality. Bill Moyers is right: the search for what it means to be spiritual is the story, not just of the decade, but of the century.

And that *is* the story—spirituality, to know God and to be known by Him. That's the issue here, not church attendance. Church attendance has relevance only because it is a means to that end. At least it was intended to be. I'm afraid that, for too many, participation in a church or ministry has not produced that outcome.

As a result, some have left. Millions of others—and I do believe their number is in the millions—remain in the institution but endure what I described in chapter 12 as a low-grade virus of discontent. On the whole, they are disappointed with their spiritual experience. Likewise, they are not particularly satisfied with their church. Yet they are not dissatisfied enough to leave—until some crisis comes along that forces the issue.

I had a common experience while working on this project. As I described it to people who were active in their local churches, they often voiced disapproval of people who would forsake the community of faith. They frowned on the disloyalty involved, and they wondered how anyone could grow spiritually apart from a body of believers.

Yet later, when talking about their own church experiences, they often vented their frustrations with the pastors or the people or the programs and said that they were seriously thinking of looking around for a different church, or that they stayed only because there was no other church, or that they were just hanging in there in the hope that things would get better.

In that way I came to realize that there is not so much difference as one might suppose between the disillusioned Christians walking out and the disillusioned Christians staying put. In other words, the issue is not church attendance. It is spirituality. It is meaning. It is knowing God. The church was always intended as a means to those ends.

"But you'll never find the perfect church!" How often I've heard that comeback thrown in the face of the discontented as if to silence all complaint. That is, if there are problems, they must be with you, not with the institution. In fact, I've actually heard people complete the thought: "You'll never find the perfect church, and if you do find one, don't join it, *or it won't be perfect anymore!*"

But what are we really saying when we admit that there is no perfect church? Does that mean people should stop bothering with the extent to which the organizations of Christendom help them along in their spiritual progress? Should they accept mediocrity and worse in the institution that Christ gave to develop them into His image?

By way of analogy, I'm reminded of the old saw about democracy: "It may not be the most perfect form of government, but it's the only government we have." OK, but how much imperfection should we be willing to tolerate?

We are a nation of immigrants, virtually all of whom came to this land seeking freedom, that incredibly wonderful ideal paid for with an incredible legacy of sacrifice. And the ideal continues to inspire. Every week, new stories emerge of people risking their lives in flimsy boats, stifling railroad cars, even the underbellies of commercial airliners, in a desperate bid for freedom.

Is that what they and their children find when they get here? Well, yes—*sort of.* They are free to move about, they are free in regard to worship, they are free to say as they please, and so on. Yet life in their new land is far from perfect. Having perhaps literally passed under the Statue of Liberty, they come into streets where it is increasingly common to be stripped of one's wallet, one's health, one's dignity, even one's life. Is that the America for which they risked everything? Don't they and their descendants have a legitimate complaint when they question a system that delivers only "freedom, sort of"?

I'm afraid the same is often true of the church. It's the institution that stands for the faith, and for that reason it draws people. Yet many of those people end up wondering about a system that often seems to deliver "spirituality, sort of."

Perhaps you're among them. You're not really expecting the perfect church; you'd be satisfied with a "good enough" church. A church with limitations, to be sure, but a church that is at least honest about those limitations. A church that stands for the highest biblical ideals, but one that also displays humility when it falls short of them and also extends grace when, despite your best faith and efforts, you fall short as well. A less than perfect church for less than perfect people in a less than perfect world.

By the way, it's not true that you'll never find the perfect church. It is true that you won't find it in this sinful world. But this world tells only the middle of the story, not its ending. How will the story come out? No one knows exactly. But sometimes you get a glimpse in those occasional moments when you and other believers enjoy a connection, a oneness in Christ that you never want to end.

For many of us, those moments are all too rare. We long to experience them all the time. But we can't right now. Neither we nor our world are ready for that kind of intimate "communion," to use an old-fashioned but still valuable word. That's why I believe moments of shared spirituality are gifts to us, "rumors of glory" that keep a profound hope alive—that Christ will deliver on His promise to take us, His people, on to perfection.[2]

We're not there yet. The end of the story has not yet been told—which also means that the stories in this book are not yet complete. That's important to remember as we read them. It should keep us from judging. It also should give us hope for ourselves, whose lives are likewise unfinished.

Of course, how things come out depends in large measure on our own choices. Which brings us back to the present. How do we live as less than perfect people with a less than perfect church in a less than perfect world? I will offer my perspective. I want to speak primarily to anyone who identifies with the people in this book. My assumption is that you have walked out the back door. You have not necessarily left the faith, but you have backed off from the community of faith. Now you are nurturing your spiritual life more or less on your own. Here are some things I think worth keeping in mind:

You are responsible. One of the recurring issues for my interviewees was control. It seems to me that much of their trouble with the church revolved around the question of who was in control of their lives. For most of them, this was not a problem during their early years in the faith. They seemed satisfied that the church or ministry knew more about spiritual matters than they. So they went along with the program—effectively giving control to their spiritual leaders.

Fast-forward many years later, as they are exiting the church. In virtually every case, they describe a growing realization that they need to reclaim their power. They need to make choices. They need to think for themselves. They need to protect themselves. They need to speak their mind. In some cases they need to say no. In short, they need to assume *responsibility* for their lives, including their spiritual life. I wonder how differently things might have turned out had their spiritual leaders helped them learn that kind of responsibility early on?

Spiritual authority is a very complex and sensitive subject, and I can't discuss it in detail here. But I will say this: in the end, every person needs to take responsibility for his or her own spiritual life. That is especially true if you are on your own, apart from a community of faith.

Part of the reason is because of a change in our culture. I once visited an Anglo-Catholic church in Boston on All Saints Eve. The church followed the custom of reading through the names of all its departed members down through the years of its existence. It was a historic church, so it probably took us an hour and a half or more to get through all the names.

The experience reminded me that years ago, people often were born, lived, and died in the same community. As a result, a church had continuity with them over their lifetimes, and sometimes over generations of the same families. It could pastor them from birth to death. It knew their history. It helped them mark their milestones. And it preserved their legacy for generations to come, as was evident at the church in Boston.

That's no longer the case. Today, with people relocating every few years and with congregations changing pastors frequently, church has become a commodity. You move into town and "look around" for a church. Which one will it be? You select among the options and plug in. If it works out, fine. If not, you try something different. It's the dance of a marketplace.

Let's assume that a particular church fits, so you start putting down roots. Then *bam!* your company decides to transfer you to another city. New town. New church. New pastor. New friends. And no continuity.

Of course, it doesn't have to be you who leaves. If just a handful of those with whom you are close move on, your notion of "church" can change completely. The same is true with a turnover in pastors.

So what does this mean for your spiritual nurture? It says that you can no longer rely on a church or any other institution to supply cradle-to-grave support. In all likelihood, no one is going to track with you over the course of your spiritual pilgrimage. I'm not saying no one cares. I'm just pointing out that long-term responsibility for spiritual development has shifted from the church to you as an individual believer.

And now you have no church. Tradition holds that you cannot grow apart from a church. How, then, will you proceed (assuming that you want to proceed)? A few of the people I interviewed have moved forward by standing tradition on its head and taking spiritual sustenance wherever they can find it—from books, magazines, television and radio ministries, a sympathetic friend or two, perhaps the arts and music, maybe volunteer work. Over time, they've become quite resourceful at finding ways to meet God apart from a local church.

Nobody says this is ideal. But then, we've already established that they are living in a less than perfect world. I think the only way they do it is by accepting the fact that if they don't, no one else will. So, driven by spiritual hunger, they keep looking high and low for ways to nourish themselves.

It's interesting to analyze their approach. To the extent that they can, they seem to create surrogates or alternatives to the things they ordinarily might find in a church. For example, worship: instead of attending a Sunday morning service, they may tune in to a broadcast service, or gather with two or three friends for prayer and holy Communion. Or instruction: instead of attending a Sunday school class, they may work their way through some writings of Thomas Merton, or perhaps obtain a video or audiotape on some aspect of the Christian life.

As for fellowship, the non-church-attenders who seem to be going on spiritually invariably find at least one but usually a handful of kindred spirits to whom they turn for support, prayer, celebration, and, in its own way, accountability.

Is this a model to follow? Of course not. There are no models when it comes to trying to grow as a Christian outside the institutional church. It is total improvisation. Certainly none of the people with whom I spoke recommended it, even if that was their circumstance.

But one thing they did stress: the need for personal responsibility. Whether you are inside or outside the church, your walk with God is your own to either nurture or ignore.

You have a unique relationship with God. Frequently in this book I have pointed out that spirituality is a function of how God has designed us as individuals. Thus, no two people have quite the same relationship with Him. It's not that there aren't common elements. But each of us experiences those elements uniquely. As a friend of mine puts it, God comes to us in the way He has made us. My friend happens to be someone who is motivated to come alongside others and help them understand things and get to where they want to go. That motivational style is reflected in his spiritual life. When he prays, for example, he often finds himself asking God to help *him* understand things or get things done, because those outcomes have meaning for him.

Another person I know, who currently is not attending a church, has discovered that she uses music to express her emotions and thoughts. So when she wants to talk with God, she often puts on a recording of some piece that particularly expresses her mood toward Him—as well as His posture toward her.

These are simple examples, but they point to something very profound: God knows your name. He wants to relate to you as you, not as someone else. And although it's true that knowing God is the key to knowing yourself, the reverse is also true—knowing yourself is the key to knowing God. There are *two* persons in the relationship; it flows both ways.

So who are you? That's a threatening question for which you may have no confident answer. So let me rephrase it: What is your story? I've written up a couple dozen stories in this book. If I had interviewed you, what would I have heard? What is your background? Into what sort of family were you born? What is its history and heritage? How did you get started in the faith? Why did you come to faith in the first place? What has been the "plot" of your life, the course of events? How do they connect together? What pieces don't seem to fit (yet)? What have been the key turning points? Who have been the major characters in the narrative? Where is your life right now? Where do you see it headed?

Now, backing off from all of that: What is the *story*? What is going on? How would you summarize the plot of your life? And then this question: Knowing what you know about God, how do you suppose He might speak into that story? How has He interjected Himself so far? What's the history of His participation in your life? When has He spoken or acted? What has He said or done? How does that fit with the rest of the story?

I think if you sat down with someone you trust and told your story out loud, you would come away with a great deal of self-knowledge that might prove useful. I say that because that was usually the case with my interviewees. Some of them were reluctant to talk with me at first. But by the end of the interview, they often expressed a profound sense of surprise at how much *they* had learned. Perhaps as a result, their spiritual lives will take into account some of that insight.

One of the most important things you can ever learn about yourself is how you learn. The New Testament calls those who follow Christ *disciples*, literally "learners." What kind of disciple/learner are you?

In chapter 19, I mentioned that people learn in very different ways. I happen to be an adaptive learner. That is, I collect information in almost whatever form it's given. My preferred styles are reading and observation. My brother, Bob, by contrast, is an imitative learner. He prefers to watch someone do something one time and then take it from there.

This difference in learning styles has resulted in very different approaches to education—and spirituality. If I want to know something, I usually start at the library or bookstore. If Bob wants to know something, he usually asks, who can I talk to who is an expert on this? Likewise, I arrive at meaning through words. My brother arrives at meaning through relationships. Neither approach is better than the other. It's a matter of how God has made us.

So how do you learn? Perhaps you're a problem-solver who only gets interested when there's a problem to be solved. Perhaps you're an explorer who needs to turn everything into an adventure. Maybe you're a tinkerer who likes to tear things down to their component parts and then put them back together—not necessarily in the same configuration. Maybe games are how you learn; you require a sense of play and chance. Perhaps you demand a group setting if you're going to learn anything.

There are countless styles and variations. The independent learner. The hands-on approach. The mental map-maker. The purely creative, out-of-thin-air type. The doubting Thomas. Or one of the most common—the conversationalist.

The point is, knowing how you learn has a direct bearing on your spiritual development. Spiritual growth is a process, but it's largely a process of learning. So the more you know about how you learn, the better you'll be able to design an effective strategy for cultivating your spiritual life.

Christ is the center. When I think back to people I have known who really went off the deep end, so to speak, in terms of their faith, I think their troubles most often resulted from losing their perspective on Christ. They may have been attracted by some novel approach to doctrine. They may have fallen prey to temptation. But somehow they became focused on something other than Christ.

This is a clear and present danger for any person who has walked away from the church. Certainly it can happen even to those who remain in the church. But it's a definite possibility for the non-attender. With no regular reminder of what the faith is all about, he or she can forget what is central and what really matters.

One reason I say this is that I have used the term "spirituality" somewhat loosely in this book. In doing so, I may have created the impression that any sort of spirituality will do. If so, let me state emphatically: Jesus Christ is the center of Christianity; therefore, spirituality without Christ at the center is not Christian spirituality, whatever else it may be.

For example, a few people told me that they had visited Unitarian churches. They liked some of the things they found there. But I was relieved to hear that they ended up not pursuing that option. I have nothing against Unitarians as people, but I am strongly opposed to Unitarianism as a system. As I see it, it is nothing but the ethics of Christianity without the doctrines of Christianity. As a result, it supplants Christ (along with the Holy Spirit) while trying to hold onto His benefits. In my opinion, it's a counterfeit.

I think it's hard to go wrong if you keep Christ at the center of your spirituality. But in saying that, I am not encouraging you to deny your very real doubts, questions, concerns, and feelings. I found the candor and realism of my interviewees to be refreshing. Now, if they can just translate that honesty to the way they relate to Christ! Likewise for you: if you pursue ruthless honesty in your relationship with Christ, I believe you'll stand a far better chance of keeping Him at the center.

Thank God for disillusionment! In chapter 19, I made the observation that spirituality is a process. I also said that disillusionment is a process. Finally I suggested that they are in many ways the same process. How can that be?

Well, consider the nature of disillusionment. Before you can be *dis*illusioned, you must have an illusion. By definition, an illusion is an image, a mirage, a fiction. It is something that seems real but is not.

The very word "illusion" derives from the Latin *illusio*, "mockery," a derivative of *illudere*, "to make fun of." So if you accept an illusion, you are buying into a mockery of the truth. In short, a deceit.

God never wants us to relate to Him on the basis of a lie. We tend to think of the lies of non-Christian worldviews such as materialism, atheism, pantheism, and most New Age thinking. Certainly God wants us to reject the deceptions in those philosophical systems.

But we Christians practice our own forms of deception when it comes to who God is and how we relate to Him. Admittedly I'm on thin ice in saying this, and I run a great risk of being misunderstood. Yet listening to my interviewees, it became evident that during their early years in the faith they picked up ideas about God that later had to be discarded. No one intentionally deceived them. And the falsehoods were hardly on the order of rank heresy. Nevertheless, they either caught or were taught illusions about God and how to relate to Him.

So God had to break through those illusions. I believe He has to do that for every one of us. Why? Because it is not good enough to relate to Him on the basis of who we think He is or who we would like Him to be; we must deal with Him as He really is. Thus spirituality is in part a process of losing our illusions, of making "a pilgrimage from appearance to reality."[3]

That process is invariably painful. As T. S. Eliot observed, "human kind cannot bear very much reality."[4] In the experience of the people I interviewed, God kept knocking out the props until they had nowhere else to turn but Him. Only then did they see Him and experience Him for who He really is.

"My illusion was to be unconditionally loved and accepted in the church," Jennifer said. "When all the relationships around me were falling down and being torn apart, and there was nothing but hurt and pain and heartache, where else was there to go [but God]?"

John told me, "For the better part of my Christian life, I was moving from bandwagon to bandwagon, from approach to approach. And finally what happened was that God in His mercy swept them all aside and none of them made any sense anymore."

"I want to know what the truth is," Sheila declared. "Finding the truth has been the story of my life. I went through so many different cultural manifestations of the church, thinking that the truth was there. Then one day I realized: I am involved in learning how to worship a *culture* and not being challenged to seek a *living* God. 'Seek the living God as long as you seek Him.'"

These statements and the many others like them in the interviews lend strong evidence to an ironic fact: disillusionment can be invaluable for one's spirituality. Indeed, it may be inevitable, for change is how we grow. Business consultant Charles Handy says, "Ask people, as I have often done, to recall two or three of the most important learning experiences in their lives, and they will never tell you of courses taken or degrees obtained, but of brushes with death, of crises encountered, of new and unexpected challenges or confrontations.

"They will tell you, in other words, of times when continuity ran out on them, when they had no past experience to fall back on, no rules or handbook. They survived, however, and came to count it as learning, as a growth experience. Discontinuous change, therefore, when properly handled, is the way we grow up."

I wouldn't give up on the church. Earlier I pointed out that the end of your story has not yet been written. The same is true for the church. No one knows what the church will be like in even five years, except that it will be different. So there's hope.

In the meantime, I would beware of cynicism and judgment. Those two attitudes have a strange way of making one miserable. And in the end, there's always the possibility of dining on crow.

"When I first became a Christian," C. S. Lewis wrote to a friend after fourteen years in the faith, "I wouldn't go to the churches and Gospel Halls; . . . I disliked very much their hymns, which I considered to be fifth-rate poems set to sixth-rate music. But as I went on I saw the great merit of it. I came up against different people of quite different outlooks and different education, and then gradually my conceit just began peeling off. I realized that the hymns (which were just sixth-rate music) were, nevertheless, being sung with devotion and benefit by an old saint in elastic-side boots in the opposite pew, and then you realize that you aren't fit to clean those boots. It gets you out of your solitary conceit."[6]

There's no getting around the fact that the church is just a collection of imperfect and actually sinful people—like you and me. It may be that some of those sinners saved by grace have thoroughly abused you, misled you, or rejected you, such that you now will have nothing to do with a church.

I don't blame you for walking out, and I feel sorry for what has happened, especially if it's been done in the name of Christ. In fact, while it may not be my place to do so, I feel some obligation as a member of Christ's body to offer an apology. You deserved better. You deserved Christ. So if, instead, you have been mistreated and hurt, I want to acknowledge your pain. It's a terrible thing to carry. When it's time, I hope that you can it lay down and walk on in peace and grace.

Perhaps it will help to remember that not all churches or believers are the same. Furthermore, not everyone is dissatisfied with their church. A great many people remain who derive tremendous spiritual benefits. So it does "work" for some. Maybe someday you can find a community of faith that "works" for you. My advice would be to keep looking.

You can't have it all. By now I hope I have redefined our understanding of the old bromide "You'll never find the perfect church." No, in this life you never will. But therein lies the grief: *this life*, life in a fallen world.

In chapter 11, I spoke of the Ecclesiastes Factor, the quality of *hebel*, which makes life fleeting and futile, like smoke in the wind. Perhaps the grandest of illusions is that Christians are exempt from that futility. We are not. Don't misunderstand: Christ has saved us from sin. There's no question about that. But He has not yet delivered us entirely from the curse.

Consequently, even though our salvation is secure and we derive untold benefits from life in Christ, we still experience *hebel*, that sense of frustration and disappointment. That's why, as Paul puts it, we "groan" inside.[7] We long to be with God, but for reasons of His own He leaves us in this troubled world. It hurts.

The result is that not only will we never find the perfect church, we will never find perfect spirituality. We may taste a sample of it from time to time; we can never have it all. Not in this life.

So what's the point? Why keep trying if, despite our best faith and efforts, we never get there?

The only way to answer such a question is with a story, of course. So let me close with one more story, that of Heman the singer.[8] I should point out that he lived during the Old Testament period, and few people today are familiar with him. Yet his life speaks to anyone who has ever felt disillusioned with the church and dissatisfied with his own spiritual experience.

In English, the name *Heman* means "faithful." And so he was, a reliable, rock-solid presence in Jerusalem, where he served King David as an astute and trusted counselor. Later, under David's successor, Solomon, Heman continued to be treated with great deference as an elder statesman, numbered among the "wise men."

But it was not so much Heman's proximity to kings or even his impressive wisdom for which Scripture remembers him, but his music. Like David, he had grown up singing, composing, and performing. In fact, the two men shared such similar artistic tastes that when David finally centralized Israel's worship at Jerusalem, he commissioned Heman and his family to be permanent overseers of the musical responsibilities.

This position was in effect the musical counterpart to a very active poet laureate. Heman was given control over all compositions, arrangements, instrumentations, and performances at court and in the temple. He was the designated musical leader in a country where painstakingly scripted ritual and worship served political and national ends as well as religious and cultural purposes. During his tenure, a fountain of music gushed forth that has never been equaled in Israel's history. Indeed, the body of work became the backbone of Judeo-Christian liturgical forms.

So which of Heman's many compositions does Scripture choose to include? Ironically, only *one*: Psalm 88. I invite the reader to look it up. You will find that it begins on a somber note:

> O Lord God of my salvation,
> I have cried day and night before thee:
> Let my prayer come before thee:
> Incline thine ear unto my cry (KJV).

In effect, the psalmist is asking, "Where are You, God? I've been calling for You day and night!"

From those melancholy lines, the mood of the song, already dark, turns positively black. Heman composes in an agony of complaint, frustration, and loneliness. He feels as though God has abandoned him; or worse, that He has become a God of affliction instead of comfort. Heman finds himself questioning God, even accusing Him. Deep, painful memories and associations well to the surface, as if his life is a vessel holding nothing but ill health and ill fortune. Like Job, he does not give up on God, but he does wonder whether God has given up on him.

No one knows the circumstances under which Heman composed this song of despair. But the piece suggests a gnawing uneasiness deep in the composer's soul, a disturbing sense of living under God's abiding wrath. For reasons not revealed, his life is marked by suffering without end and without explanation.

It just doesn't seem to fit. Here is a man enjoying great popularity and success as the court composer in a kingdom basking in peace and prosperity. The spiritual and moral life of the nation is at an all-time high. The people are united. God is apparently pleased. Yet Heman's soul is "full of trouble" and his spirit is "in despair."[9] The logical question is, why?

I can only guess at an answer. But one place to start is with a closer look at Heman's name. On the face of it, naming a son Faithful was unremarkable for a Jewish family of that day. Yet Faithful was actually an ironic name, given Heman's background.

His grandfather was Samuel the judge, the same Samuel who anointed Saul as Israel's first king. As it turns out, Heman's father was largely responsible for that unfortunate choice.

Samuel had two sons, Joel (Heman's father) and Abijah. In the later years of his life, after he had brought relative peace to the land, Samuel realized that sooner or later he must turn over leadership to his sons. He must have guessed what sort of snakes those two would turn out to be. So he set them up at the extreme southern limits of the territory in a border town called Beersheba, where they could do the least harm.

Yet in the end they did great harm, both locally and nationally. Living in relative obscurity, unhindered by any form of accountability, they used their position to personal advantage, lining their pockets with bribes and kickbacks and deciding cases by whim.

Eventually, word of their abuses made its way back to the leaders in the north. I suspect that most of those officials ignored the situation. After all, corruption among Israel's judges had become legendary. But there were those who wanted to transform the nation into a kingdom, and here was an opportunity. Bringing the matter before Samuel, they appealed for change. They were no longer satisfied with judges; they wanted a king. It was this request that led to the tragic reign of Saul, a man who might have lived a successful and fulfilled life had he not been forced into a job beyond his capacities.

How interesting, then, that Joel should have named his son Faithful, for Joel was anything but faithful. Could it be that he was thumbing his nose at his own father, Samuel, the leader of a system he seems to have despised?

Of course, in many ways Joel was merely living out the family's heritage, in which faithfulness to God had been more the exception than the rule. For example, if one traces the line all the way back to Jacob, the ancestor, one finds that he was remembered as much for his deceit as for his ties to Abraham, the patriarch. And not unlike their father, the first ten of Jacob's twelve sons proved to be virtual cut-throats.

Generations later, another ancestor, Korah, followed his cousin Moses out of Egypt. Once in the Sinai, God appointed Korah's family to manage and maintain the tabernacle, Israel's mobile worship center. But that wasn't enough for Korah. Backed by 250 others, he rebelled against Moses and Aaron, demanding equal access to all forms of leadership. God decided the matter in dramatic fashion: the earth opened up and swallowed Korah and most of his family alive!

We can only speculate as to what sort of man Heman was. But how could the family's legacy and the behavior of his father and uncle not have left a profound impact on him? He must have felt shame every time he heard his name: Faithful. It is likely that he was disgusted with his family, for as far as we know, he refused to join in their crimes. My guess is that he turned inward, brooding on the dark nature of his ancestors and the continuing instability of his country's leadership. And it seems reasonable that music might have become a refuge for him from the corruption he saw in his youth and later in the politics and intrigue of the royal court.

Admittedly, I am speculating here to a large extent. But it would take some kind of person like the one I've described to produce a work as deep and dark as Psalm 88. And that is why I bring in Heman's story here at the end of this book. Psalm 88 and the little we know of the man who composed it are bits of evidence about the search for spirituality in a less than perfect world—a fallen world, as a matter of fact. [10]

The story tells us that in a fallen world, even the quest for meaning and the pilgrimage of faith are going to be marked by the Ecclesiastes Factor: we can't have it all in this life. We want to see God; we only get glimpses. We want to find answers; we mostly get mysteries. We want to be good; we must settle for grace.

Do you find that a bit sad? I do. But I do not find it hopeless. By no means! For although life may be less than perfect, it is far from pointless. It is headed somewhere. And that's another reason for bringing up Heman. His story forces us to ask, what's the point? We try to make sense of his story—and for that matter, the stories contained in this book or our own stories—because we feel they ought to make sense. There ought to be a meaning to them. There ought to be more than randomness and chaos. And there is.

That's why the stories in this book are so valuable. They help to clarify not only what the search for spirituality is all about but where it is headed. The people living these narratives are like modern-day Hemans. They have met with disappointments and disillusionments (and for some, even disasters) along the way. But look how their journeys all point in a very definite direction. We've been privileged to hear about their travels so far. I look forward to the time when they can tell us what they found at the end of the road.

NOTES

1. As related by Robert Coles, *The Call of Stories: Teaching and the Moral Imagination* (Boston: Houghton Mifflin Company, 1989), 30.
2. Ephesians 5:26–27; see also 4:12–14.
3. Dame Iris Murdoch, *Metaphysics as a Guide to Morals* (London: Allen Lane/Penguin, 1993).
4. *Murder in the Cathedral*, Part II
5. *The Age of Unreason* (Boston: Harvard Business School Press, 1990), 11–12
6. "Answers to Questions on Christianity," *God in the Dock* (Grand Rapids: Eerdmans, 1970), 61–62.
7. Romans 8:22–23.
8. The story of Heman can be pieced together by studying a number of passages in Scripture, including: Numbers 16:1–35 (Korah's rebellion); 1 Samuel 8:1–9 (Samuel's appointment of his sons to judge Israel); 1 Chronicles 6:33; 15:16–17; 16:41–42; 25:1–8; and 2 Chronicles 5:12.
9. Psalm 88:3, 15.
10. Only a few short years after Heman's death, the kingdom was divided, the leaders had turned away from God, and his songs were forgotten, except for the one.

Moody Press, a ministry of the Moody Bible Institute,
is designed for education, evangelization, and edification.
If we may assist you in knowing more about Christ
and the Christian life, please write us without obligation:
Moody Press, c/o MLM, Chicago, Illinois 60610.